R. H. Crozier

The Confederate Spy

A Story of the War of 1861

R. H. Crozier

The Confederate Spy
A Story of the War of 1861

ISBN/EAN: 9783337246594

Printed in Europe, USA, Canada, Australia, Japan

Cover: Foto ©ninafisch / pixelio.de

More available books at **www.hansebooks.com**

THE CONFEDERATE SPY:

A STORY OF THE WAR OF 1861.

By R. H. CROZIER, A. M.,
FORMERLY CAPTAIN OF COMPANY I, 33D REGIMENT MISSISSIPPI VOLUNTEERS.

"Verily there is nothing so false that a sparkle of TRUTH is not in it."
Tupper's Proverbial Philosophy.

LOUISVILLE, KY.:
PRINTED BY JOHN P. MORTON AND COMPANY.
1871.

Entered, according to act of Congress, in the year 1866, by

H. H. CROZIER, A. M.,

In the Clerk's Office of the District Court of the United States for the Middle District of Tennessee.

JOHN P. MORTON & CO.,
STEREOTYPERS AND PRINTERS,
LOUISVILLE, KY.

DEDICATED
TO THE
Surviving Members of Loring's Division.

"They left the plowshare in the mold,
The flocks and herds without a fold,
The sickle in the unshorn grain,
The corn half garnered on the plain,
And mustered, in their simple dress,
For wrongs to seek a stern redress:
To right those wrongs, come weal, come woe,
To perish, or o'ercome the foe."

PREFACE.

It is with extreme diffidence that the author of the following pages ventures before the intelligent public in the character of a novelist. Whoever writes any thing in these days, when the press is already teeming with ephemeral literature, must suppose that the effusions of his mind are above the thousands that come forth every hour. But the author of this unpretending little volume has too much modesty to lay claim to any such superior excellence, especially in a *first effort*. He does not publish the book with the humble hope that it will rank with even the ordinary works of mediocrists in the world of romance. The author has only one object in view. He submits the book to the judgment of the patriotic southern public, with the hope that it may help to supplant the poisonous northern literature which has for so many years flooded the South, and villified the southern people and their institutions. The time has now come when there ought to be a change. The South must have a literature of her own. If we could not gain our *political*, let us establish at least our *mental* independence.

We appeal, therefore, to the southern people; to their dignity; to their sense of justice to themselves; and we ask them no longer to encourage the *yellow* and the *red-backed* trash of the North, in which the attempt is made to hold up the South as the butt of the civilized world. Soon thousands of tales will come forth from the vile den of New England, containing scandalous caricatures of our beloved South, and of the misfortunes of our late Confederacy. Do not buy them, southern reader! Do not insult the memory of your noble dead by enriching northern writers, who make sport of their bloody graves! If you must read novels, we ask you, for the sake of your dead heroes, to read those which do not abuse and villify your ancestors, yourselves, your institutions, your religion—all that you hold dear and sacred!

The following story is founded upon facts, or rather it comes nearer being a narrative of facts. We have dealt with living characters. The main errors in our book, taken even as a history, consist chiefly in points of chronology and locality. The author confesses that he has taken advantage of the privilege allowed to all novelists, in this respect, and has located and dated scenes in order to maintain the connection of the story, and preserve its unity. The author claims no great credit for the construction of the plot. Unfortunately, *it constructed itself*. We are indebted very slightly to our imagination. The incidents herein related are nearly all actual occurrences, however horrible they may appear. Perhaps an apology is due to the reader for the profanity which so frequently occurs throughout these pages. All we have to say is, that the Yankee character can not be correctly delineated without it.

Southern reader, you now know our object. Will you sustain us? Will you encourage southern writers? If so, "prove your faith by your works."

THE AUTHOR.

PANOLA COUNTY, MISS., May 27, 1865.

THE CONFEDERATE SPY.

CHAPTER I.

"There was a soft and pensive grace,
A cast of thought upon her face,
That suited well the forehead high,
The eyelash dark and downcast eye."

IN the extreme north-eastern portion of the "dark and bloody ground"—or, in other words, the State of Kentucky—there stood in the year 1860 a stately residence. It was a tall, square, two-story building, similar in size, shape, and appearance to hundreds of others scattered throughout the heaven-favored land of the "sunny South." There was therefore nothing peculiarly remarkable in the construction of this dwelling. Nevertheless, rearing itself, with its snow-white walls and tall stone chimneys, amid a grove of scattered oaks, that were green and shady in spring, but bare, leafless, and somewhat melancholy during the bleak days of winter, it presented from the distance a picturesque and romantic appearance. The surrounding scenery was unsurpassed in loveliness. The top of the eminence upon which the house was situated contained several acres, that lay spread out in level smoothness for more than two hundred yards; then gradually declined in all directions, till arrested by hills on one side, and lost on the other in a bottom. In the rear of the residence tall hills arose in majestic splendor; in front, at the distance of half a mile, there flowed a large creek, or perhaps it would be better to call it a small river, whose clear, transparent waters rolled on in solemn silence, until, mingling and commingling with other streams, all were finally introduced, through the channel of the grand old "Father of Waters," to the wide bosom of the Gulf of Mexico. An immense tract of the river bottom had been made subservient to the purposes of cultivation, and the consequence was, a broad plantation spread out, whose monotony was broken by fences and cross-fences, that reached to the hills far on the other side of the stream, which were bedecked with tall, waving trees, crowned with deep cerulean blue. The house was approached from the direction of the river through a long avenue, either side of which was decorated with all varieties of trees and shrubs. At the foot of this avenue ran a road, which, from the observatory on the house-top, could be seen, for a long distance, winding along the little hills that bordered on the river bottom.

Every thing in the vicinity of this magnificent dwelling evinced the refined taste of the owner. The broad plantation with its tall, strong fences, the comfortable negro-quarters, the neat barns and stables, the orchard with its delicious fruit, the white palings, the yard variegated with all descriptions of flowers, made it manifest, if external circumstances can furnish any indication of character, that this was the habitation of a person of elevated feeling and cultivated mind.

We do not wish, however, to tax the patience of our reader with too much description, nor to force upon his attention too many objects that can claim no essential pertinency to our story. We will therefore commence without further preface, prelude, or preliminary, as Horace says, *in medias res* (to translate which three words literally signifies, in the middle of things), and at once introduce the characters destined to figure throughout these pages. Then we will commence as we have said.

Joseph Burrell, at the time this story begins, was an old man, active though even at the age of sixty-five. Having possessed an ample fortune from early youth, he had enjoyed immunities from the ordinary cares of life that so much trammel the actions, harass the feelings, and sour the tempers of the greater portion of mankind. Major Burrell, and we call him major not because he had been in military life that we ever heard of, but had obtained this title, like many other people do, from the possession of a great quantity of worldly wealth. We are disposed in this country to bestow high-sounding military titles upon millionaires and nabobs. But Major Burrell, with commendable prudence, had vastly improved the magnificent inheritance handed down by his ancestors. At the age of twenty-three, when both his parents had gone to that "bourne whence no traveler returns," he quietly settled down at the old homestead like a wise young man, married the woman of his choice, and had lived happily many years, instead of strolling about through the world without any definite object in view, and wasting his splendid bequeathment in idleness, extravagance, and dissipation. The reader, when he learns the part Major Burrell is to play in this little history, will agree with me that it is not necessary to enter into all the particulars of his character. We will simply say that he was a stout, hale, hearty, active old man, in his dotage, as will be seen in due time. The outside world will be better satisfied when we add to the catalogue that he was *rich*. And now, reader, by the by, you and I know full well that wealth has its advantages as well as its cares and encumbrances. It confers many blessings and privileges upon its fortunate possessor. It brings power, political and social influence; it supersedes the necessity of a lifetime of labor; besides many other advantages, things, and circumstances, which it will not be proper now to enumerate. But beyond this its power may be said to cease. The seeds of disease and the shafts of death are scattered broadcast among rich and poor, without distinction or discrimination. The "green monster" seizes, without much warning, upon Dives and Lazarus. And, reader, this circumstance is a great consolation to us poor sinners, who are struggling day after day, toiling night after night, for the means of subsistence, and yet by the most strenuous efforts can barely keep the corporeal system in a good, comfortable condition, and the mind in a calm, tranquil state; for if riches could ward off the attacks of man's chief enemy, and enable one to escape the "ills that flesh is heir to," there could be but little enjoyment beyond the simple pleasure of exercising the organs of respiration in a world where there would be only one grand, mighty, desperate, and protracted struggle for "filthy lucre." And now, with this brief digression and this little moralizing, which we hope will be received in a spirit of kindness, we will proceed with the story.

Major Joseph Burrell, although surrounded by every thing in the shape of physical comforts which the human heart could in reason desire, was nevertheless subject to the penalties of mortality, and had been called upon to mourn the loss of a wife and four children. One by one they had been snatched from the stage of action, till only two now remained to console him in his declining years: the elder, a son, who, at the time our story commences, was a student in the military institute of West Point; the younger, a daughter, who, with the reader's permission, will be more particularly noticed.

Eighteen years had flown over the head of Emily Burrell. We will commence the description of Emily by asking the reader if he or she, as the case may be, ever saw an ugly young lady? We never did. Nearly all young ladies are good-looking, if not handsome and positively beautiful. The term ugly therefore is a modifying adjective, which is not at all applicable in the description of the "fair," especially one of young and tender years. We mean to insinuate by this that Emily was no exception to the general rule. Indeed, she could lay claim to the very highest order of beauty. Her dark hair hung down from a classically-shaped head, in jet black tresses, to shoulders that vied with alabaster in point of pure whiteness. A pair of large, black, brilliant eyes, that flashed and sparkled under the influence of aroused feeling, evinced the possession of a mind and heart that could be wrought to the highest pitch of excitement. Above the eyes arose a pure, white, broad, open, smooth forehead, whose inequalities nevertheless were sufficient to redeem its owner from the suspicion of possessing a phrenologically well-developed head without the intellect to sustain appearances. Her nose was, we say without hesitation, unlike Solomon's description of his bride's (we do not know which one of them he had reference to) nasal organ—"as the tower of Lebanon which looketh toward Damascus." (Between you and me, reader, *inter nos*, and speaking without irreverence or profanity, I always associated Solomon's description with the idea of a *pug* nose.) It is sufficient to say that Emily's was not a *pug* nose, and that it was duly proportioned to her other features. Add to these lineaments rosy cheeks, red lips, a pretty mouth, white, pearly teeth, a symmetrical figure of medium size, beautifully proportioned, and graceful in all its motions and movements, and you have before you one whom Juno (I believe there is no law, moral, civil, or military, against taking the name of a heathenish divinity in vain) might have envied, even when she, according to Virgil, stalked through the heavens in her pride and vainglory, with the high-sounding, world-wide banter, *incedo regina*, issuing from her ambrosial lips.

But, strange to say, Emily, with all these external recommendations, was not a proud, vain, self-conceited girl, as the reader might be inclined to suppose. At a very early age she had manifested a taste for literary pleasures, and was deeply read for one of her age. Emily was a student—a student of nature—a thorough lover of knowledge. She loved solitude, and had early felt, in the language of a great poet,

> "There is a pleasure in the pathless woods,
> There is a rapture on the lonely shore;
> There is a society, where none intrudes,
> By the deep sea, and music in its roar."

Often had she wandered along the banks of the limpid river, sat in the cool, shady grove, listened to the unaffected music of nature's warblers, and reflected profoundly upon subjects which might have been considered beyond her years. Calm, sober, intense thought had solidified her mind and purified her nature. Her life thus far had been spent principally in an ideal world. Having had few companions of her own sex from childhood, she almost lived upon thought. She could with Shakespeare exclaim:

> "The shadowy desert, unfrequented woods,
> I better brook than flourishing peopled towns;
> There can I sit alone, unseen of any,
> And to the nightingale's complaining notes
> Tune my distresses and record my woes."

However, the record of Emily's real "distresses and woes" would have been somewhat summary. Thus far few disappointments had embittered her existence. Aside from the ordinary troubles and cares incidental to, or rather inseparable from, mortality, she may be said never to have suffered. Smooth and even had been the current of her young life. Far from the busy haunts of noisy cities, she had lived in the forests—a student and a child of nature. She must not be supposed, from the description we have given, destitute of sensibility, nor a follower of Plato, nor a member of the church of passionless Stoics. Indeed, she was warm-hearted, enthusiastic, kind, generous, benevolent, and would have loved madly and wildly could she have met with her *beau-ideal*. But she was not a character to lavish her affections upon an object recommended only by the beauty of exterior organism. She was one who could love only where moral excellence and solid worth would first command esteem, respect, and admiration.

It is evident that a girl possessing all these physical and mental attractions, besides being prospective heiress of an immense fortune (which last qualification is not overlooked by some people), could not forever remain in obscurity. Some poet has beautifully said:

> "Full many a flower is born to blush unseen,
> And waste its fragrance on the desert air."

But such was not always to be Emily's destiny. Up to this time, which is something remarkable, she had bestowed few thoughts upon "love, courtship, and marriage;" and yet she was blessed, if blessing it can be called, with numerous admirers and lovers. But to none of these had she ever given the slightest encouragement to persevere in their attentions. With something akin to good-natured submission, she had endured the numerous visits of the silly fops that flocked to her father's house from the little town not far distant, and listened cheerfully to their silly chat upon silly subjects. But not one of these had ever awakened in her heart a sentiment bearing the most remote resemblance to love.

One evening a small party of these young gents had congregated in the counting-room of a mercantile house in the little town to which we have already alluded. One of the number had just returned from Major Burrell's. As the conversation which took place on this occasion may save us the trouble of a long description, and as it was connected with our story, we will record so much of it as is necessary. We, however, warn the reader in time, that this chat was similar to that of most young men enlivened and exhilarated by the influence of the god Bacchus.

"Well, Bill, how's Miss Emily?" said one to William Jones, as he entered the apartment.

"She's well enough, I guess," replied the person addressed,

in a tone that plainly showed he was not as well pleased with the visit as usual.

"You need n't be so crusty about it, old fellow; you are not the first that ever got his *walking papers* at the same house," said the first speaker, with a wink to his companion.

"You are mistaken there. I did not get my papers; but I rather guess we are all done for at the old Major's."

"How's that, Bill?" said Tom Wilkins. "Tell it all at once."

"Very little explanation will suffice. I have just returned from the old Major's, as you know, and Miss Emily is terribly smitten with an awkward relative of hers—a sort of fifteenth cousin, or something of the kind—just kin enough to make courtship interesting. He is not to be grinned at, though, for he is a darned good-looking fellow, notwithstanding he's so gawky; and I'll bet ten to one carries off the prize: and there goes another five hundred thousand!"

"Egad! that's what sticks you. But what's his name?"

"His name is Gallam, Hallam, Ballam, or something that way. I do n't recollect now."

"Where does he come from, and what kind of a fellow is he? Tell it all in a lump."

"Well, then, he lives about one hundred and fifty miles from this place, I understand. His height is, I should judge, in the neighborhood of five feet ten. His hair is black; eyes of the same color. His complexion is on the Ethiopian style; nose large and fashionable; mouth somewhat less than Tom Wilkins's, there."

"Darn it," said Tom, "never mind my mouth; you have always got something to say about my features. By jingo! I wish you would find something else to talk about."

"Boys! I've got a good joke on Tom; and, since he's so darned testy and cross, I'll tell it."

"Tell it and be d——d!" said Tom, angrily.

"Well, last week Tom and I called on Miss Emily. I thought I would keep it a secret for his sake, but I declare it's too good to be lost. While we were sitting in the parlor, Miss Emily excused herself and retired for a few moments. During her absence Tom walked to the mantel-shelf, and very unluckily upset an inkstand, and spilled its contents on the hearth-rug. Tom quickly jerked out his pocket handkerchief, wiped up the ink, and put it in his pocket. Just then Miss Emily came in. Tom was somewhat confused; but, to hide it, I suppose, he picked up a book of poetry.

"'Miss Emily,' said Tom, 'here's a beautiful piece of poetry;' and he read four lines. 'I wrote them down, and here they are:

> 'Fair oldest child of love, thou spotless night!
> Empress of silence, and the queen of sleep,
> Makest lover's eyes enamored of thy beauty.'
> Who, with thy black cheek's pure complexion,

"But the beauty of the performance was, when Tom was reading the third line, he snatched out his handkerchief and wiped it over his face till his own cheeks were as black as midnight.

"'I think, Mr. Wilkins,' said Miss Emily, when Tom paused, '"thy black cheek's pure complexion" is a splendid idea; and you have pronounced it and illustrated it with an emphasis that is calculated to make a decided impression.'

"I was so tickled I laughed outright, and so did Miss Emily. Tom looked at us in surprise, but he happened to catch a glimpse of his face in a mirror, and he was the most woe-begone chap ever I saw. If he blushed, his face was so black nobody could see it. By Jove! boys, he just made one snatch at his hat, and ran out like the very devil. I never saw Miss Emily laugh so much in my life. I thought she never would stop."

"By dad! Tom must be *kangarooed* for that," said one, while the party was in a perfect roar of laughter.

"Guilty or not guilty, Tom?" asked another.

"Go to h—ll!" answered Wilkins, rising and leaving the room. The whole party roared louder than ever.

But we have promised not to worry the patience of our kind readers with long descriptions of scenes which are disconnected with the story. We have introduced the above characters merely to bring forward a personage with whom we must become more intimately acquainted. If the reader can form any idea of Emily's cousin—that is, his personal appearance—from William Jones's description, we are satisfied. We will, therefore, leave the party, discussing for a few moments in regard to Emily's fortune, and the probabilities of a marriage with her cousin, and introduce that gentleman himself, and let the reader form his own opinions, and draw his own conclusions. As we do not like to jumble up events together, and crowd so many different circumstances all into one place, and thereby confuse and distract our readers' attention, we will commence a new chapter. The reader is now at liberty to drop the acquaintance of Bill Jones and Tom Wilkins, as they will not make their appearance again in this little history.

CHAPTER II.

"Let us love temp'rately; things violent last not;
And too much dotage rather argues folly
Than true affection."

WALTER HALLAM, the person to whom allusion was made in the last chapter, was the descendant of parents in moderate circumstances. Appreciating the advantages of education, they had sent Walter to school until he was graduated. Though a young man of some "parts," he gave but little promise of distinction, at least in the literary world; and yet he was somewhat of a student in his own peculiar way. Knowledge to him was valuable only so far as it could be made available in the achievement of some definite end, and was practically useful. Abstract science was his utter detestation. However, Horace, Virgil, and all the other Greek and Latin authors who are the beloved companions of the true scholar, had no sympathy from young Hallam, with their "ridiculous nonsense," as he termed it. "Milton," he would say to his fellow-students, "is a bombastic old fool; and I confess my surprise that sensible men should be so taken with his silly descriptions of hobgoblins, and his desperate battles between angels and devils, and his foolish contradictions in general. Why, by the gods! how could a battle ever terminate between parties, the members of which could not be killed. The idea of spirits tearing up hills and mountains by the roots, hurling them through space at one another, and playing the devil generally—it's simply absurd and ridiculous—all sheer nonsense and child's stuff. Now there's that other old dotard, Ovid—a good match for Milton—

with his metamorphoses—changing women into trees, and trees into women; turning the color of mulberries from white to red; driving the chariot of the sun round the world; scorching the African till his hair was kinked, and the devil knows what all—it's so unnatural and puerile that a child would blush at his follies."

At the conclusion of such criticisms he was generally greeted with a burst of hearty laughter from his fellow-collegians. He took it all good-humoredly, but still could not be convinced by any process of reasoning that there was beauty in poetry. Walter had never experienced an emotion of sublimity in his life. A landscape was beautiful to him only as it could be converted into a farm. The croaking of a frog was as fine music to him as the intonations of a mocking-bird, or any air that ever trilled on harp, flute, violin, or guitar. And yet, notwithstanding all this, Walter possessed a poetical power, of which he himself was unaware, or if he was he seemed to undervalue it. This power showed itself sometimes in his language, when Walter appeared not to know it.

The reader need not suppose, from what we have said, that Walter Hallam is a black-hearted villain of the first cast. In the annals of fiction especially it is too much the case that the characters are all either semi-angels, beautified and adorned with superhuman virtues and graces, or John Murrells, doubly steeped in vice, crime, and villainy. Whether Walter was a natural villain, we will leave the reader to conclude. We deem it sufficient merely to say that upon first acquaintance he would be pronounced a plain, blunt man, with good, ordinary sense, who placed a value upon things and principles in accordance with their adaptation to the practical purposes of life; and such was his external character at the commencement of this story. If he should grow worse than he is here described, it may probably be attributed to the fault of surrounding circumstances, rather than his own nature.

Young Hallam received his degree in a Kentucky college at the age of twenty-three, in the year eighteen hundred and sixty; and before commencing the battle of life in earnest, and, besides, his father desiring him to attend to some business in the town of ——, he was paying a visit to Major Burrell, his father's cousin. This relationship was sufficient, as William Jones insinuated, to cover the object of his visit (if indeed, he had any other object at first than that of a friendly, social visit) under the guise of family connection. It is certain, though, that Walter had availed himself of this circumstance so far as to have remained about two weeks under his cousin's hospitable roof. Emily had received and welcomed him with sisterly affection. She had treated him with the politeness and familiarity due to a relative. It is strange, though, that in this land of enlightened liberty, where society is characterized by so many agreeable features, the "fair sex" is sometimes subjected to the mortification of having any extension of warm friendship construed into a feeling which was by no means intended. This is the case to such an extent that when a lady, especially a young lady, entertains the company with a ballad containing any sentiment bordering upon love, each young "lord" in the room will probably regard it as peculiarly applicable to himself. It is not surprising, therefore, if Walter, being a good-looking, rather handsome young man, should begin to consider his cousin's little attentions as prompted by feelings warmer than those justified by the ties of consanguinity. Still less will it be surprising, that Emily being a really beautiful and accomplished girl, attached to a splendid inheritance, he should honor her with a due reciprocity of emotion. His affection, however, was not of that wild, ardent, fiery kind that makes the lover sometimes fall on his knees before his adored one, and vehemently say:

"Doubt thou the stars are fire,
Doubt that the sun doth move,

Doubt truth to be a liar,
But never doubt I love!"

Walter's love was strictly in keeping with his character; that is, it was of the practical kind. Whether Emily's worldly prospects contributed any thing to the agitation of his tender feelings, we will leave the reader to judge. The following soliloquy of Walter's will show in what channel his thoughts were flowing:

"My cousin Emily is a right pretty girl—rather bookish, though, and inclined to be visionary. She will, nevertheless, with proper training, make a very good wife; and I flatter myself that she *likes* me hugely, if nothing more. As for love—this puppyism of modern times—she can indulge in to her heart's content. As for myself, I shall love with calmness, moderation, and judiciousness, contemning as I do the silly ways of petty coxcombry. Love—this spiritual essence, this imaginary passion, which exists only in the brain of moonstruck poets—is one of the grand humbugs fit only for women. Love or no love, a fortune of five hundred thousand and upward does not fall into one's hands every day of the year. It is certainly worth an effort. Probably Emily will inherit the old homestead with all its appurtenances; if so, all parties consenting, I see no good reason why a marriage can not be brought about, and I and my pretty cousin settle down at once in our young days, live happily together through life, and die peacefully in a good old age, as our ancestors have done. By the gods! I will try the experiment."

This was a pleasing picture to Walter; and he was no builder of air-castles. Having once resolved to secure his cousin and her fortune to himself, he furthermore formed the doughty resolution to broach the subject to Emily on the first opportunity. Having transacted the business which had brought him to the town of ——, and protracted his stay much longer than was his original intention, he deemed it high time to put in practice a portion of his brave resolves. We will, however, do Emily the justice to say that she was totally unconscious and unsuspicious of the intended honor, and of her cousin's premeditated attack on her single-blessedness. The opportunity which Walter desired soon presented itself.

One bright, lovely evening, in the early days of the fall of eighteen hundred and sixty, Walter and Emily were mounted on two spirited chargers, and riding down the avenue that led to the road. Turning down the river, the two rode slowly and in silence. Emily was gazing around, lost in admiration at the transcendentally lovely scene that lay spread out in every direction, and had wandered far in thought from her present company. Walter seemed not disposed to interrupt her in this pleasing employment, busied as he doubtless was with his schemes of temporal prosperity, which might have appeared to some as the vagaries of a wild dream, but to him as eminently feasible, and deduced from the calm conclusions of a practical judgment. Emily, presently recollecting herself, turned to her companion, and spoke with her usual gayety and cheerfulness of disposition:

"What are you thinking of, cousin Walter?"

"It would be difficult to tell exactly what," Walter replied, slowly. "Nothing, though, of any great importance at the instant you spoke."

"Probably you were thinking, like I was, of the scene before you—of the river, the hills, the trees, the birds, the flowers, and a thousand other things that furnish a view worthy the painter's pencil and the poet's pen."

"No, no; I assure you I was thinking of none of these things. Your painter's pencil and your poet's pen have no charms for me, except as the one executes a substantial signboard, and the other writes a good, business-like hand. Painters, poets, and all other characters of that description, I look upon as the mere butterflies of life—perfect drones in the great bee-hive of society—men who attempt to avoid honest labor, and gain a livelihood by palming off their foolish written trumpery on their fellow-creatures."

"Why, cousin Walter, I am utterly astonished at you! You are surely jesting. Do you never read the poets?"

"Yes, sometimes I do, but mainly to see with what jingling gimcracks mankind can be pleased."

"How do you like Milton? You certainly must have been highly entertained with 'Paradise Lost.'"

"Milton was a poor, blind old man, in dotage, who gathered up the superstitions and idle tales that pass current among negroes and children, and culled an absurd story from this heathen nation and that barbarous people, and then fashioned it into one methodical mass, and threw it on the world as the greatest work of ancient or modern times. I never could see any sense or beauty in 'Paradise Lost.' There is something about it too untangible. It is too much like the dreams of a sick man or the strange whims of a lunatic. If the imaginings of a child were clothed in the language of poetry, you would see as good a poem as can be found in the ridiculous nonsense of Milton."

Walter was in earnest in what he was saying, and Emily was very much surprised, as well as amused, at this, the severest stricture she had ever heard upon the prince of English poets.

"What do you say to Byron?" asked Emily, with a quizzical expression.

"Byron! Byron—that dandified upstart, who swore like a trooper when the whiteness of his hands was soiled. Why, cousin, what could you, or I, or any body else think of a man who has pandered to the worst passions and appetites of human nature as he has? What could I think of a man who would, either for the means of subsistence or for the sake of notoriety, expose the depravity of his own heart to the gaze of the world, and then laugh at the sensation the exhibition created? What could I think of a man who has turned loose upon the world a stream of corruption that has tinged the sentiments of the youth of our land with low vulgarisms that a pure-minded being would blush to utter in respectable society? I will agree that there are some flights of fancy in Byron that seem to be pleasing to certain minds, but it is like wading through a sea of molten lava to gather a perishing flower."

"Well, I declare, cousin Walter, you are really eloquent in censure; and you talk like a preacher. I love to listen to your elegant criticisms, even when you rail at my favorite authors."

"I should be sorry to think, Emily, that Byron is your favorite. If he is," continued Walter, with plain bluntness, "I would at least exclude that infamous character, Don Juan. But as I am not remarkably fond of eloquence, music, poetry, and the like, and as I am no preacher, and do not wish to put you out of humor, I will no longer meddle with your favorites."

"Cousin Walter," said Emily, recovering from a momentary confusion, "do you recollect that oft-quoted sentiment of Shakespeare—

> 'The man that hath no music in himself,
> And is not moved with concord of sweet sound,
> Is fit for treason, stratagems, and spoils.'"

"Why, yes, I recollect the substance of it. But what of that?"

"Well, I am afraid," said Emily, laughing gaily, "as Nathan said unto David, 'Thou art the man.'"

"Now, my beautiful cous, you are becoming rather personal," said Walter, not over-well pleased with this application.

"My dear cousin, I meant no offense; I only said it as a pleasantry. I will take it all back, and beg your pardon. But now, tell me, do n't you really think this is beautiful:

> 'Eternal Hope! when yonder spheres sublime
> Pealed their first notes to sound the march of time,
> Thy joyous youth began; but not to fade
> When all thy sister planets had decayed.
> Where, wrapt in fire, the realms of ether glow,
> And heaven's last thunder shakes the world below,
> Thou, undismayed, shalt o'er the ruins smile,
> And light thy torch at Nature's funeral pile.'

What do you think of that, cousin Walter?"

"It sounds to me just so," said Walter: "smile, pile, mile, file, quile, tile, style, vile—jingle, rattle—about as musical as the bell on yonder cow, that knows not a syllable of poetry."

"Well, now, cousin Walter," she continued, more for amusement than any thing else, "did you never walk by moonlight, gaze up at the blue, arched vault of heaven, and feel in your soul some such sentiment as this:

> 'The sky
> Spreads like an ocean hung on high,
> Bespangled with those isles of light
> So wildly, spiritually bright!
> Who ever gazed upon them shining
> And turned to earth without repining?
> Nor wished for wings to flee away
> And mix with their eternal ray?'"

"I would much rather mix with my fellow-creatures, cousin Emily, and employ the means of locomotion intended for man by nature. I imagine stars would be rather dull companions, to say nothing of the unsubstantial food furnished by their rays."

"Walter Hallam!" said Emily, with a mischievous smile, "you are the most incorrigible Diogenes I have ever met with. *Odi profanum vulgus et arceo*," she continued, tossing her head in mock disdain. "I presume you have read Horace?"

"Why, certainly; every school boy has read 'Old Falernian Wine.'"

"Well, Walter, I believe I will give you over to hardness of heart and reprobacy of mind."

"Now don't do that, my dear cousin, for I am now going to convince you I am not hard-hearted, though I can not repeat a line from Shakespeare, Milton, and your other favorites;" and he hesitated as if studying how to commence.

Emily was totally unsuspicious of Walter's intentions, so she said, with smiling good humor:

"Well, proceed, Walter; I shall be happy to listen to any arguments that shall convince me you are not lost to all sensibility."

"Will you allow me to preface in the shape of a question?"

"*Certainement, avec plaisir, qu'est ce? Donnez moi encore la langue Francais, s' il vous plait.*"

"*Je Francais meprise,*" said Walter, who was not much of a French scholar. "Let us speak in English."

"*Comme il vous plaira.* Proceed."

"Well, then, do you ever think of any thing but birds, flowers, trees, stars, moonshine, poetry, and the like?"

"Of course I do."

"Did you ever—but I will come to the point at once—do you ever bestow a thought upon the subject of matrimony?"

"I can not say," said Emily, supposing Walter was talking in a sportive way, "that that has ever been much the subject of my meditations. It is a plain topic, easily comprehended, I imagine, and one upon which I will have ample time to reflect. I am only eighteen yet."

"I am aware, cousin Emily, that you are young yet. But I ask you, would it not be wise to devote a little time to reflection upon a theme which might, in time to come, force itself somewhat painfully upon your mind? By postponing it now you may hereafter be necessitated by the mere force of circumstances to enter upon married life as a relief from your own troubles and sorrows. Your father, you know, is now fast becoming old, and must, in the ordinary course of nature, soon leave you without a protector. I say without a protector, for your brother is your senior but by a few years, and, like the majority of young men, will in all probability be disposed to ramble over the world, leaving you solitary and alone in your desolation. And I imagine the pleasure of being an old maid will scarcely compensate for the care and trouble absolutely inseparable from such a condition. To live alone in the world; to struggle alone among the giddy throng, where all is strife and confusion; to buffet alone the waves that rise on the sea of life—such a lifetime, I imagine, cousin Emily, will furnish but few reminiscences upon which memory can dwell with pleasure."

"Why, cousin Walter, you do talk so like a gray-headed philosopher; you make me really sad; and in anticipation of being an old maid," she continued, in a spirit of playfulness, "I feel like repeating—

> 'Alas for my weary and care-haunted bosom!
> The spells of the spring-time arouse it no more;
> The song in the wildwood, the sheen in the blossom,
> The fresh-swelling fountain—their magic is o'er!
> When I list to the streams, when I look on the flowers,
> They tell of the past with so mournful a tone,
> That I call up the throng of my long-vanished hours,
> And sigh that their transports are over and gone!'

It would have been such a beautiful conclusion to your harangue, cousin Walter."

"Harangue, the devil!" said Walter, in a tone of some vexation, and not noticing the uncouth expression which had escaped him. "I wonder, Emily, how you can call plain, common conversation a harangue!"

"I beg a thousand pardons," exclaimed Emily, quickly,

"I did not intend to wound your feelings. I humbly crave your forgiveness."

"I can easily forgive, if you will not quote any more poetic gibberish. It is just as easy, and much more pleasant, I am sure, to converse in plain unadulterated English."

"I think, my good kinsman, you are much more of a poet and an orator than you are aware of. The very images you occasionally throw out show that you are not altogether destitute of the 'faculty sublime.' Take, for instance, 'the waves that rise on the sea of life:' it is indeed a poetical idea, in proper meter too, and would go with boiling, raging, tumultuous with strife. Now there is poetry, one line of which you composed yourself. Don't you see plainly you *are* a poet?"

"I am neither poet nor orator, and if you can manufacture poetry out of my plain, blunt English, all I have to say is, much good may it do you. I do not know that I feel particularly complimented in being compared to poets, all of whom I look upon as mere ciphers in human society. I would much rather be called a good brick-mason."

"I am so sorry, cousin Walter, you have such an aversion to *vis poetica*. I thought, when you first came, we would have many a mental stroll into those lofty regions, where, it is said, one 'soared untrodden heights, and seemed at home where angels bashful looked;' but I am disappointed."

"Never mind that now; I would be obliged if you would postpone this pleasurable poetical employment until some more fitting time. Come now, be serious for a short time, and listen to me."

"I can be serious enough, Walter, if you wish it; but I should like to know for what reason."

"For a very obvious reason, my dear cousin. Do you know I love you?"

"Why, I hope so, cousin Walter. I love you," said she, looking at him rather doubtfully.

"That is the way to talk—right to the point. I thought I was not mistaken; and now, both being of one mind, when shall we consummate our happiness by a speedy marriage?"

"O, cousin Walter!" she now quickly cried, comprehending it all, "I—I did not mean that; you have utterly misconstrued my language. O, I did not mean that!"

"Mean what? Did you not say you loved me?"

"Why, yes, certainly: as a sister should love a brother—as one relative should love another. That was my meaning."

"That is meaning enough, my dear Emily. If you love me as such, you can love me as a husband distantly related; that is all I will ask. I shall not require you to make me an idol. I am no believer in puppy worship."

"O, cousin Walter!" said she, in surprise, embarrassment, and confusion, "do you, can you mean what you are saying? Is it possible you are in earnest?"

"I was never more so in my life, dear Emily. And why should I not be? I see nothing at all inconsistent or improper in our union. We are both young, and we can settle down quietly in our youthful days; live like rational beings, contented and happy, and loving each other, as you will have it, as relatives, if nothing more. Is it not a pleasing picture, and can you not enjoy life with me, who am sober, steady, and honest, as well as with any of the contemptible gewgaws, I will call them—town dandies—that bow, and cringe, and whine around you, with a servility as despicable as it is deceitful."

"Why, we are cousins, Walter, and I have an utter abhorrence of family marriages. Besides, you would not marry a person who does not love you, and whom you could not love?"

"I would not marry one, Emily, whom I could not respect and esteem. If you mean that sickly, sentimental stuff, which the morbid sensibility of a puny-minded novelist would call love, that represents sensible men and women as fondling puppies and kittens, I fear I have none of it; if, however, by love you mean admiration of a sensible man or lady, lasting regard and profound respect for their excellent principles and qualities of mind and heart, I profess to have a due share of it; and I here bestow it all on my fair and lovely cousin."

Emily was now silent in painful embarrassment. It was utterly impossible for one of her ardent nature to love such a cold, passionless, insensible creature as her cousin Walter Hallam appeared to be. And it was so palpable that his love, if he could be said to be inspired with any portion of that sacred feeling, was so entirely secular in its character that she shuddered at the bare thought of such an unholy union. He was her relative, however, and she must spare him, and extricate herself from this unpleasant dilemma with as little pain as possible to his feelings. She was revolving in her mind the most judicious way to do this, when Walter asked:

"And what says my dear Emily to this proposal?"

"I fear, cousin Walter, we could never agree."

"And why not, my fair one?"

"Why, the conversation we have had this evening shows very plainly there is no congeniality of taste and feeling between us."

"How do you make that out, Emily?"

"Well, then, to illustrate," said she, playfully, "I will suppose a case. Suppose we were united, as you desire, and commence to 'settle down,' as you call it. *Imprimis*, we would build a nice little cottage in some pleasant spot. Then may be I would say, 'My dear Walter, here is a spot so nice for a flower garden; let us have one.' Your reply would very likely be, 'No, no; I intend this for an Irish potato patch, or a turnip patch.' Of course I should feel considerable disappointment, and be inclined to pout. I would want our yard decorated with shrubs and flowers; you would want it planted in water-melons. I would want a nice little library, where you would desire a wardrobe, or may be a cupboard. You would have a fence where I would wish white palings. I would ramble by moonlight, and you would walk in sunshine. I would be gazing at the stars, while you would probably be nodding. You would want your buttons sewed on, while I would be reading the poets. I would want to sing, with my guitar, while you may be would desire to call the hogs. I would be engaged with my painting, when you would want me to milk the cows. O, cousin Walter, don't you see we never could agree?"

"Certainly not, if yours is a true picture."

"It may be somewhat exaggerated and overdrawn, but in the main it is correct—quite correct."

"I should be sorry to think so, Emily. You may depend upon it I shall not attempt to deprive you of a single pleasure you may desire. You can have as many flower gardens as is agreeable to you. You can sing, play, and read as much as you please without fear of disturbance from me. You must not take me to be a perfect old curmudgeon. I am not as indifferent as you seem disposed to believe to amusements—rational amusements. I like singing, playing, reading, and the like well enough—all in their proper places and at the proper time. But I can see no good sense in devoting one's whole life to abstractions. What good can possibly result from always gazing at the stars and forever reading poetry? And why should life be spent in the pursuit of such useless follies, when so much can be done for the good of our fellow-creatures? I imagine it is not my duty to be forever poring over the extravagances of Milton, or any other poet, when I might cause the wilderness to blossom and bring forth good fruit, and thus contribute to the relief of suffering man. Why can you not take this view of the subject?"

"I own there is some good sense in what you are saying, cousin Walter; but then you are too much of a philosopher, too practical, too matter-of-fact for one of my disposition. I

must have some one to love—some one to *worship* and *adore*
Men may do very well without this folly, as you think it, but

> 'Alas, the love of woman! it is known
> To be a lovely and a fearful thing;
> For all of theirs upon that die is thrown,
> And if 't is lost, life hath no more to bring
> To them but mockeries of the past alone.'"

"I would be much obliged to you, Emily, if you would talk to me in prose. I can understand it better than poetry."

"Now that goes to illustrate further what I have said," replied Emily. "For I should sometimes—very frequently, perhaps—repeat poetry; and if now you chide me, or even signify your displeasure, you would, when married, give me a positive scolding for every offense of that kind. O, we never could agree, cousin Walter—we never could agree."

"I am not so certain of that, Emily, as you seem to be. I think we could agree, at least, as well as other people do. We are not to expect perfect happiness. I do not, and I presume you do not, expect to find a paradise on this earth. We could live happily, contentedly, and agreeably together, and that is about as much as one need calculate on in this life."

"You probably might live happily, cousin Walter, but I could not. O, when I marry, if I must marry, my husband must be idolized in my heart. He must be next to the *Creator* in my affections. He must be one whom I can lean upon in perfect, trusting confidence—one who can feel some sympathy with the wild emotions that struggle in my breast for utterance—one into whose listening ear I can pour the tale of my little, womanish sufferings, trials, cares, and anxieties, without the fear of meeting a stern rebuke or reproof."

"Probably you already have such a one in your mind?"

"No, Walter, I will be candid with you; I have not. In fact I have rarely ever thought of this subject, at least in a serious way. But I do assure you I will never surrender my hand and heart to any, unless it be to such a one as I have feebly and briefly described. I can imagine no worse fate to poor woman than to be linked, in the closest intimacy, with a person whose presence she can tolerate only for the sake of his solid and manly virtues. He should be the light of her existence—a part of herself, whose absence would be like the deprivation of one of her limbs. But I have said more on this subject than I intended. Come, let us change it; for it is any thing but a pleasant topic to me. I would much rather talk of Milton, Shakespeare, Byron, or some literary subject."

"I will not insist on your answer now, Emily. But I hope you will reflect seriously upon my proposal, and give me a favorable reply. I do not utterly despair from what you have said. I know women are strange beings, and often mean the very reverse of what they say."

"And I know," replied Emily, "that men are often very presumptuous and bigoted; and sometimes, under an appearance of candor, conceal the worst form of hypocrisy and deceit."

"That may be so; but we will not quarrel about the virtues and vices of the two sexes. Think about what I have proposed, and give me an answer as soon as you have decided."

"I can tell you now what that answer will be."

"I would rather not hear it now, because you have not weighed the subject with the care and attention it merits."

Emily made no reply. She thought her cousin was very dull of comprehension, or very obstinate not to have discovered her resolution and her meaning at once. But she had too much respect for her practical relative to wound his feelings unnecessarily; and she now determined to wait, and devise some lenient means to persuade him to desist from his purpose. She thought he was a strange being, and practiced a kind of strange courtship, but Emily was too kind-hearted to obey, at this stage of proceedings, the Scriptural advice of Solomon—"Answer a fool according to his folly."

After a brisk ride they had now reached the house. That night Emily reflected seriously upon some circumstances which Walter had said might, nay, must ere long occur, and her dreams were troubled. She saw her aged father lying upon his death-bed, and Walter Hallam standing near by, imploring the old man to make his will. The will was made. Hallam was handing to Major Burrell a pen to sign the instrument, when a stranger abruptly entered, snatched up the paper, and disappeared. The whole scene then faded away, but not until it had made an impression upon her mind which she did not soon forget. The impression was disagreeable in its character, and unfavorable to Walter. The next morning, therefore, when she arose, it was in vain she attempted to banish the thoughts which disturbed her mind, and assume her usual appearance of cheerfulness.

CHAPTER III.

"Along the woods, along the moorish fens,
Sighs the sad genius of the coming storm;
And up among the loose disjointed cliffs,
And fractur'd mountains wild, the brawling brook
And cave, presageful, send a hollow moan,
Resounding long in listening fancy's ear."

ABOUT ten o'clock the next day subsequent to that upon which Walter Hallam had made a proposal of marriage to his cousin, a solitary traveler might have been seen slowly riding along the road that ran in front of Major Burrell's residence. The horseman was distant nearly two miles from the house; and halting upon an eminence that commanded a view of the country for a great distance in all directions, he gazed around in speechless admiration at the splendid scenery. There stood the tall, white dwelling, looming high amid the grand old oaks, which had escaped the woodman's ax, and withstood the storms of centuries. The gentle breeze, creeping from leaf to leaf, had sighed among their venerable branches, that bore marks of past resistance to the rude attacks of time. But now not even a light zephyr caused the green leaves to rustle. There was the clear river rolling slowly on in mournful silence, as if its pellucid waters were reluctant to leave a scene so calm and bright, and mix with the turbulent surf of the sea. There were the beautiful hills rising, one after another, in seemingly studied regularity, marshaled in the order of a solid phalanx as if for sturdy combat, stretching out far in the distance, till the eye beheld a blue streak linked with the horizon; then crossing the river, and forming a complete circle, and thus enclosing as lovely a scene as could be found under the wide canopy of heaven. A bright sun looked down from fairer than far-famed Italy's smiling skies, pouring forth his fructifying rays, enlivening and cheering nature, throughout all her various ramifications. It was one of those calm, quiet, mysterious hours, when scarcely a sound disturbs the dead, solemn silence. All nature was hushed. Not even a bird, with its shrill carols, agitated the awe-imposing stillness. It seemed as if creation were buried in profound slumber.

A close observer would have discovered in all this and in other signs the unmistakable precursor of a sudden change in the weather; but the horseman heeded them not. He still paused, and seemed apparently lost in thought, and unobservant of a small black cloud that was now beginning to rise slowly and darkly above the horizon. A weather-spy would merely have glanced at these silent indications of an approaching hurricane, and then, proving his faith by his works, would have rapidly betaken himself to some place of shelter and safety. But the horseman was not weather-wise; or, if he was, he manifested indifference in regard to the matter, and sat on his horse, unconscious, in appearance, of natural events transpiring in the physical world, while his faithful steed was leisurely cropping the tender grass that grew by the roadside. He gave loose reins both to the animal and to his thoughts. If our readers should feel any curiosity to know the nature of the reflections in which the traveler was absorbed, he can read as follows:

"O, who can look upon such a scene and not say, in his heart, 'In wisdom hast thou made them all?' Who can comprehend the purposes of the Eternal Mind, that called this vast universe into being? Why are so many beauties scattered throughout the earth? Why do the wild flowers bloom in the uninhabited wilderness? Why does the landscape spread out in peerless splendor? Why do the hills and mountains rise in unequaled majesty? Why does the blue sky stretch out its vast covering, bedecked at night with myriads of glittering gems? Why does yon glorious orb of light pursue, with faithful regularity, his trackless course through space—bring joy to the heart of suffering mortality? Have all these objects been created for man—poor, puny man? Indeed, 'what is man, that thou takest knowledge of him, or the Son of man, that thou takest account of him?' Can it be possible that this vast universe was shaped for the pleasure of such a weak-minded being? He passes through the earth unmindful of the numberless grand mysteries that crowd around him at every step. The volume of nature lies open before him, but he reads not a line. The earth exposes her millions of treasures to his gaze, but he passes on in sinful indifference, gathering up trifles that afford but a momentary pleasure to his body, and rarely bestowing a thought upon the eternal future, and his own destiny in relation thereto. Strange, incomprehensible being! how inconsistent are thy ways, considered in reference to thy eternal destiny!"

We have penned these disjointed reflections to demonstrate two facts: first, that the subject of this chapter was a young man, and second, that he was inclined to be *religieux*, as the French say—both of which facts we think the reader, if he be thoughtful, can deduce from the preceding thoughts.

The storm was coming on, but still the traveler changed not his position. Cloud after cloud had now arisen in murky and ominous gloom, until a quarter of the heavens presented a threatening aspect. They rolled up, mixing and mingling, as if combining their force and uniting their strength for a frightful attack on the earth below. A low, muttering, heavy sound could now be heard murmuring feebly in the distance, and a light gale rustled for a moment among the trees, and then died away. The reader need not suppose our traveler was afflicted with deafness, because he heard not these slight sounds. Whether he was or not, he continued to pursue pretty much the same train of reflection:

"I wonder how man, with his mighty powers of intellect, could ever have worshiped senseless, graven images! It seems, though, that the human mind naturally clings to the idea of a divinity—naturally forms the conclusion, from a sense of its own dependence, that homage and gratitude are due to some intelligence of a higher order than itself. Even inanimate idols, fashioned and shaped by man's hand, are supposed to possess virtues and powers which divine truth teaches can be attributed only to God. Nevertheless, heathen mythology, with a god or goddess representing every virtue, vice, and passion, notwithstanding some of its palpable absurdities, is a beautiful system. Jupiter with his thunderbolt—Neptune with his trident—Vulcan with his forge—Juno, the proud queen of the skies—Venus, the beauty—Diana, the embodiment of chastity—are all beautiful conceptions of the mind, which could not be bettered in the absence of eternal truth. Yet how utterly insignificant when compared with the present great system of Christianity, which, by the force of its own internal evidence, appealing to the heart and reason of man, has banished the superstitions and myths of ages! The idea of a Supreme Unity, combining all the elements of power, greatness, and grandeur, could never be deduced from any evidence of nature. It required a direct communication, a revelation traced by the finger of the One himself, to furnish man with the true history of his own existence. And the Bible with all its mysteries, its peremptory commandments, its inimitable parables, its striking metaphors, its glorious imagery, its"——

The thought was not completed; for at that moment a strong gust of wind burst upon the traveler in all its fury, and carried his hat a short distance up the road. Thus suddenly recalled to himself, he looked up in astonishment at the change which had taken place in so brief a space of time. The whole heaven was now black; the thunder roared terribly; the lightning flashed with blinding effect; and gust after gust howled madly on. The traveler hastily dismounted, leaving his steed unfastened, seized his hat, and had turned to remount, when a large dead oak fell with a deafening crash immediately behind him. A few of the scattering fragments struck the faithful horse, that now reared and plunged, and then, deserting his master, flew up the road, like a frightened deer, with the speed of the wind. The traveler seemed a little perplexed, but he thought of old Timon, and the idea appeared to amuse him to such an extent that he suddenly jerked off his hat, and exclaimed aloud:

"'Blow wind, and crack your cheeks! rage! blow!
You cataracts, and hurricanoes, spout
Till you have drench'd our steeples, drown'd the cocks!
You sulphurous and thought-executing fires,
Vaunt couriers to oak-cleaving thunderbolts,
Singe my *black* head! And thou, all-shaking thunder,
Strike flat the thick rotundity o' the world!
Crack nature's moulds, all germens spill at once,
That make ingrateful man!'"

The *quondam* horseman, now become a pedestrian, then clapped his hat on his head, and made rapid strides in the direction which his horse had taken.

The storm soon began to rage with perfect fury. The heavens became intensely black; the forked lightnings, in zigzag form, flashed athwart the dark clouds, and was then followed by thunder so loud, harsh, and terrific, it seemed as if the very foundations of nature were tearing up in convulsions, and that the artillery of heaven, doubly charged, was playing on a doomed world. The Æolian cavern had been opened, and the winds, laboring under no restraint, came raging, tearing, and howling on, sweeping down sturdy trees in their mad career, bearing on birds which had been rudely disturbed in their lofty retreats, and whose wild, piercing notes could be distinctly heard above the din and confusion of the storm. The attack had begun in earnest. It was a fearful manifestation of heaven's power. O, who has not in such an hour felt a sense of his own insignificance and utter dependence, and his own inability to exist, for even a single moment, without aid from on high? Who has not felt in his heart, amid the wild commotion of such a storm, that "God reigneth?" The scoffing skeptic, amid the howl of the hurricane, methinks, would offer up a silent prayer, and promise himself, if spared, to show more reverence in future to Him "who plants his footstep on the sea, and rides upon the storm."

Some such thought as this was in the mind of the traveler, who now, after the lapse of twenty-five minutes, had nearly reached the foot of the long avenue that led to Major Burrell's residence. He continued to walk rapidly on. But now a few big drops began to descend, and in a moment afterward the rain poured down in liquid torrents. The traveler, whose aim was to reach the dwelling before him, was forced to take shelter under the boughs of a broad-spreading oak that stood hard by the road-side. He had scarcely taken a position that afforded some protection against the drenching rain, when a blinding streak momentarily relieved the partial darkness, gleamed for an instant among the clouds, but halted not. Its mission was not there. Cutting through the air like a merciless missile of death, it bolted straight as an arrow to the tree that sheltered the weary footman. Striking near the top, it burst the tough old oak to the roots. A sharp, keen, appalling crash followed in its wake, and the poor traveler lay stretched out as a dead man. It was fortunate for him, however, that the noble tree, notwithstanding the severe treatment it had received, yet stood in shattered splendor and injured majesty. Otherwise his own mother might not have recognized the mutilated form of her son. With something like pitying kindness it still held out its overhanging branches above the head of the senseless man; and the big drops that dripped from its boughs on the poor prostrate child of earth seemed like tears for the fate of a stranger, whose life it had interposed its own huge body to save.

The storm raged and the rain continued to pour down in unabated fury; but at the expiration of one hour, however, it began to show evident signs of weariness. Its malice was gratified; the wind was hushed; the rain slackened by degrees, and then entirely ceased. Only an occasional distant growl of the thunder could be heard rumbling amid the clouds, which began to break and disunite, and then to sail rapidly away, like the discomfited forces of a flying army. The sun—grand source of light—soon shone out clear and brilliant from a smiling sky. The birds came forth, rejoicing in their glad songs that the contest was over. Nothing now remained to indicate the visit of the storm, except the drops glittering like gems in the sunshine, which fell lazily from the boughs; and the trees, which, lying here and there, had yielded to the fury of the stubborn attack, and lay like the dead left on a gory field of carnage; and the remains of a disappearing rainbow which had expanded across the dome of the world—God's own immutable promise to man, written in the skies, that no more shall the earth be submerged amid the deluge of waters.

Our poor traveler still lay at the foot of the tree perfectly motionless and unconscious. He had fallen on his back at full length. His hat, which had been knocked off by the terrible concussion, had been blown into the middle of the road. The right arm lay across the fallen man's breast—the hand on his heart; the other was clutching in a death-like grasp a low bush that grew at his side. The eyes were closed, and his pale, colorless face was upturned to the bright blue sky. His white teeth could be seen through his bloodless lips that were but partially closed. If he breathed at all, it could not be perceived. Reader, we have only to conclude this chapter with—

"God moves in a mysterious way
His wonders to perform."

CHAPTER IV.

"———Death should come
Gently to one of gentle mould like thee,
As light winds, wandering through groves of bloom,
Detach the delicate blossoms from the tree;
Close thy sweet eyes calmly and without pain,
And we will trust in God to see thee yet again."

It was one o'clock. Major Burrell, Walter, and Emily sat down to a sumptuous repast, which was dispatched in silence on the part of the two younger persons. The Major, however, rattled away, with the usual garrulity of age. Hallam seemed disposed to listen, and Emily was making fruitless attempts to banish the disagreeable dream which she had had in reference to her cousin.

"I should like to know," said the Major, "whose horse that was which I had put up in the stable—a most noble and well-formed animal. I am fearful some traveler has been caught in the storm, and thrown from his horse. The animal reminds me of one which I once owned, when a young man like you, Walter. He was a large, coal-black, well-built horse, and powerfully muscled. I have n't seen such an animal in many a day. He had a bow neck, a large fiery eye, and wide expanding nostrils. Well, I lost him in just such a storm as we've had. I recollect it as well as if it had happened but yesterday; it was the 24th day of April—my birth-day, by the way—and I was twenty-two years of age. I had started out that morning—it was bright and gay—to see a little girl who lived not far from here. All boys, you know, Walter, have sweethearts, and so I had one. Well, I was riding along the road in a nice little lope, when I was suddenly overtaken by a storm. How the wind did blow! I spurred my noble horse to his full speed. He went flying along like lightning, when a dead tree, standing by the road, fell right across my poor horse's neck. On I went, and was thrown about thirty feet from my fallen charger. The faithful creature was instantly killed, and I was considerably bruised. I could not help shedding tears for the fate of that horse; and I had him decently buried."

In much the same strain the Major rattled on till the meal was finished. Then Emily retired to her own room, reflecting how she should rid herself of her cousin's addresses without inflicting pain to his feelings. It seemed to her that he considered their ultimate marriage as a sort of a settled thing, when such an idea was quite remote from her thoughts, and was any thing but agreeable. He went about his courtship in so cold a manner—so much like it was a mere civil contract of partnership, in which feeling and affection were to be ignored—that she shuddered with holy horror at the prospect of such a worldly alliance. Then his feelings and his tastes were so utterly incompatible with her own. He appeared not to relish a single thing that could furnish pleasure to one of her sensitive mind. The more she reflected, the more determined she was to tell him plainly and flatly and positively, in such a manner that her meaning could not be mistaken, that his attentions in that way were quite disagreeable and unpleasant; and that the sooner they were terminated the better it would be for all the parties concerned; that they never could be any thing to each other more than cousins: lovers—never, never.

About three o'clock Emily was aroused by a gentle rap on her door. Arising and opening it, she, in some embarrassment, beheld her cousin Walter. She could not but think of the old saying, "Speak of the devil and he'll appear;" for she was and had been thinking of her unceremonious kinsman.

"I thought, cousin Emily," said he, "you would like to ride this evening; so I have had the horses saddled, and have come to let you know they are ready. I presume you wish to ride?"

She readily assented, thinking this would be a favorable opportunity to carry into effect her resolution if the subject of marriage should be adverted to. Hastily donning her riding-habit, she announced herself ready; and the two were soon seen pacing down the avenue. Nothing was spoken till they had reached the road, when Emily said:

"There has been a dreadful storm, cousin Walter. Look at the trees lying around in every direction. I was so busily engaged when it came on that I had no idea such a havoc was taking place."

But Walter made no reply to this remark. He was looking intently at a dark object in the road, to which he called Emily's attention.

"It is a hat," said Walter, dismounting as soon as he had reached it. "Some traveler has lost it in the storm. I expect some accident has happened. I will warrant this belongs to the owner of the horse that is now secure at the house."

"O, heavens! Look, cousin Walter, look!" exclaimed Emily, pale with sudden fright, and pointing to the prostrate form of our still unconscious traveler. Walter hastened to the fallen man and examined his pulse.

"Quick, Emily, quick! he may be saved if treated properly. Run to the house and send help."

Emily, with the instincts of true benevolence all alive, turned and almost flew to the house. In a few hurried words she explained to her father what had happened. The old man summoned three or four domestics, and then went rapidly to the relief of the sufferer. He soon reached the spot to which he had been directed, and found Walter busily endeavoring to restore the poor man to life.

"Does he still live, Walter?" asked the Major, approaching.

"Life is nearly extinct, sir; but he may be saved."

"My God!" exclaimed the old man, when he surveyed the fine form before him; "what a pity! He must be saved, if possible. Here, Dick, build a litter; and you, Walter, mount and run for Dr. Johnson."

"You forget, Major, that I never saw Dr. Johnson in my life, and have no idea of his locality."

"That's a fact, boy, to be sure. Jim, mount that horse and fly for Dr. Johnson! Quick — like the very devil was after you! Do you hear, boy?"

"Yes, sar;" and the black thus addressed jumped on the animal, and, taking his master at his word, went dashing and splashing, indeed, as if his Satanic Majesty were in full pursuit, with a whole legion of sooty followers. The rude litter was soon constructed, and the youth, more dead than alive, was gently placed thereon, and then borne with as much rapidity as his condition and the circumstances would allow. Arriving at the house, the body was deposited on a clean, soft bed, and such restoratives as the medical experience of Major Burrell, which was rather limited, suggested were immediately applied. The young man, however, lay still, and exhibited no signs of returning consciousness. The Major walked the floor uneasily; now going to the door to see if the physician were coming, and then returning to the bedside of the unfortunate traveler. Two hours had now elapsed. The Major had completely exhausted his store of medical knowledge, and still Dr. Johnson had not arrived. Major Burrell, for the fiftieth time, felt the pulse of his patient.

"So help me God, Walter, the young man is dead!" exclaimed Major Burrell, in a tone of the greatest excitement.

Walter, who had been sitting silent all this time, hastily moved to the bedside. He felt the pulse, and then the heart.

Both were apparently still; and the hands, feet, and, in fact, whole body were cold.

"You are correct, sir; he is indeed dead."

Both now examined more carefully, but not a sign of life could be detected. They were satisfied he was no more.

"What a pity that one so young and handsome should die, unknown and unrecognized! But search the pockets, Walter; probably something may be found, by means of which he can be identified. His friends should know, if possible, his untimely fate."

Walter did as he was requested, and, feeling in the vest pockets, drew forth a small miniature and a letter. It was in a plain, round, and to him strikingly familiar hand. He read the direction aloud to the Major—"Mr. Henry S. Winston, State University, Oxford, Mississippi."

"I do declare," exclaimed Major Burrell, "I believe it's the nephew of old General Winston! I heard him say, a few days ago, that he was looking for his nephew to visit him. Poor old man! how awfully will he be affected! But I must let him know it at once. If you will remain here, Walter, I will drop a line to the General." Then spreading a snow-white sheet over the corpse, he left the apartment.

Walter sat down leisurely, and slowly opened the miniature. He started in amazement. No, he could not be mistaken; the features were plain and well-defined. He beheld too truly the picture of his own sister, who had been dead but a few weeks. He now tore open the letter, and recognized at once his sister's well-known handwriting. He perused hastily the contents, which were as follows:

"OAK GROVE, KY., August 16, 1859.

"MR. WINSTON: I can not call you dear Henry, as I formerly did. I do not know why I should write you this letter, unless it be to try to relieve my aching heart. O, how I have suffered! God only knows what I have felt. I have never breathed a single syllable of our unfortunate love to a living mortal. I have suffered all alone—alone! They treat me as if I were *mad*, Henry; and it may be I am. Sometimes I know I act very strangely, even to myself. O, Henry, how you would pity me if you could see me wandering all alone in the grove, and playing such mournful airs! O, how it makes me weep! Tears are such a blessed relief. Do you ever weep? I acknowledge I acted rashly, but it is too late to apologize now. I thought you were going to *deceive* me. O, I loved *you*—how deeply and truly! My heart was so true to you that it was *false* to itself and God! You know not how I loved you! But you frightened me so on that dreadful occasion. I can never be happy again in this world. Your image on my heart was the God I worshiped. I ought not to say this, Henry, but it matters not now. I am still true to you, though I should not confess it now. But, Henry, before this reaches you, I shall be in the cold grave. I am dying by inches. I feel it in my heart. I shall welcome death. I long to die, and join the sweet angels, whose songs I can hear sometimes ringing out so clear and beautiful. I want to be with them, Henry; and I know I shall soon be one of them. I will then watch over your pathway, and try to guide you on to the heavenly land! Can't you sometimes think of poor Carrie? Won't you remember her sometimes when you stroll by moonlight as we used to do? I can't write any more, Henry. This sheet is all stained and blotted with my tears; and my poor head swims so. Now, Henry, farewell *forever*. I bid you an eternal adieu. May God and his holy angels bless you; and may we meet in the bright world above.

"CARRIE HALLAM."

Walter deliberately refolded the document, and thrust it into his pocket.

"This, then," thought he, "accounts for the strange freaks of my poor, mad sister. Her letter bears the unmistakable marks of a deranged intellect. Poor thing! she died, within a few days after it was written, of a *broken heart*. She seems to have forgotten that this young man had left Oxford, for I see the letter was forwarded, on the 30th of the same month, to Holly Springs, Mississippi, his probable place of residence.

I always suspected that my sister's affections were strangely entangled; but, as she says, not a word escaped her as to the cause of her melancholy and her madness. And this man that now lies before me, cold and rigid, was the cause of her untimely death. It is probable the thunderbolt struck him down in the bloom and beauty of youth as a just retribution for the atrocity of his conduct. It may be after all the unfortunate man is not so much to blame as I believe. My sister, in her disconnected letter, does not directly charge him with faithlessness. There is, though, something mysterious about the whole affair, which I do not understand. What is meant by 'that dreadful occasion' I have not the slightest idea. My sister, however, was a delicately organized girl, and serious disappointment of any kind would have discomposed her intellect. I do not understand the matter; but there is no use in speculating concerning it. They are both dead now, and I hope have met where that happiness can be enjoyed which was denied on earth. Though I lay no claim to religion myself, I hope they are both in heaven."

He was here interrupted in his thoughts by the entrance of Major Burrell, who, seating himself and remarking that he had sent for General Winston, asked:

"Did the letter contain any thing of importance, Walter, or have you read it?"

"I have, sir. It contains nothing of the least interest to any body except the person to whom it was written and the friends of the writer."

Major Burrell was satisfied with this reply, and asked no other question. A profound silence now reigned throughout the chamber of death. Twilight was creeping slowly on, gradually chasing away the fast-fading remains of the departed day. The noises without—the lowing of the cattle, the noisy cackling of poultry seeking the roost, the loud, boisterous songs of the field hands returning home from their daily labor—all contrasted strangely with the deep stillness within.

The corpse had been carefully laid out on a wide plank, either end of which rested on a chair placed near the middle of the room. Not far from this sat Major Burrell and Walter Hallam, both seemingly buried in thought. Their meditations were doubtless of a serious character. However, all at once a loud, piercing scream was heard from the boughs of a stumpy oak that stood not more than thirty yards from the house. Major Burrell started.

"Confound the owl!" said he; "I never could endure them, Walter, since the death of my good mother. She died just about this hour in the evening. I remember it so distinctly. I was thinking of the unhappy circumstance when the shriek of that hateful bird brought the sad event more forcibly and painfully to my mind. The company that were sitting with my mother's corpse were seized with consternation at the wild, unearthly shriek of an owl that had alighted unseen in the window. It made my blood run cold. Since then the hoot of that bird has always appeared to me to forbode evil."

Walter was about to make a remark in reply, but at that moment a venerable old man, with long, gray hair, abruptly entered the apartment. His look was wild, and his aged form, now somewhat bent with the weight of years, shook and trembled with agony and anguish truly pitiable. Major Burrell arose.

"General Winston," said he, offering his hand.

But the person thus addressed saw him not. His eyes were riveted on the inanimate form before him, that lay cold and still in the embrace of death. . Hastily advancing, he raised the covering, and gazed for a moment on the rigid features of the corpse in speechless horror; then, falling on his knees, he cried, in tremulous accents:

"O, God, have mercy! It is my poor boy—my nephew!

Lord, pity a miserable old man! I can hardly bear this. O, Henry, my poor, poor child, it is hard to give thee up!"

The wretched old man wrung his shriveled hands in a paroxysm of inconsolable grief. Great tears chased each other down his wrinkled cheeks, and then bedewed the pale face of his senseless nephew. It was deeply affecting to witness the poignant sorrow of age, tottering from the ravages of twelve score seasons, over beautiful youth stricken down on the threshold of blooming manhood. Major Burrell was deeply moved. He, however, suffered the old man to indulge in his feelings of anguish till nature should produce that calm which invariably follows the outbursts of violent grief. Presently taking him by the hand, he said, kindly:

"My dear old friend, I deeply sympathize with you in your distress; but you must be reconciled to this sad bereavement. Arise and be seated;" and he led the old man to a chair.

"O, Major, this blow will nearly kill me!"

"I know it, General; it is sad and distressing, and I wish I could offer you consolation."

"I am now," continued the General, in a trembling and broken voice, "I am now entirely alone in the world. This poor boy was all that was left to me, and now he is gone. I once had, you know, Major, a blooming family. I rejoiced and thanked God in my heart for giving me so many blessings. O, how cheerful, contented, and happy we were! But I worshiped my wife and little ones too much. God would not suffer me to adore human idols. My dear, blessed wife soon died of the measles; and then my sweet babes — little innocent things — followed, one after the other, and now they are all gone, all gone!" And the General sobbed like a child.

"I know, General, what you feel. I can sympathize with you; for I once, like you, had a family around me, and they left me, one by one, as yours did, until only two remain to comfort me in my old age." And the Major, thus recalling these sad events of the past, could not refrain from tears.

The two old men, both now tottering on the verge of eternity, wept together over the bereavements which each had sustained. Walter Hallam arose and left the apartment.

"There were only two of us," said General Winston, after a moment, "there were only two of us—my brother John and I. He removed to Mississippi when a young man. I had scarcely recovered from the first effects of my own sorrows, when I was stunned by the intelligence that my brother's family had all died of yellow fever, except one; and there lies that one now, a corpse. O, God, have mercy!" After a brief pause the grief-stricken man continued: "I have nothing now to live for. This poor boy was coming to my home to glad my old heart once more before I should die; but God, in the fullness of his wisdom, has deprived me of that pleasure. I am a poor old man now—all alone—not a single relative in the world. It is wicked to wish to die, Major, but I hope God will see fit to soon take me from my miseries. I have endeavored to serve him faithfully for many years now; I have fought with the true Christians under the banner of the Lowly One, and I hope soon to join the host that has crossed the flood. God in his mercy will not permit the old soldier long to survive his companions who have all fallen victims to death. I trust I shall be ready to meet the summons when it comes. O, I long to rejoin my dear ones, who have slept for years now in the old church-yard, but whose souls, I hope, trust, and believe, are praising the blessed Redeemer around the eternal throne. God have mercy on me, and enable me to bear my burden with Christian resignation."

The two men, who were sitting with their backs to the door, were so entirely absorbed in their own thoughts and afflictions that neither noticed the entrance of Emily into the room. She was preparing to seat herself when she observed that the face of the body was uncovered, and she hastened to spread the sheet over it. A small table stood at the head of the corpse, and on it were placed a candle, and several bottles and vials containing medicines which had been used for the restoration of the dead youth. In her haste she overturned one of the vials, and the contents spilled directly in the face of the corpse. She was terror-stricken at the accident, and was attempting to repair the damage she had done, when, to her utter amazement, the eyes of the dead man flew wide open, and an audible groan escaped. Emily shrieked and fell to the floor. The two old men started up in amazement.

Is it not strange, reader, this fear of a corpse? Why do we dread to be left alone with a senseless mass of clay? We stand around the death-bed of our departing friends; we watch with extreme grief their dying struggles; and when the last faint gasp is over, then we instantly feel that their spirits are freed from the tenement of earth and are hovering in the room as spectators of our sorrow. When all becomes still, and the pale man is "laid out," then, if the slightest movement is made in the vicinity of the corpse, how we start as if we expected the dead one to pounce upon us and drag us down to the tomb! Even the gentle breeze that steals through the apartment, and rustles the snow-white covering that conceals the lost one from view, will make us look around with trembling fear, and prepare to fly for life. And should our acquaintances or friends, who had been prepared for burial, happen to disappoint us, and conclude to cheat the grave of its due, and then suddenly pop up into a sitting posture, we would doubtless fly with indescribable apprehension from their presence, and leave them, until reason should remount the throne, to recover in the way they thought proper from partial death. It is not surprising, therefore, that Emily should have acted as she did, nor is it a matter of very great astonishment that the nasal organs of the corpse could not endure without flinching the knock-down propensities of ammonia. At least it was more than Henry Winston could tolerate without manifesting some sign of disapproval.

The two old men were extremely surprised at this sudden turn of affairs, but Major Burrell comprehended it all at one glance. The eyes of the corpse remained open for nearly a quarter of a minute, then closed with a frown, and another groan was distinctly heard.

"Great God! he lives, General, he lives!" exclaimed Major Burrell. "Lord God! what shall we do?" and he ran from the room in a fit of terrible excitement, like a distracted maniac, scarcely conscious of what he was doing.

General Winston stood for a moment almost stupefied. There is no knowing how matters would have terminated had not a third party appeared upon the stage. Just as Major Burrell reached the front door his ear caught the sound of the hoofs of a couple of flying steeds clattering up the avenue. The horsemen were at the door.

"Dr. Johnson, as I live! For God's sake, Doctor, quick! lose not a moment! The man lives—just come to himself. For God Almighty's sake, hurry, Doctor, hurry!" and the physician was absolutely dragged from his horse and pushed into the apartment.

"Save him, Doctor, save him, and you shall be trebly repaid!" exclaimed General Winston, as soon as he saw the physician enter.

Dr. Johnson seemed surprised at the looks of terror and dismay depicted on the countenances of the two men, and at Emily, still sitting on the floor, recovering from her swoon. He, however, spoke not, but went to work like an experienced disciple of Esculapius. It is impossible to describe the breathless anxiety with which General Winston and Major Burrell looked on. They watched narrowly every movement of the Doctor, and then looked at the face of the corpse, to discover any signs of returning life. Dr. Johnson examined the body very carefully a moment.

"The young man has been terribly stunned," said he.

He seized his saddle-bags and was soon applying proper remedies.

"Is there any hope, Doctor?" said General Winston, after the lapse of a few moments.

"I can not say yet, General. I will tell you in a quarter of an hour."

The Doctor worked faithfully with his patient for another five minutes; then the eyes were again opened and closed, and a breath drawn with great pain and difficulty.

"Thank God! thank God!" cried the General.

"Hurry, Doctor, hurry, for God's sake!" exclaimed Major Burrell.

The doctor could not repress a smile at the old man's impetuosity, but he continued to work rapidly. Ten minutes sped away; then respiration commenced heavily and irregularly. Five minutes more and the young man was breathing more freely. Dr. Johnson paused for a moment, then spoke:

"General," said he, "the young man will live."

"Thanks be to God!" exclaimed General Winston, grasping him warmly by the hand.

"Three hours since," continued the Doctor, "I could have saved him without any difficulty. I was some distance off when I received the summons, and have had a long, hard ride. But tell me why you have laid the young man out as if for burial?"

"We found him about three o'clock," replied Major Burrell, "and labored for nearly two hours to bring him to life; at the expiration of that length of time every spark of life seemed to be extinct. We had not the most remote idea that he lived till just a moment before you came, when Emily entered the room, shrieked, and fell fainting to the floor. We then looked up, and discovered the General's nephew with his eyes wide open, and heard him groan. In a moment afterward you very fortunately arrived."

The physician cast a look at Emily, which she interpreted as one of inquiry in regard to the part she had played in this semi-tragical drama, and she answered:

"O, Doctor, I very awkwardly upset a vial of medicine in his face."

"The young man, then, is doubtless indebted to your awkwardness for his life, Miss Emily. I see it was ammonia. A few minutes longer and I doubt not he would have been beyond my skill. But the patient must be removed from this plank."

Young Winston was placed again on the bed. Another hour soon passed, and then Dr. Johnson pronounced the patient out of danger.

"Now," said he, "I must be gone; I have other patients that require my attention. The young man will probably not be conscious till some time to-morrow. As soon as he speaks give him this," holding a vial of medicine in his hand, "but do not by any means suffer him to talk. He will doubtless, before this time to-morrow evening, be able to relate his own story in regard to the accident."

"I am under lasting obligations to you, Dr. Johnson," said General Winston. "You can not imagine how sincerely I thank you."

"You are under no obligations to me, General; and it affords me ineffable pleasure to see you relieved from what I know must have been your distress. You are as much indebted to Miss Emily as to my humble self. But I have no time to talk. Good night." So saying the worthy doctor gathered his hat and saddle-bags, and was soon gone to the relief of other sufferers.

We will leave the reader to imagine the joy of General Winston, in which Major Burrell and his lovely daughter sincerely and heartily participated. The old General must needs kiss Emily for her "timely awkwardness," he said, and she submitted with a very good grace.

That livelong night the two old men sat in the room of the General's nephew. They talked merrily for awhile of the good old times of the past, and then sadly of their early friends and acquaintances who had long since departed from the stage of human action. Then they would pause for a long time, as if by mutual consent, each recalling scenes and incidents of youthful days that now lay buried amid the decaying waste of memory. The night crept slowly on, and the soft zephyr, laden with the perfume of the fast-fading beauties of summer, sighed amid the branches of the tall, stately oaks; then died away almost as slowly as the last rays of the sinking sun. But still the sufferer reposed in apparent unconsciousness. No perceptible change was discovered in his condition till toward the dawn of the morning, when his respiration was evidently performed with much less difficulty. The patient was safe.

After breakfast, Emily persuaded her father and General Winston to take some rest, promising that she would watch by the bedside, and if any change for the worse should take place she would inform them at once. Accordingly they retired and left her alone, the Major saying he would send Walter to assist her.

Emily took her position at the bedside. She had not sat more than fifteen or twenty minutes, listening to the heavy breathing of the patient, before he suddenly opened his eyes, and stared wildly around the apartment and at her.

"I see how it is," he at length said, in a feeble voice: "I have died, and thou, beautiful creature, art an angel, come to conduct me to the spirit-land. Is it not so?"

"You are not dead, sir," said Emily, quickly interrupting him; "neither am I an angel, but a poor mortal like yourself.

But the doctor said you must not talk, sir, and that you must take this medicine."

He rubbed his bewildered head, then swallowed the dose without another word, and very soon afterward fell into a deep and refreshing slumber.

Emily now examined more closely the features of the sleeper. She viewed before her a young man, apparently twenty-five years of age. She saw his raven black hair, his bold, high forehead, his Grecian nose, and his firmly-set mouth. His eyes, she had seen, were of a dark blue. Emily thought it was altogether the most beautiful and handsome countenance she had ever beheld, and was gazing into the young man's face with an eagerness which we will justify by calling it the natural curiosity of woman. She was merely looking at the face like a lover of art would examine a fine picture or piece of sculpture. She did not all this time observe her cousin Walter, who was standing in the door, looking at this spectacle with no feeling of pleasure. At last he spoke:

"It seems to me, Emily, if the young man were conscious, he would feel highly flattered with the earnestness of your inspection, which is certainly closer than he could reasonably expect upon so short an acquaintance."

Emily started, and she appeared all at once to comprehend the impropriety of her action; then she colored at being detected; then her eyes flashed with anger at being reproved. Walter knew it not, but he had planted in Emily's breast the seed of sudden but deep detestation of himself. Women sometimes hate for very slight causes. But Emily checked her rising indignation.

"You are unjust, cousin Walter—very unjust and suspicious. But I will make no apology for my actions; and as there is no particular necessity for my presence here, if you will remain I will retire." So saying, she left the apartment.

CHAPTER V.

> "He says he loves my daughter;
> I think so too; for never gazed the moon
> Upon the water, as he'll stand, and read
> As 't were, my daughter's eyes: and, to be plain,
> I think there is not half a kiss to choose
> Who loves another best."

It will be best not to fatigue the reader's patience by entering into minute details in regard to Henry Winston's recovery. It is sufficient to say that he did recover, and that without any accident, incident, difficulty, or event, more than might be supposed to attach naturally to a condition of short sickness. We will further say that the tedium of the sick-room was considerably relieved by Emily, who frequently read to young Winston, at his request, from his favorite authors. Two persons of such similar tastes soon formed a warm friendship—a friendship founded on mutual respect and esteem. As to any other sentiment beyond friendship, "deponent saith not." Byron, I believe, says "friendship is a dangerous word for a young lady." Be this as it may, in six days the young man changed his quarters to his uncle's—General Winston—but not without a warm invitation from Major Burrell to visit at his house whenever it should be agreeable.

Three weeks had passed away. The reader will, of course, like to know what our hero was doing all this time. It would be useless to state how frequently Henry and Emily met; how often they sat in Emily's bower, situated on one side of the avenue, and sang with the guitar, or conversed on the great works of great minds; or how often they rode out and enjoyed the pleasures of natural scenery.

The reader, we are aware, has already imagined the *denouement;* and we will not deny that the effect of this continued association with a man of Winston's personal appearance, and intellectual and moral qualifications, can not be easily imagined upon a young girl of pure heart and refined sensibility. Sometimes she would detect herself looking down the avenue long and anxiously when she was alone; then a deep blush would play over her beautiful features. What caused it she hardly knew; but she knew from some strange cause that she felt extremely miserable in Winston's absence; and she knew, furthermore, that in his company she felt very happy. The poor girl, ignorant of some of the passions of the human heart, persuaded herself that her curious feeling originated from a cause connected with the intellect. Sometimes, however, a feeble inkling of the truth would rush to her mind, especially after looking down the avenue for a long time (and somehow it seemed a *very long* time to her) she would see Winston coming; then she would suddenly close the window curtain, and seat herself in a dark corner of the room; then she would suddenly steal to the window, to see if she were mistaken, and if Henry were really in view. Had any one told Emily in plain terms that she was most desperately in love with young Winston, she would have denied it emphatically. She did not acknowledge it to herself. She supposed and persuaded herself that she loved Winston's company for the sake of the intellectual pleasure it afforded. They generally conversed upon subjects connected with science and art. Winston had never, by the most distant hint, intimated that he was inspired with any other feeling in regard to Emily than pure respect and esteem. Her modesty and natural purity of character would, therefore, have prevented her from bestowing her love where it would not be appreciated. But day by day she become more entangled, more infatuated, and more miserable. Like a defenseless ship in the maelstrom, she was moving slowly but surely, and perceived not clearly the point to which she was drifting. Old Major Burrell watched both the young people with a father's anxiety. From all the indications, which are well known to those who have passed through the fiery ordeal of love, he believed all would be right in the end. So he looked on and smiled.

Emily knew not the depth of her affection, till one day Winston, after a long conversation, said:

"It is frequently a sad thing to part, Miss Emily; and it will be trying to me to leave the kind friends whose acquaintance I have formed during my visit to this country; but, as much as I regret it, the trial must soon be undergone."

It had never occurred to Emily that they must part; and now the sudden thought that she must give up Winston sent the crimson tide almost curdling to her heart. She knew then that the intellect was not so much concerned with her feelings as she had supposed. She felt vexed and perplexed, but she attempted to choke down her emotions and reply in a tone as cold and indifferent as she could assume.

"I was not aware you were going to leave so soon."

"Yes, Miss Emily; I can not prolong my stay much longer. But before I go I must express my obligations to you for the many happy hours which you have been so kind as to devote to my entertainment. I have, indeed, derived much pleasure from your society. I do not say it to flatter you, Miss Emily, but I have never met with a lady in my life whose young mind is so well stored with all that can dignify woman's nature, or one who worships with so true devotion at the shrine of nature."

"Thank you for the compliment, Mr. Winston. I appreciate it very highly, coming from the source it does."

They talked on for awhile; then Winston was heard repeating the following lines from Campbell, in reply to something Emily had said; what it was we know not. The lines appear to have been misapplied, judging from what Emily remarked when Winston concluded the quotation:

> "Till Hymen brought his love-delighted hour,
> There dwelt no joy in Eden's rosy bower!
> In vain the viewless seraph, lingering there
> At starry midnight, charmed the silent air;
> In vain the wild bird carol'd on the steep,
> To hail the sun, slow-wheeling from the deep;
> In vain, to soothe the solitary shade,
> Aerial notes in mingling measure played;
> The summer wind that shook the spangled tree,
> The whispering wave, the murmur of the bee,—
> Still slowly passed the melancholy day,
> And still the stranger wist not where to stray;
> The world was sad, the garden was a wild;
> And man, the hermit, sighed till woman smiled!'"

"That is a digression from the subject, Mr. Winston. I had no reference to such a topic."

"I know it, Miss Emily; and I would not do you the injustice to construe your language otherwise than you intended. But the lines will serve as an introduction to something I must say before I leave you."

Emily hung her head in spite of all her efforts to look dignified and indifferent. She felt that the "something" to which Winston alluded would not be unpleasant; but she said not a word.

"I can not, Miss Emily, allow this opportunity to pass, whatever may be the result, without telling you what a lasting impression you have made on my heart. If I am speaking to one whose affections are pre-engaged, she, I hope, will have the kindness to spare me the mortification of feeling which must always accompany an avowal to a preoccupied heart."

She replied in a low tone, and her low words could be heard only by Winston. They could not have been unfavorable, for the young man immediately said:

"Then I must now know my doom."

After a short pause, he moved nearer to where Emily sat, and, seizing her trembling hand, he continued:

"My dearest one, I love thee. Language has no power to express the unutterable emotions of my heart. I would you could read at this instant the workings of my soul. When I first saw you standing by my bedside, I recollect I took you for an angel; but I was afterward glad to find you were mortal. I felt that very moment that my fate was sealed. I loved you then better than life. You have been ever since in my thoughts by day, and in my dreams by night. Whether sleeping or waking, you have been absent from my mind scarcely a single moment. My dearest Emily (suffer me to call you such), I love you madly! I adore you! Only the God of heaven can know the wild emotion that now thrills through every fiber of my being. O, I can not find words sufficient to express myself! It is useless to try it. But, now I have told you all, can I, dare I hope for any return of my warm, ardent affection?"

"This declaration, Mr. Winston," said the blushing Emily. "has taken me by surprise, and was entirely unexpected to me; but I do assure you I feel highly flattered by it."

"And is that all?"

"Why, what more could you expect me to say? But, if you desire it, I will say you have my esteem and respect, and may always claim my warmest friendship."

"Friendship is but a poor return for the inexpressible love I feel for you. I would far prefer never to have seen you than to possess nothing but your friendship after forming your acquaintance. You ask what I want you to say. Now, Miss Emily, I understand you saved my life, for which I thank you; but I would to heaven I had perished in the storm rather than now leave this spot without an assurance of your love! Will you not, then, be the light of that life God made you the instrument of preserving?"

Women are strange beings. In matters of love it may be safely asserted they are more deceitful than the "lords of creation;" but, be it said to their credit, modesty makes them so. As Shakespeare says:

> "Maids in modesty say *No* to that
> Which they would have the profferer construe—*Aye*."

Emily loved Winston with her whole soul, and listened to his burning words with the delight which women only can feel, but she had too much modesty to surrender her heart without some show of resistance; so she replied:

"I have not thought on the subject, Mr. Winston; and I think our acquaintance is rather limited. But, if it were otherwise, you could not wish me to say I loved you, unless I did?"

What she meant by making such a reply, and adopting such a *modus operandi*, we will leave to the "fair sex" to say. Winston, however, answered:

"No, Miss Emily, I could not require you to make such a sacrifice. As much as I love you, I would scorn an alliance in which all the love would be on one side, and in which I would claim a heart that could beat no response to mine. It could furnish me little pleasure to see the tender vine withering on the oak. And were you the queen of the world— could you command the wealth of land and sea—I would despise myself, I would lose my own self-respect, could I desire for one instant to share a prosperity which would bring but misery without the smile of love. Rather than be one of the parties to such an unholy contract, I would prefer to drag through a wretched existence, solitary and alone, the only comforter of my own sorrow and misery. If you love me not, say so; I shall take it as an act of kindness. I shall not attempt even to persuade you to bestow your affection upon me. I would throw from me in contempt love that should be brought about only by persuasion. I want only that warm, wild emotion that bursts forth spontaneously from the heart, and makes an idol of its object. I want that love which clings with an undying tenacity to its idol, and bids defiance to time and death. With such a being, O, I could live happy anywhere—in the deep, dark dungeon dank, where the light of the sun never comes—in the wild wilderness—on the burning desert—in the palace of the nabob or the hut of the poorest beggar. If you love me not, say so, and let me prepare to meet my fate. I can not forbear saying, though, that if your answer is unfavorable to my wishes, I would to God I had died under the boughs of yonder oak, where you found me at death's door. Miss Emily," continued the young man more vehemently, "I am the best friend you have on earth; I would lay down my life for thee—I would cheerfully die for thee, my dearest girl. You are the only one on the earth to whom I could confide the secret thoughts of my heart. My relatives—father, mother, brothers, sisters—have all gone to the spirit-land. They have left me alone to guide my frail bark through the tempestuous sea of time. With the exception of my good, kind old uncle, there breathes not a being in the wide world connected to me by the bonds of blood-relationship. But the love I had for them all is not the one thousandth part of that I feel for thee. Speak, then; let me know my doom."

Emily did want to speak, and intended to. She was pleased with Winston's vehemence and the thrilling language of his love. But she knew not in what manner she ought to make known the true state of her own heart.

"I have had no time for reflection, Mr. Winston; and I do not know that I am fully prepared to answer."

"The human heart," replied Winston, slowly, "is not such a cold, dull thing that it knows not at once its own emotions. I must say I do heartily despise the custom of society which requires the fair sex to demand time to reflect whether they love or not—just like there could be any mistake about it. True, generous love, warm from the heart, makes no cold calculation, but overleaps the bounds of reason, and fastens upon its object, utterly regardless of consequences and of the opinion of the world. It gushes forth like the mad torrent down the steep mountain side. It never mistakes its object; and you know now, Miss Emily, whether you are willing to become mine, as well as you would by reflecting upon it a month. Will you, then, be mine?"

Winston paused, and Emily remained silent. She no longer had an excuse for not giving a candid reply, but still she hesitated. It would be difficult to tell what varied thoughts were working in her mind. But she seemed all at once to recollect herself, and suddenly withdrew her hand, which Winston had been holding. The young man changed his tactics.

"Miss Emily, I must take that, then, as my answer. Farewell, and may God bless you!"

As he rose to leave, Emily's countenance turned deathly pale, and Winston knew he could not be mistaken. He moved back to her side.

"Emily, my dearest, I am not mistaken; you do love me. Say so, and consent to be mine."

"*Henry, I will!*"

Winston heard the whisper, and the next thing the blushing girl was clasped in her lover's arms. Reader, the curtain falls.

CHAPTER VI.

"Farewell, thou hast trampled love's faith in the dust;
Thou hast torn from my bosom its hope and its trust."

WALTER HALLAM, notwithstanding the length to which he had already prolonged his visit, still lingered, reluctant to part with Emily and her fortune. We will, however, do him the justice to say that he loved his cousin with as much ardor as it was possible for one of his stoical turn of mind to feel. He had not again mentioned to her his proposal since the day before the storm, but had watched with a jealous eye the growing intimacy between Emily and Henry Winston. The latter, he had concluded, since his recovery, was an unmitigated scoundrel—had jilted and trifled with his sister, and was now attempting to deceive his cousin in the same way. Even if this were not the case, it was not his intention that Winston should step between his cousin and himself, and bear off in triumph her vast fortune. He had no idea of such a thing; yet he felt somewhat apprehensive when he saw the evident partiality which Emily manifested for Winston's company. It would be an act of kindness, an act of justice to his cousin to inform her with what kind of a character she was dealing. It would be an easy matter, he thought, to put an end to proceedings in this quarter by merely showing to Emily the letter his sister had written to one who must have been her lover. The time had now come when this duty ought to be performed; because, for the last two or three days (that is, after the event narrated in the last chapter), he by no means relished the familiarity with which Emily treated his rival. He must now discharge his duty. So the third day after Emily had listened to the impassioned words of Henry Winston, which had made the world wear a different and more pleasing aspect—(what young maid does not feel this same buoyancy and elasticity of spirit when the idol of her heart can be unreservedly worshiped?)—she found herself alone with Walter Hallam. Emily was silent; and she was thinking of her lover, who was this very evening to consult with her father; and, all parties consenting, the twain were to be made one the first day of the next year. She was so busy with her own reflections that she was scarcely aware of Walter's presence. He was the first to break the silence.

"Will you listen to me a few moments, cousin Emily?"

"Why, certainly, Walter; but from your tone of voice I presume I am to hear a lecture. Is it not so?"

"No, Emily, no. Lecture the devil! I want to talk to you plainly for your own good; I want to advise you."

"I can not conceive of any emergency or contingency in which I would need your advice, cousin Walter. It is true I am young and inexperienced, but when I am in such a condition as to need instruction or advice, I can apply to my father."

"Then, Emily, I want to *warn* you."

"O, well, go on, cousin Walter," said Emily, in a tone of indifference; "I will listen."

"I will come to the point at once then; this young Winston "—— Emily colored.

"Well, what of him?"

"There may be no necessity for my warning, Emily, unless certain events have transpired, which I think not improbable."

"Don't speak in riddles, cousin Walter; I am no hand at unraveling enigmas. A thousand circumstances may or may not have occurred, whether you think them probable or not. I do not understand your meaning."

"You affect not to understand me. Very well; I will put

this plain question, which you can not misapprehend: Which do you prefer—myself or Winston?"

"Prefer—yourself or Winston? What do you mean?"

Walter felt a little nettled at Emily's apparent ignorance of a simple interrogation.

"You seem to be quite dull of comprehension to-day, Emily. But I have the vanity to believe I can make myself understood. Which, then, do you prefer as a lover—myself or this devil Winston?"

The black eye flashed fire, and the red lip trembled with indignation.

"Walter Hallam, if you can not use more respectful language, I shall be under the necessity of avoiding your company. This is the third or fourth time you have thrown out expressions which would not be tolerated in respectable society."

"You are becoming very particular, all at once. I am not aware of having violated the rules of etiquette."

"If you are not, so much the worse for you then."

"But that is no answer to my question, Emily."

"I do not recognize your right, sir, to question me as to my likes or dislikes or preferences."

"I suppose, though, you can answer the portion of the question which relates to myself? You have not forgotten that you have kept me in suspense for several weeks?"

"It was not my fault. But, if that is all you want, I can answer you at once."

"Well, then, when shall our marriage take place?"

"I can answer that in one word, Walter—*never!*"

"And that is your positive and irrevocable answer?"

"It is useless to multiply words on the subject. I have answered your question plainly, and I meant what I said; but, if you desire it, I can repeat; and I say—*never, never!*"

"And you prefer Winston to me?"

"I said no such thing, and had I never seen Hen—Mr. Winston—my reply would have been the same."

"Emily, its no use trying to deceive me that way."

"I am not trying to deceive you, sir; I have spoken nothing but truth."

"I am fully persuaded, Emily, you would have married me if this finical upstart had not interfered."

"Then I can inform you that you are flattering yourself with a delusion. I never would have married you."

"Can you deny that you are carrying on a *puppyism* with this man Winston?"

"Mr. Hallam, I shall not answer your unbecoming questions."

"You are so very fastidious to-day, I will put the question in another form. I will ask you, then, if you are not in love, as you may call it, with Winston?"

"And if I should be, what have you to do with it?"

"I almost knew it, Emily; and I see it will be of no use advising you; but I will show you what I have to do with it. I shall not suffer you to be deceived any longer by such a d—d scoundrel as he is."

"Walter Hallam," said Emily, rising, "I will not stay to hear such indecent language."

"O, well; go on, Emily, if you can not listen to reason and common sense. I was going to make an explanation; but go on, if you want to. I will do you the kindness, though, to break off your unbecoming intimacy with this consummate villain, even against your consent; no doubt you will thank me for it at some future day."

Emily was so enraged that she stayed not to hear another word.

"The girl," said Hallam to himself after she was gone, "is perfectly infatuated. But I will not suffer her to be imposed on by this d—d poetical hypocrite. I shall see him this very evening, if he comes here, and let him know that some of his past villainies have come to light. It is strange to me, and always has been, how women can prefer the canting gibberish of popinjays to the talk of sensible men. They would at any time rather listen to a pitiable piece of 'Pop-goes-the-weaselings' than the best chapter from Adam Smith. Let any darned fool, with barely sufficient brains to recognize his own mother's son in a crowd, only black his mustachios, twirl a walking-cane with a hand covered with brass rings, and spout his d—d nonsense about moonshine, and the silly things gather around him like a set of chattering monkeys. Let a man enter company with the assurance of an emperor, bow and scrape like a bobbing duck, rear back in his chair, and roll out his bird-and-flower phrases, and the more silly he talks the more will the giggling girls 'fall in love,' as they call it, with the 'dear angel!' Love! the devil! A more contemptible piece of folly was never invented by the brain of man. But my cousin Emily is a good girl, and shall be saved from this match. When he is gone, she will be disposed to reconsider the matter, and take me for a husband. Women often say no when they mean yes. They are as changeable and fickle as the winds anyhow. But may be all will yet be right."

That very evening Henry Winston, according to promise, was walking leisurely in the direction of Major Burrell's. His thoughts may be better imagined than described. Nothing is more embarrassing to a well-bred young man than the necessity of asking the consent of the "old folks" to his contract of partnership, in all things temporal and spiritual, with their lovely daughter. Winston was thinking in what manner he should broach the subject to Major Burrell. He had studied up twenty different ways and twenty different forms, but they had all been rejected, one after the other. At last he concluded to wait, and speak on the spur of the moment, according to the humor he should find the Major in. He had now nearly reached Emily's bower, when he thought he distinguished voices. Drawing nearer, he paused and listened. Emily was singing that simple little air:

> "'When other friends are round thee,
>   And other hearts are thine;
> When other bays have crowned thee,
>   More fresh and green than mine—
> Then think how sad and lonely
>   This wretched heart will be,
> Which, while it beats, beats only,
>   Beloved one, for thee!
>
> Yet do not think I doubt thee,
>   I know thy truth remains;
> I would not live without thee
>   For all the world contains.
> Thou art the star that guides me
>   Along life's troubled sea;
> Whatever fate betides me,
>   This heart still turns to thee.'"

Winston felt a thrill of pleasure stealing through his frame as he thought these beautiful words were all intended for himself; but the next moment his joy was changed to anguish.

"I think you have improved very much in singing, my dear Emily, since I left," said a deep voice, which made Henry start like a cannon had exploded at his feet. "But, Emily, what about this young man Winston? I understand that you are very dreadfully in love."

Emily reddened, but with sparkling eyes she replied:

"*I do not love Henry Winston.* I——" Then, as if ashamed of the intensity of her feelings, she suddenly paused.

"You what, my dear?"

"Well, never mind," she cried, "*I love you, and have always loved you;*" and she threw her arms around the gentleman's neck, and imprinted a kiss upon his cheek.

Henry Winston was thunderstruck. He stood for a moment stone-still, then he suddenly decided his course of action. He stayed to hear no more; the demon of jealousy had entered his heart, and the proud man was stung to the quick with the thought that he had been duped by a curly-haired girl, who would now make sport with her true lover over the secret sentiments of his heart which he had uttered to Emily. It maddened him, and he rushed from the spot. The world appeared dark and gloomy, and he was walking as if he were attempting to leave it forever. The reader will think this was a strange course for an impetuous lover to pursue; but he is not sufficiently acquainted with the character of our hero to understand his motives. There are few men in the world who would have acted exactly as he did. It would have been better for his peace of mind, and Emily's too, if his propensity to eavesdrop had been more strongly and fully developed; for, after a momentary pause, the conversation was continued:

"But, Emily, what do you mean by saying you do not love Henry Winston? I know you do."

"Brother James, I will hide nothing from you. I do not *love* him; it is more than that—I *worship* and *adore* him." And she hid her face in blushing confusion.

"O, that's it, is it? Well, come, sister, don't be ashamed. But when can I see your divinity?"

"Now, directly; I am looking for him every moment."

"And that is why you have brought your guitar here."

"Yes; Mr. Winston is very fond of music, and we sing together very frequently. O, I know you will like him so much when you see him."

"I hope so, Emily, since you desire it. But, changing the subject a little, what do you think of our cousin, Walter Hallam? You say very little about him in your letters."

"There is little to say about him."

"I infer, then, you do not like our kinsman as well as you do your new household god?"

"I will express no opinion concerning him; you can see him, and form your own opinion."

"Well, let us go to the house then; I wish to see our father and become acquainted with Walter Hallam."

The reader will readily understand that the person with whom Emily was so familiarly conversing was her brother, James Burrell. He had come home upon a short leave of absence, and was to return to West Point in a day or two. It will not be necessary to honor him with a longer description. We will notice Hallam.

Walter was standing in the doorway when Winston turned into the avenue. As soon as he saw this, he abruptly left the house at right angles to the direction in which his hated rival was walking, and proceeded to the road which he knew Henry must travel, with the intention of meeting him, on his return, as if by accident. He sat down close to the road-side with the patience of a beast of prey watching for its unsuspecting victim. He had sat thus but a few moments on the wayside, when, to his great surprise, he saw Winston approaching, with a speed which was truly astonishing and unnatural to a man who had just left a lovely intended *la fiancee*.

"The devil must be to pay now," thought Walter. "I wonder what can have happened."

But he had little time for reflection, for Winston's rapid gait soon brought them together.

"Whither so fast, Mr. Winston? I do not think you usually travel so rapidly. Are you ill, sir? You look rather pale."

In Winston's state of mind the voice seemed to come from the throat of a demon. He halted abruptly, and stared at Hallam vacantly, as if he did not understand clearly what was spoken. He knew the words, whatever they were, were uttered in rather a tone of sarcastic insolence, which had a tendency to arouse his anger. Upon second thought he concluded not to notice Hallam's impudence, and was preparing to pass on, without deigning to reply, when Walter again addressed him:

"If you are not too much pressed for time, Mr. Winston, I would be glad you would make an explanation I have to demand."

"Well, speak fast then, Mr. Hallam."

"I am usually in the habit of coming to the point at once, and "——

"Well, say on, man. No *ands* and *ifs*, nor prefaces; if you have any thing to say, speak out quickly, and let me be gone."

"Well, then, sir, you recollect a letter addressed to you by one who now sleeps in the grave, and a small miniature"——

"Letter? Miniature? Whose?"

"You seem to be in a devil of a hurry, sir; but the letter was from my sister, who died shortly after it was written."

"And I would to God," exclaimed Winston, in a wild, sad voice, "I, too, slept in the grave!"

"Mr. Winston," said Hallam, in astonishment, "your conduct appears to me inexplicable. First, you deceived my sister; then you may be playing the same part a second time; and now, when asked for an explanation of your strange and unaccountable conduct, you wish that you were dead. How is that, sir?"

"When I learn that I am responsible to you for my actions, I will make any explanation that may be deemed necessary; but, until then, all I have to say is, I never spoke two dozen words to your sister in my life. I have no time to explain further; I am in no humor for explanations."

"I must say your mind does appear to be wandering, Mr. Winston."

"I have no time to tarry. So good evening."

"Mr. Winston," said Hallam, placing himself directly in front of the former, "your statement is not at all satisfactory. I must have an explanation, sir. My cousin, Miss Burrell"——

Winston's eyes flashed fire.

"You attempt to detain me by force, eh? Well, we will see."

Almost before the words were out, and before Walter could divine the intention of his enraged rival, he received a blow upon his forehead which felled him to the ground. Henry scarcely turned his head, but walked on like a madman. He had made but a few strides, however, before he heard Hallam exclaiming, in an angry voice:

"You shall repent this, sir; and, unless you are a coward, we will meet again soon."

But the object of this threat seemed not to hear him, or at least seemed to think his prostrated enemy unworthy of further notice. He moved on like a maniac, and at a rate which soon brought him to his uncle's residence. The General was not at home, and did not arrive till late at night. Going up to his room, Henry threw himself on the bed and lay still for a few moments, with his face hid in his hands; then rising, he rapidly paced up and down the room.

"Who would have thought," said he to himself, "it was possible for so much deceit to be connected with one of her apparent gentleness and candor. No, I can not be mistaken; I heard it distinctly—'*I do not love Henry Winston;*' and then she said to her lover, '*I love you, and have always loved you.*' I wonder who the fellow is. What an arrant fool I have been! How easily duped! But if she did not love me, she acted the coquette and the hypocrite to perfection. One thing I can not be mistaken about—*I loved her.* I would rather die than lose her. I will make one more effort to secure her. I will demand an explanation. What! an explanation after hearing her say with her own lips that she did not love me! No, I will not be such a fool. I will have more manliness and independence. She might laugh in my face. O God! what a blow *here!*" placing his hand over his heart. "But I will suffer in silence. O, how I love her still, though I have been so terribly deceived! When her head lay upon my shoulder, and I felt her heart beat against mine, and she even sealed her vows with her tears, how could I doubt? I had not the slightest suspicion of her infamous and unjustifiable duplicity. I never saw a person seemingly more truthful, artless, and candid in my life. She certainly *does* love me. But how can I be so foolish as to doubt the evidence of my own senses? Did I not hear her with my own ears say she *did not love me?* It was no dream. Would to God it were! I heard it without any possibility of mistake. Probably she can explain it. Pshaw! what is the use of asking her to explain a thing as plain as one of the axioms of Euclid. No, I will leave the country at once. I will fly from her presence and endeavor to forget my unhappy passion. I will rise superior to this misfortune. I can not deny that the blow has shocked and staggered me, but it shall *crush* me—*never, never!* If I mistake not, I see in the political firmament signs of a gathering storm, which will soon shake the world to its center. The South will never submit to the domination of an abolition President; and, as soon as the first alarm is sounded, this arm shall be raised in her defense, and shall strike for Mississippi's honor till it be palsied in death. Amid the scenes of carnage and bloodshed that shall consecrate every hill-top, I may perhaps drown my own deep-rooted sorrow. Then,

'Welcome, rough war, with all thy scenes of blood
Thy roaring thunders, and thy clashing steel!'"

All that night a candle burned steadily in the room of Henry Winston. He was seated at a table busily writing. General Winston returned home about ten o'clock, but immediately retired to his bed. As Henry was a student, it was no unusual thing to see a light in his room till midnight. The young man's actions showed, however, that this night at least his reflections had little to do with science. Occasionally he would cease, lay his head on the table, sit for a few moments as if wrapped in thought, then suddenly start from his seat and take a turn across the apartment. Again, advancing to the table, he would seize the paper upon which he had been writing, gaze at it for an instant, and then deliberately hold it to the light till it was entirely consumed. Then he would walk to the window, thrust himself half-way out, as if he had been suffocating. Returning to his writing, he again seized his pen, but paused.

"I must," thought he, "write something. Yes, she shall know that I am not ignorant of the part she has been playing. I shall not attempt to *deceive her*. I will tell her that I did love her, and that I do even *now*, though I will endeavor to tear her faithless image from my bleeding heart. Yes, she shall know it all."

And the young man, whose feelings were in a mingled tumult, sat for an hour at his desk. At the expiration of that length of time he folded a well-filled sheet, inclosed it in an envelope, and directed it to Miss Emily Burrell.

"Now," thought he, "one to my good uncle, and then I leave *forever!* I can not bear to see the old man, and part from him in my present state of feeling. My poor old uncle—the only living relative I have on earth—may the great God bless him and protect him in his solitary gloom!"

And the young man's tears—the first he had shed—flowed unrestrainedly down his cheeks. After a few moments, however, he was calmer.

"O, why did I ever meet Emily Burrell? My happiness has all vanished like an empty dream. But it is folly to indulge in useless grief. I will endeavor to be a *man*. The world shall never know what I am suffering. Even though my very heart should burst, I will endure it, like a Spartan, without a murmur. And now, my poor old uncle, a line to you, and then I go from a spot upon which I would be intolerably miserable should I stay near it another hour."

He wrote rapidly for a short time; then, his note being finished and directed, he lighted a fresh candle, gathered up his hat, and walked out of doors, leaving both letters in a conspicuous place on the table. Going hastily to the stable, he bridled his faithful steed, that recognized him by a low neigh, and led him to the rack in front of the house. He then again went into the house. Advancing noiselessly and cautiously to his uncle's door, which was partially open, he listened an instant to the deep breathing of the hoary-headed man, but he quelled the strong appeals of nature, which at first urged him to arouse the old man, and make a candid statement of the whole affair. He concluded not to disturb the sleeper; so he turned on his heel, left the house with an aching heart, mounted his horse, and rode silently away. He was compelled to take the road that led by the spot which had been the scene of his love and his triumph. O, how his heart beat when the tall building which contained one around whom his warmest affections and thoughts had clustered loomed up in sight! Approaching nearer and nearer, he at last saw a light in Emily's room, and, looking closer, he could plainly see her lovely form by the window. He halted abruptly; and here ensued another struggle of the heart. Love swelled in his heaving breast, and seemed about to force him to that solitary light, which appeared to possess the fabled charms of the *ignis-fatuus*. It was a struggle of love against jealousy and folly. All the resolutions of our hero were about to be scattered by a single breath of the blind god. Should he even now, in the stillness of the night, go to Emily, and ask her to explain her contradictory words? Might there not, after all, be some mistake? Reason said go, but pride revolted at the idea, and folly triumphed.

"O God!" he cried, "I can bear this no longer. If I remain here another instant my manhood will desert me!"

Putting spurs to his horse, he flew clattering down the road, and turned his head away from the light, that he might not behold the fair siren tempting him to an act of unmanly humiliation. Emily heard the unusual noise, and listened with an unaccountable anxiety till it died away in the distance. She knew not why, but the clattering hoofs of that flying steed seemed to strike her very heart. But the horseman went dashing on and on, till the first faint streaks of light were dimly visible in the east. His feelings were in such a state of excitement that he was scarcely aware of the rapid gait in which he had been traveling. He slackened his speed. but still pushed on. That morning, when the brilliant sun arose in splendor, and the birds were singing merrily and hopping from branch to branch, the poor excited youth was many miles away from the light he had seen in the room of Emily Burrell; but still the form in the window was stamped in the vivid color of fire on the aching heart of Henry Winston.

CHAPTER VII.

"In vain she seeks to close her weary eyes—
Those eyes still swim incessantly in tears;
Hope, in her cheerless bosom, fading, dies,
Distracted by a thousand cruel fears,
While banished from his love forever she appears."

THE morning following the night of the precipitate flight of Henry Winston his uncle arose as usual, and his nephew not having made his appearance, he inquired of a domestic if the young man had arisen; but the servant knew not. After waiting till the breakfast hour, and no one having seen Henry, the old man started to his room.

"He has probably overslept himself," said the old General, as he was going.

He was, however, met on the way up the stairs by a servant, who gave him the startling intelligence that the bed in "Mas Henry's" room had not been occupied, and that a candle was still burning on the stand. The General hastened into the room, walked up to the table, and saw the two letters left by his nephew.

"What can it mean?" said he, as he adjusted his spectacles and proceeded to an examination of the epistles.

He read the contents of the one addressed to himself, which were as follows:

MY DEAR UNCLE: I know you will be astonished and grieved when you find I am gone. You must excuse my abrupt and unceremonious departure. I knew, my kind uncle, if I stayed, you would endeavor to adjust a matter which will admit of no compromise. I refer to the relations which once existed between myself and Miss Emily Burrell. You will be surprised to learn that all connection is now broken off between myself and that young lady. I assure you I had good reasons for the course I have adopted. She proved *faithless*, and I asked no explanation of her conduct, from the simple fact that my own senses furnished me with all the evidences of her duplicity that I could have required. Please send to her the letter you will find with this note. Believe me, my dear uncle, it grieved me to leave you thus; but if you had known my feelings, I know you would now exculpate me from blame. As I could not see you, I take this opportunity of bidding you an affectionate farewell.

Your nephew,   HENRY.

"There is some mistake about this," said the old man, after reading the note a second time; "there is some mistake about this, and I wish the poor boy had not acted so hastily. The letter to Emily shall be sent at once, and I shall learn from her what the difficulty is. I am satisfied it is some trifling lover's quarrel, which will amount to nothing. I have set my heart on this match, and it must not be broken off by mere trifles." So saying, he forwarded the letter as directed.

Emily had sat up nearly the whole night upon which her rash lover was flying along the road like a wild man. It was the first disappointment to her new-born love, and she felt it keenly. She had never learned that "the course of true love never did run smooth." She could imagine no reason why Henry had not visited her the previous evening, according to promise. Whenever, before this time, he had not complied with his promise, he always gave the reason of his failure by letter. If it had not been a visit whose object was to seal the contract of marriage, she would not be so uneasy. Hour after hour she had watched for him, until the heart was "sick with hope deferred." Late that night, when she heard the steed lumbering along the road, it sounded in her ears as a fearful foreboding of evil. Then she began to reflect upon what her cousin Walter had hinted at the day before. He had wished to warn her, and she had left him in a fit of anger. It could not be possible, she thought, that Henry was trifling with her feelings. How could he be so base and ungrateful? Had he not vowed, again and again, that he would be true? Yea, had he not even sworn, and invoked the wrath of heaven on his head, should he prove false? She then began to think that Walter Hallam was interested himself, and probably he had something to do with the non-appearance of Henry; may be Walter had *murdered* him, and his mangled body was now lying hidden in the forest. She shuddered. But how could she be so foolish as to suppose her cousin would be guilty of such a heinous crime? Henry was sick, perhaps; but then he would have sent her word.

While thus these distracting thoughts were rushing through her mind the morning after her lover's flight, a letter was placed in her hands by one of General Winston's servants. With a trembling hand she tore the seal, and read:

MISS EMILY: I am gone from you *forever!* [The poor girl sickened and almost fainted; after awhile, however, she summoned up her courage, and read it to the end.] If we meet again, it will not be my seeking. It will not, I suppose, be necessary to state my reason for my conduct, as your own sense must suggest at once that I have discovered your heartless designs in regard to myself. I am at a loss to conceive of any motive which could have induced you to play the part you have, unless it be but the vain and frivolous wish of a thoughtless flirt to trample upon the feelings of a human heart. I would not have believed it had I heard it from a third party. Though you have trifled with my affections, I shall not attempt to conceal the fact that I loved *you;* and if this confession can furnish any gratification to your vanity, much good may it do. I will say more: I will even say that I love you *now;* but I hope to utterly tear your image from the depths of my bleeding heart. I loved you devotedly, Miss Emily, and with sincerity. I lavished all the affections of my whole soul upon you; and what return have I met with? But I trust I shall be able to forget you, and I will remember the many happy hours I have spent in your company as but the vagaries of an indistinct dream O it will be a severe struggle thus to banish from my mind an object once the center of all my thoughts and emotions. I once hoped that you would become the guide-star of my life—the beacon-light of my existence; but that hope is gone, and I am left alone to wander in the darkness of blighted love. When you read these lines I will be far away, and it will be accidental if you ever hear of me again. Notwithstanding the treatment I have received at your hands, I hope your pathway through life may be smoother than I dare wish mine to be. May kind angels watch over you and attend your every step. May all the blessings which I dare not hope for myself be showered on you. *Farewell forever!*

HENRY S. WINSTON.

We can not attempt to describe Emily's feelings when the perusal of the letter was finished. Perfectly innocent of the charges alleged against her, and ignorant of the grounds upon which they were based, she could not imagine in what thing she could have given cause for even suspicion of faithlessness. One stern fact, however, stood prominently before her, and that was, her lover was lost to her *forever*. When she thought of the cruel, cutting words her lover used, she shed bitter tears of anguish. But, after awhile, when nature was somewhat exhausted, and her feelings were more calm, and she was again endeavoring to find some clew to the mysterious event which had happened, the conviction suddenly fastened upon her mind that Walter Hallam was in some way connected with the disappearance of her betrothed. The above-mentioned individual, at that very moment, was standing in the door, watching, with intense interest, her every movement.

"Cousin Emily!"

She started as if she had been stung by an adder.

"My dear cousin, what distresses you so?" he said, kindly.

The question maddened her, because she was now convinced that she was indebted to Hallam for her present trouble.

"Walter Hallam!" said she, looking up with swollen eyes and a flushed face, "I will no longer attempt to conceal the opinion I have of you; I will speak out; and I will say I believe you are the cause of my present distress."

"How is that, Emily?" asked the young man, in surprise.

"Walter, do not pretend to be ignorant of an event which you yourself brought about. You shall gain nothing by it."

"Emily, for God's sake, explain yourself. What do you mean?"

"Can you deny," she said, with angry, flashing eyes, "that you prevented Mr. Winston from coming here yesterday, and that you were the cause of his abrupt departure last night?"

"Emily," said Walter, with more than usual earnestness, "I swear by the heaven above us I knew not till this moment he was gone! You accuse me wrongfully, cousin."

"You made threats in regard to Mr. Winston yesterday?"

"True; and I had some words with him yesterday evening on his return from here, and"——

"He was here yesterday, then?" cried Emily, interrupting him.

"Why, did you not see him?"

"No, I did not."

"There is something strange about this. I saw him enter the avenue, and I immediately left the house to demand an explanation of his conduct, when he should return home. He came tearing up the road in a few moments after I reached it. He appeared to be crazy. But tell me, what is the meaning of all this?"

"Walter!" said she, in a firm, determined voice, "I will speak candidly; *I love Henry Winston*, and we were betrothed lovers. This morning I received a letter, stating that he was gone *forever*. And now, to speak plainly, I believe you had something to do with his leaving."

"All I know about it is, he struck me yesterday, and ran

like a sneaking coward. I told you the fellow was a damnable villain, and he has proved it beyond all controversy."

"Walter," said Emily, rising, "I will not stay to hear you apply such epithets to one before whose face you would not dare to use such language. I will leave you."

"Cousin Emily," said the young man, with a reddened face, and standing before her, "read this before you go, and if he be not what I say, then you may call me what you please." And he handed her the letter from his sister to Henry Winston.

After perusing the letter, she was painfully puzzled and perplexed. She sat, with her head down, without speaking.

"Emily," said Walter, after a short pause, "I desired to show you this yesterday; but you left me in a very angry mood."

"Walter," said she, starting up as if a sudden idea had struck her, "this is a *ruse* of your own. You forged this letter! You did it to shake my confidence in Mr. Winston!"

"If I did, may God strike me dead on the spot! I found it in his pocket, with this miniature. You know I could not have forged the picture. This man Winston, my dear cousin," said Walter, with some show of tender feeling, "is the *murderer* of my sister, and has sought to destroy your peace of mind. I wished to warn you, but you would not let me."

"O Walter! forgive me. I do not know what I am saying. I am so wretched."

"I speak but the truth," resumed Walter. "I say he is a d—d scoundrel, and deserves the gibbet, if any murderer ever did. You should be thankful you have escaped the hellish monster. I am sorry he has made such an impression on your mind."

"Let us drop the subject, if you please," said Emily.

"I will never mention his name to you again, Emily. But there is *one* whom you can trust—*one* you need not fear—*one* who will anticipate your every wish—and one who will endeavor to make you contented and happy through life. And now, I again ask you, if you will cast off such a friend? My dear cousin, give me your hand and heart. I"——

"Walter Hallam!" she quickly cried, "if you do not wish to forfeit my friendship, never mention that subject again. O God! I can never love any body! I wish I could die! Leave me, Walter, leave me instantly!"

Walter gazed at her for an instant in seeming sorrow and surprise; but he concluded it would be the best policy not to urge his cause at present; so he left the apartment.

In a moment afterward James Burrell entered the parlor, where she was still sitting, in painful thought.

"O brother!" cried Emily, throwing herself into his arms; "I am so miserable!" and she sobbed aloud.

"Emily," said the brother, kindly and tenderly, "my dear sister, what does this mean? What troubles you so?"

"Read this, James; read it," she said, handing him a letter.

James, after hastily reading and returning the document, remarked:

"It is incomprehensible to me. But General Winston is waiting for you in the front parlor. Come, dry your tears; he can probably explain it all to your satisfaction."

The poor girl was too wretched and troubled to care for outward appearances. So quickly leaving her brother, she hastened into the parlor, with the undried tear glittering on her pale cheek. The old General stood before her.

"Emily, my poor child," said the old man, taking her by the hand, "I am sorry to see you thus. You have been weeping, child."

"O General Winston!" and she sank into a chair, and covered her face with her handkerchief.

"Emily," said the General, in a kind voice, "we must talk plainly. There is no necessity for concealment. Talk to me like you would to your own father. Now, what is the difficulty between you and my foolish nephew?"

"O, sir, I know not. I should ask you that question."

"There is a mistake somewhere, or somehow, Emily. The foolish boy left last night without even bidding adieu to his old uncle. I know he would not have acted so had he not been in deep distress of mind. This morning I found in his room two letters—one to myself, the other to you. I presume you have read yours?"

"I have, and I can not comprehend it."

"He seems to think you have been trifling with him."

"I know it; but, as God is my witness, I am not aware of ever having given the slightest cause for suspicion."

"I knew that, Emily; I knew you were true; but the boy is laboring under a terrible mistake of some kind."

"He, sir," said Emily, hesitatingly, "may have been trifling with *me*."

"Do not accuse him, Emily, of such perjury. I *know* better than that. A more high-minded, honorable boy does not breathe than Henry Winston. He loved you as truly as ever man loved woman. I know there is some mistake about this. Is it possible you can have no idea in regard to it? What took place yesterday between you and him?"

"I did not see him at all yesterday; though I understand he was seen in the avenue."

"Strange—very strange!" said the old man, as if talking to himself. "Emily," said the General, rising. "I shall write to my nephew to return immediately. I am satisfied he has made a most foolish mistake. Until I can hear from him, let me ask you not to suppose him, for one moment, *false* to you. I know he loves you, and I trust, in a short time, to see the wayward boy kneel at your feet and ask pardon for his conduct."

"I hope, General Winston, you will not lower me in the

estimation of your nephew by mentioning this to him as at my request."

"Fear not, my child; I shall write in my own name." Saying which, the General took his leave, and was soon wending his way homeward. Arriving at home, he seated himself and wrote a letter to Henry—telling him he had committed a great blunder from some cause or other; that, to his own certain knowledge, Emily still loved him, and was seriously disturbed on account of his rash conduct; that he had not the slightest reason to doubt her sincerity; that he must return at once and fulfill the contract, etc.

This letter, owing to the exciting events which soon afterward occurred, was never received by the person to whom it was addressed.

The next day James Burrell departed for West Point, and Walter Hallam, finding it was useless to remain longer, left for his home.

Poor Emily was left alone to weep over her sorrow and disappointment. Many, many unhappy hours did she spend. Henry (though she could not account for his strange conduct) she still loved, with that true devotion which alone woman can feel. His image was impressed indelibly upon her heart, and she cherished it with a feeling approaching almost to madness. Time rolled on; but amid all its changes it brought no consolation to the bleeding heart of Emily Burrell.

CHAPTER VIII.

"Then banners rise, and cannon-signal roars,
  Then peals the war-like thunder of the drum,
  Thrills the loud fife, the trumpet-flourish pours,
And patriot hopes awake, and doubts are dumb."

THE 20th day of December, 1860, had now come. The storm which had been gathering for years past was about to burst forth in sudden fury. A President had been elected by a party opposed not only to the social institutions of the slaveholding states, but to the fundamental principles which underlie the government itself. This party, which had been steadily increasing in numerical strength for years, now raised a howl in the wildest fanaticism and frenzy, and, taking advantage of an unfortunate division in the political organizations of the country, elevated to the chief magistracy a man of their own choice, and of their own destructive principles. It had been predicted long before by the far-seeing John C. Calhoun, that whenever any party should seize the reins of power, and inaugurate an administration upon the principle of centralization— or, in other words, that the several states sustain the same relation to the General Government that counties do to a state government—a dissolution of the Union would be the inevitable consequence. The time had now come for the verification of Calhoun's prediction; for Mr. Lincoln asserted the very identical political dogma which he declared would lead to the destruction of the government. The prophecy of the great advocate of state sovereignty was literally fulfilled. On the 20th of December, 1860, South Carolina, claiming her right as a mere partner in the Federal compact of Union, and conceiving her dignity outraged, and the security of her rights threatened by the election of a President whose principles were so antagonistic to hers, passed the ordinance of secession. Public sentiment was ripe for revolution, and it required but a bold leader to put the ball in motion. On the 9th of January, 1861, the star of Mississippi's destiny glittered side by side with that of South Carolina. One after another the southern states wheeled into line, under the banner of defiance, ready to repel any invasion of their practically claimed rights, or to meet the opposite party in a spirit of friendship and form a treaty of peace. But that party chose rather to adopt the suicidal policy of coercion, and expressed its wrathful determination to apply physical force for the restoration of a Union which had become hateful and intolerable.

The "Peace Congress" met. Proposition after proposition was made for reconciliation; compromise after compromise was offered; but were all rejected. The Republican party would hear to nothing but absolute submission, and an unconditional restoration of the Union to its previous condition. The Congress adjourned without accomplishing any thing.

On the 4th of March the new President took his seat. The inaugural address was eagerly and anxiously looked for. It, however, disappointed the feeble hopes of those who expected the adoption of a pacific policy, and declared that the integrity of the government should be preserved, and that the "stars and stripes" should float in triumph over every foot of soil which the United States had claimed. Seventy-five thousand volunteers were called out for the suppression of the rebellion. All hope of compromise was now destroyed, and the Union was indeed dismembered.

The Confederate Government was immediately organized, and steps were hastily taken to meet the formidable preparations making in the North. Without almost any of the usual and necessary appurtenances to a regular government, the Confederacy was born to be baptized with blood in its infancy.

The civilized world seemed to look on in apparent indifference as to ultimate results; or if any emotion was manifested, it was akin to a feeling of rejoicing over the downfall of republicanism. Crowned heads considered the dissolution but as the legitimate and necessary consequence of the experiment of self-government. They thought it would now be incontestably demonstrated that monarchy is the only form of government adapted to the wants and requirements of society. If any real sympathy at all was shown for either party, it was decidedly in favor of the North. It is true, a strict neutrality was early declared by England; but yet the United States was treated as a superior power endeavoring to crush a rebellion of stupendous magnitude. France placed herself in the attitude of an ancient seeress, so that in whatever manner the great struggle should terminate, she would be in a position to treat favorably with either or both parties. All our claims to recognition, and our right to admission into the community of nations, which, if our social institutions had been acceptable to the fastidious taste of false philanthropy, would have been at once acknowledged, were totally disregarded. The Confederacy stood absolutely alone—a mark for the shafts of a hostile world. Without a treasury, without a navy, without an army, she quailed not before the angry frowns of kingdoms, principalities, and powers. Relying on nothing but her own strong arm, the indomitable spirit, the stubborn patriotism of her people, she stood forth like a solitary giant, ready to vindicate her rights against the attacks of northern vandalism and the moral power of combined Europe.

Preparations for our subjugation were made on a grand scale in the North. It was the intention to march straight through to Richmond, "rough-shod" over the "ragged rebels." Wagon-loads of handcuffs came rattling and jingling along in the splendid train; and with these Confederate officers were to be manacled and paraded in triumph through the streets of the Federal Capital. Fine ladies, dressed and bedecked in the gay, gaudy colors of northern fashion, who had come to witness the signal victory, were seen amid the well-organized host. What a splendid procession! On and on they went, in the pomp of their pride and the glory of their strength, with hearts swelling in anticipation of the magnificent performances and exploits that were to immortalize the heroes of the 21st of July. They reached the plains of Manassas. Then they rushed, with yelling impetuosity, against the solid ranks of the stubborn southrons, expecting the frightened rebels to give way and fly in terror at the mere sight of Yankee valor and chivalry. But what was their surprise, astonishment and chagrin when the "Grand Army" was seen flying in disorder and confusion to the fortifications of Washington City! The rebels prevailed. God, in his wisdom, did not permit *this* horde of vainglorious braggarts to trample down the vindicators of human liberty and the rights of man. Five hundred thousand men were now called for by the Federal Government, with the intention of crushing the infamous rebellion by overwhelming force. The Confederacy raised an army of corresponding magnitude, and the great struggle now commenced on a scale so extensive that the whole world looked on in amazement. Armies were raised with a celerity, battles were fought with a rapidity, that completely puzzled the military chieftains of Europe. No four years in the annals of this world can present a history marked by so great a diversity of bloody scenes and gory events.

But, as the reader is familiar with the history of the late war, or rather as it is not our province to write its history, we will proceed with our story.

Henry Winston, after his return from Kentucky, volunteered his services in the first call for troops. With a magnanimity which was by no means uncommon or rare in the first days of the revolution, he refused all offers of promotion and office, and attached himself as a private to a company in the 9th Mississippi Regiment, which was stationed nearly a year at Pensacola. At the expiration of its term of service the regiment was disbanded, and Winston soon after joined the 15th Mississippi—a regiment distinguished for its valor and its heroic achievements upon many a dark and bloody field.

We will now commence at the latter part of September, 1862. About that time the army under General Van Dorn took up the line of march from Davis's Mills, sixteen miles north of Holly Springs, and proceeded in the direction of Corinth, Miss. On the night of the 2d of October the troops bivouacked at Chewalla, the first outpost of the garrison of Corinth. Early on the morning of the 3d the march was resumed. When within four or five miles of the little town of Corinth, the enemy's pickets were met and driven in. Steadily advancing, the Confederate troops soon reached the outer line of intrenchments, and then both parties were engaged in the work of death. The incessant rattle of musketry and the thundering peals of the open-mouthed cannon reverberated among the neighboring hills. Amid all this confusion and horrible din could be plainly heard the shrieks and groans of the wounded and dying, the shouts and curses of the living, all mingled together in one terrible medley. But every one recollects the battle of Corinth, so disastrous to the western army. On the first day the Confederate forces fought with a desperation and stubbornness that could not be withstood, and when the sun sank to rest the enemy was driven to his last stronghold. The "stars and stripes" could be seen waving from the forts around the town. One hour more of daylight and Corinth, with its army, would have been ours. But no Joshua was there to subvert the laws of nature and check the sun in his downward course. All was lost.

The company to which Henry Winston belonged was detached early Friday morning (the 3d) and thrown out in advance as skirmishers. They were deployed, and moved slowly and cautiously through thick bushes and briars, keeping up the line as well as the nature of the ground would permit. Coming to a field, they moved through it in regularity and order, meeting no resistance, with the exception of a few shells, thrown at random, which went whizzing high overhead, and bursting far back in the rear. When they reached the opposite side of the field, and advanced a short distance through the woods, they came in contact with the enemy's skirmishers. Brisk firing now commenced on both sides; but the Federals were soon driven back to their line of intrenchments. The Confederates moved up to within one hundred yards of the breastworks, and fought several regiments. For two hours they kept up a continuous firing; but at last, seeing that they were not supported, and their ammunition being exhausted, and themselves worried, they were compelled to fall back in haste, leaving several of their comrades wounded on the field; among them was Winston. He received a wound in the left arm, but might have made his escape had he not at the same time been struck by a spent ball, which, however, retained sufficient force to knock him senseless to the earth. When he recovered, in a short time afterward, he found himself surrounded by a small squad of Yankees.

"Water, men, for heaven's sake, water!" said the suffering Confederate, in a weak and feeble voice.

Some one of the party (without reflection, of course), obeying the first impulse of humanity to relieve distress, handed him a canteen. Winston eagerly seized it, and emptied it of its contents before returning it.

"Py Got!" said one of the party, "you drinks like a hoss. You is von tam starved reb. Vere you pe from, anyhow?"

"What command do I belong to, you mean?" said Winston.

"Yesh. Got tam! vot regiment you pe from?"

"The 15th Mississippi."

"Missippi, eh? Py Got! I no like dem Missip. Vot you got in yo pocket? Any monish?"

"None that would be of any use to you."

"You have no monish—no watch, eh?"

Winston made no reply to this last inquiry, for he was wearing a fine gold watch, which he did not wish to lose. He quickly pulled his purse from his pocket, and handed it to the wretch, in hopes that his attention would be diverted from the watch.

"You got no watch? Py Got! me sees for meself. I make you give him up," said the blue-coat, attempting to search him.

"My friend," said Winston, "would you rob a wounded soldier, who has had the misfortune to fall into your hands? I am completely at your mercy—perfectly helpless; and now would you search me after I have given you my purse? Is this the way one soldier should treat another? Is this the way you fight for the Union?"

"O, Got tam! me fight for meself, too. Me find one tam reb, me take his monish and his watch. It ish confisheate. Give up de watch—me no search you."

"Come ahead, Hans," said another Yankee, "I'll help you search him, and we'll go *halvers*."

"No, py Got! me no halvers. It ish my prisoner. Me shoot his arm jes to git his watch."

"Go on, then; the feller'll pizen you, though. Them rebs carries pizen just to catch sich greenhorns as you. Ef you touch it, it will kill quicker than snake pizen."

"De hell you say! You no fool me dat way."

"Go ahead, hard-head; but I would n't be surprised to see you drop dead in five minutes after you touch the pizen."

"By Got! how can you search him den?"

"O, I understand the business."

"Dat is one Yankee trick Me scarch him meself, an if he pizen me dead, me will kill him, if he pe mine own mudher, by Got!"

Saying which the blue-coat unbuttoned the military jacket of our wounded hero, and, seizing the watch-guard, cut it with his knife, and drew forth a chronometer that caused his eyes to dance with joy. At this juncture a new comer stepped up, in the garb of a Federal captain.

"So, Mr. Winston," said the officer, with a mock bow, "I find you among the Philistines."

Henry turned his head, and beheld Walter Hallam gazing at him with a sarcastic smile, that caused a cold chill to creep through his frame. However, Winston was one who feared not mortal man.

"You find me at present," said Henry, in reply to Hallam, "among a set of thieves, who do not scruple to rob the wounded and defenseless."

"You is a tam tief yoself, mine Got!" said the Dutchman.

"Come, Mr. Winston, no hard names, sir," said Hallam. "You recollect our last meeting was any thing but agreeable. You remember how you grossly insulted me, and then fled?"

"It is a falsehood, sir. You attempted to detain me by force, and I knocked you down, and passed on."

"Passed on! You struck me, and then ran off, as none but a coward would do."

"You are an infamous liar!" exclaimed Winston, now thoroughly aroused at this insinuation against his courage.

"Cowards can rant, Winston, when no danger threatens. But I repeat, sir, you insulted me, and ran like a coward. It was adding insult to injury, for you are the *murderer* of my sister. You attempted to deceive my cousin; and when I asked you to explain your conduct, you struck me and ran, and left the country at the dead hour of night, like a d—d coward. Deny it if you dare."

"I do deny it, and if you think I am a coward, even with one arm, I will fight you on the spot."

"No, sir; I shall not allow you that chance now. I once intended to challenge you, but that time has passed. I no longer consider you a gentleman."

"Vile dastard! you make that a pretext to avoid an honorable fight."

"And you, sir, are taking advantage of your position as a prisoner to call names and apply epithets, which you would not dare do if we were equal," said Hallam.

"If you think that a protection, I will waive it willingly."

"If you should, sir, I would not place myself on an equality with one who can not claim the privileges of a gentleman."

"Sneaking poltroon!" exclaimed Winston, springing to his feet—and, utterly forgetful of time, place, and circumstances, he planted a blow in the face of Hallam—"take that for your impudence. Now challenge me, if you want to."

"Winston," said the enraged Hallam, "that blow shall cost you your life. You shall die on the spot. Seize him, boys! bind him, and shoot the d—d rebel dog."

"By Got! dat ish right," said the watch thief; "let the tam rebel pe shot. Got tam! I'll vinish im."

Half a dozen Yankees closed in around the one-armed Confederate. Poor Winston was brought to his senses.

"In God's name, men, are you going to murder me in cold blood?"

"Colt plood or warm plood, te cap'n saysh you must pe kilt. Got tam! me no likes you nohow."

"Mr. Hallam," said Winston, in a calm, firm voice, "if you are an officer, I appeal to your sense of justice and honor. I would scorn to beg for my life; all I ask is fair play. This is a private quarrel between ourselves; and if you are a gentleman and a brave man, you will allow me the privilege of a fair fight. You can not screen yourself behind your military dignity and your fastidious notions in regard to caste without degrading yourself as a man. The insult I have offered is sufficient to level all distinctions of that character. Wounded as I am, I can nevertheless fight with pistols, and this I propose to do. Now, sir, if you are not a base coward, lay aside your assumed dignity, and meet me like a gentleman. To use your rank as you propose is the climax of baseness."

"I can not put myself on an equality with a man who could strike me and run. Do your work, men."

"You are an arrant coward, as I thought; but do your worst. Heaven will yet avenge such a foul murder."

"No time to talk about heaven now. Bind him, men!"

"There is no necessity for that," replied Winston. "I can meet death without being bound, if you will murder me."

"Bind him, I say!" shouted Hallam.

Poor Winston, with his bleeding arm, was now bound. He gave himself up for lost, and, with a silent prayer, he stood calm and collected in the midst of the merciless ruffians. Seeing that it would be useless to plead with such vile wretches and pickpockets, he opened not his mouth, but awaited his fate in silence.

"Now, boys," said Hallam, when the prisoner was bound, "step back ten paces. Ready!" The feet were thrown back, and the guns clicked ominously, but Winston looked at the wretches without the change of a muscle. "Aim!"

"HOLD! HOLD!!" cried a deep voice, in stentorian tones.

Winston at once recognized it as the same voice he had heard in Emily's bower. A Federal colonel rushed between the parties with a drawn sword. With a face burning with indignation, he ordered the guns to be lowered.

"Hell and fury, soldiers! murder a wounded prisoner? And you here, Captain Hallam, the instigator of this? By G—d! sir, it is d—d cowardly! You are a disgrace to the cause in which we are fighting. You ought to be court-martialed."

"Colonel," said Hallam, stepping up to his side, and whispering in his ear, "it is that d—d rascal, Winston. Do you not remember him?"

"I care not who it is, sir. By G—d! would you disgrace yourself and our government by such an act of villainy. G—d d—n it! I'm ashamed of you. Here, Sergeant Jones, take this prisoner to the rear; and if a hair of his head is injured, by the living God, you shall suffer for it! You, Captain Hallam, return with your men to your proper place, sir."

The Yankees, thus interrupted in their bloody purpose, retired sneakingly to their intrenchment. Winston, in the care of Sergeant Jones, had not gone far to the rear toward Corinth before he heard a wild, enthusiastic shout, such as only Confederate soldiers could make, causing the welkin to ring. It was the 33d Mississippi Regiment charging the first line of the enemy's works. The fact is known to many that this charge was made without bayonets and with empty guns! The Federals lost not a man; but as soon as the gallant and daring Mississippians of the 33d were within fifty yards, several regiments of Yankees fired off their pieces with considerable effect, and then took to their heels. Winston looked back, and saw an old dirty flag, torn and rent, proudly waving on the top of the enemy's intrenchments. It was the "stars and bars." But he had no time to pause, for the discomfited Yankees, hotly pursued by the Confederates, were soon at his heels, and he was caused to "double-quick" in order to prevent recapture. On they went, pell-mell, and in a short time reached the strongly-fortified town of Corinth.

Our wounded prisoner was immediately taken to the hospital, where his wound was examined and dressed, after the Yankees had been attended to. The artillery and musketry continued to roar and rattle at intervals during the whole evening. When night put an end to the contest, the Federals had been driven in on all sides, and were now all huddled together in their last fortifications. Corinth would undoubtedly have fallen the next day had not the Yankees been allowed to heavily re-enforce during the night from the garrison of Bolivar. Many Confederate soldiers will recollect that the cars were heard the whole night long rolling into the besieged town loaded with re-enforcements.

It was about eight o'clock that night when Henry Winston was aroused from an uneasy slumber into which he had fallen, by a light shining full in his face. Opening wide his eyes, he discovered an officer, surrounded by several others, dressed in Federal uniform, gazing earnestly into his countenance.

"I think," remarked one, in an undertone, "he looks more intelligent than any of the others."

"I believe he does," replied the officer; and, after looking closely for an instant, he seemed satisfied with his inspection.

Turning to one who appeared to be surgeon in charge, he said:

"Doctor, is that man," pointing to Winston, "badly wounded?"

"His wound," replied the surgeon, "is rather severe, but not dangerous."

"He could travel, I suppose?"

"He could, sir, without any danger."

"Then send him to my quarters at once," said the officer, in a whisper, which Winston did not hear.

He then turned and hastily left the building. He had gone but a short time before a file of armed soldiers entered, preceded by the surgeon in charge.

"That is the man," said the Doctor, when they had reached Winston.

The soldiers, going to Henry, said, "You will go with us."

"And for what?" asked Winston, half-rising.

"Ask no questions, but come on," said one, sternly.

Henry, not comprehending the purpose, nevertheless obeyed without asking any further question. Let the purpose be what it might, he knew it would be folly in his present condition to resist; so he resolved, since nothing better could be done, to submit to whatever fate might have in store for him. As soon as they reached the door, the two soldiers placed themselves, one on either side of the prisoner, and pointed in the direction they were to go. Henry obeyed without saying a word, though he thought the strange movement rather a suspicious proceeding. He feared that Walter Hallam had something to do with this unusual procedure; and, if so, he had nothing to hope. His fears on this score were, however, groundless; for after a brief walk they arrived in front of a two-story building, which stood about two hundred yards north-east of the old Tishomingo Hotel. One of the guards, opening a door, motioned to Winston to walk in. Henry entered the room, and found himself alone with the officer who had left the hospital a short time before.

"Be seated, young man," said the officer, in a kind tone, motioning to a chair. "I have something to say to you. I presume you know in whose presence you now are?"

"I have not the honor of your acquaintance, sir," replied Winston, in a tone of indifference.

The officer did not seem very well pleased at this mark of *nonchalance*, but he appeared to forget it in a moment, and fell into a brown study, that lasted for several minutes. Our hero sat perfectly still, and resolved to maintain the silence as long as the Yankee should. The officer spoke.

"So you belong to the rebel army, sir?" he said, looking Winston full in the face.

"I belong, sir, to the *Confederate* army."

"I am extremely sorry," continued the officer, not noticing the stress with which Henry pronounced 'Confederate,' "that so many young men like yourself have, under mistaken notions of duty, been induced to array themselves in opposition to their country's true interest. Many have been inveigled into this rebellious movement by designing politicians. Men who once held office of profit and trust under the old government have, for the sake of attaining higher power, turned traitors, and made the southern people believe that it was the intention of the United States Government to interfere with their institutions. I trust, however, that when their eyes are opened to the true state of the case, this misguided people will return to their allegiance. To all of those who in ignorance have enlisted in the defense of the so-called Confederacy, our government offers a full pardon, upon condition of laying down their arms; and she now offers it to you."

Winston made no reply, but waited patiently to learn why he had been sent for. The officer continued, after a brief pause:

"You seem to hesitate, my friend. Well, now I ask you, as a man of sense, if it would not be well to desert a cause now, which can not but be unsuccessful, and which will bring certain ruin upon all those who will persist in upholding it? Many of the southern people have been forced into the rebel service by the odious act of conscription passed by a spurious congress. Such ought not to be punished with the guilty. But if they remain in it from a false sense of honor, they must take their chances. The United States Government is determined, and she is amply prepared, to crush this infamous rebellion; and it will be done—I tell you it will be done. Her resources are sufficient; there is no scarcity of men, money, and war materials; and, sooner or later, she will be triumphant. Mild means have been used, and will still be used, for the restoration of the Union, until it is seen that those in rebellion will accept no honorable terms. After that, fire and sword will devastate the southern land. The northern patriots will flock with sorrowful hearts from every hill

and vale like gangs of locusts, and carry desolation to every
household and fireside. But, my friend, I must be brief; my
time is precious. I think you will see as I do, and I advise
you to escape the fearful doom which awaits those engaged in
this wicked movement. Return to our time-honored flag, and
you shall have a position which you are qualified to fill, if you
will do your country a service. She demands it of you this
very night. If you will do this, you shall not only have a
position in our army, but be well compensated for your
trouble. Will you do it?"

"I can not agree to perform any service until I know its
nature and object," said Winston, who, although suffering
from his wound, nevertheless felt some curiosity to know what
he would be required to do. "What is the service, sir?"

The officer appeared satisfied that his reasoning had "had
the desired effect," and he proceeded to reveal his plan.

"Young man, be not startled or surprised when I tell you
what this service is. It is all right and fair in war. You can
accomplish it this very night, and your country demands it at
your hands. Do it and you are a made man." The officer
drew nearer to Winston, and whispered a moment in his ear.

"General Price! My God!" exclaimed Henry, horror-
stricken at the proposition. "You are surely jesting—you
can not mean it!"

"My friend, I meant what I said."

"Let me hope, for the honor of the country from which
you come, that you do not mean that?"

"I repeat it, I meant what I said; and if you will do it, I
will pay you *one thousand dollars in gold* as soon as the work
is accomplished."

"*One thousand dollars!*" said Winston, in a tone which
could be construed into surprise at either the smallness or
largeness of the amount. The officer understood the latter.

"Yes, every dollar of it, in *pure gold*."

"*One thousand dollars*," said Winston, with a curl of the lip. "You must mistake me, sir, for one of your own vile race."

"Do you know, sir, to whom you are talking?" exclaimed the astonished officer. "I am GENERAL ROSECRANS!"

"I care not who you are! My God!" said Winston, in visible indignation, "I would not thus degrade myself, and heap deserved damnation on my soul, for *one thousand thousand*—no, not for all the gold in the United States! And if this is all you have to say, you may as well send me back. I would *die* before I would do it."

"Then go and take your chances," said the officer, hastily rising and going to the door. "I expected better of you than this. But I have no time to bandy words with a stubborn rebel. Here, guard, take him back."

Thus ended the interview between General Rosecrans and our hero. Henry was taken back to the hospital, where he slept until awakened by the booming of the cannon, early next morning. The result of the second day's fight is too well known. By mismanagement and blunders, the day was lost to the Confederates. The closing scene was a heroic charge from a small portion of General Price's army, led by the lamented Colonel Rogers. It was the last effort of a "forlorn hope." Poor fellows! many of them never returned from that assault. God grant that they may reap their reward in heaven!

It was during the confusion attendant upon this charge that Henry Winston made his escape. About ten o'clock the whole army commenced a disorderly retreat, and no permanent halt was made till they arrived at the pleasant village of Holly Springs. Thus ended the battle of Corinth, which was but the beginning of a long series of disasters and misfortunes.

CHAPTER IX.

> "They that bear
> The humble dead unhonored to their homes,
> Pass now i' th' streets no lordly bridal train,
> With its exulting music; and the wretch
> Who on the marble steps of some proud hall
> Flings himself down to die, in his last need
> And agony of famine, doth behold
> No scornful guests, with their long purple robes,
> To the banquet sweeping by."

EIGHT months had now passed since Henry Winston was wounded at the battle of Corinth. The army had fallen back from Holly Springs to Abbeville, from Abbeville to Grenada, and from Grenada to Canton. It was now encamped about eight miles from the last-mentioned village, on a spot whose only striking feature was scarcity of water. The camp was situated about a quarter of a mile from a filthy little creek, with holes of stagnant water, in which the genuine liquid was concealed from view by a beautiful covering of green-colored scum. Soldiers were seen strolling along the banks of this creek, searching for a hole which might not be the habitation of detested "*wiggle-tails*," or in which hogs had not laved their burning sides. Many a Confederate general was bitterly cursed upon the banks of that same dirty stream for confining men to such a *water-tight* spot, while the "stars and wreath" was quenching his thirst from cool cisterns that were hermetically sealed to the troops; which operation was performed by hiding the handles of the pumps, or by placing a guard over the precious beverage, who was like the ill-natured "dog" in Æsop's Fables, and could neither drink himself nor suffer others to do it.

One hot summer day, in the latter part of June, 1863, when the sun in his wrath was pouring down his vengeful rays, and scorching the very earth, and the poor soldier was compelled, in order to prevent being baked alive, to conceal himself under the foliage of the forest trees, or stretch a blanket over a bush under which three or four would crouch like Esquimaux in a shower of rain in the frigid zone, a courier rode up to the head-quarters of Colonel Farrell and delivered to that officer an order. Several soldiers, smoking with heat, came creeping out from under their "bake-ovens," and proceeded to the Colonel's tent, hoping, in heaven's name, to hear an order to move to where there was "much water." Colonel Farrell, after reading the document, seemed to reflect for a moment, and then, turning to an orderly, said : "You will order private Henry Winston to report at once to my quarters."

"Private Henry Winston," being a soldier not in the habit of straggling, was readily found, and very soon made his appearance at the head-quarters of the regiment.

"Winston," said Colonel Farrell, "I have just received an order calling for a man of a certain description, and I believe you will answer to it. I shall, therefore, order you to report forthwith to General Johnston, whose head-quarters are at Canton."

Private Henry Winston possessed one quality which every good soldier ought to have—that of asking no unnecessary questions. Taking it for granted that the Colonel knew best whether he would answer to the description or not, he obeyed without hesitation, and arrived in due time at the village of Canton. He immediately reported to General Johnston's adjutant; but that officer referred him to the General himself. Going into the room, according to direction, he found General Johnston alone in a profound study. So intently was he occupied with his own thoughts, that he seemed not to be aware of the fact that an intrusion had been made on his privacy. Our hero stood for a moment; but seeing no prospect of a disturbance of the silence on the part of the officer, he concluded at last to convince the General that he was no ghost, which, it is said, can be done by speaking first.

"General," said he, "I have reported to you in obedience to orders."

The latter individual suddenly started up, in seeming surprise.

"Ah, indeed," said the General, speaking as if in a dream. "For what purpose?"

"I am not aware, General, for what purpose. I was simply ordered by your adjutant to report to you; and I have done so."

The officer spoke not for the space of two minutes; but examined the soldier from head to foot with a scrutiny which Chesterfield would have considered highly improper in one's ordinary intercourse with society. He appeared to attempt to read the very heart and soul of Winston, who, however, stood the test without a change of countenance or the movement of a muscle. When he had scrutinized the subject to his satisfaction, the General again spoke:

"What is your name, sir?"

"Winston—Henry Winston."

"Winston? Are you related to General Winston, of Kentucky?"

"I am, sir; he is an uncle of mine."

"Be seated, then, Mr. Winston. I think you will do. I am well acquainted with your relative, and I know he is true to our cause. I can, therefore, trust you with important business."

"I hope, sir, no one can doubt my loyalty."

"No, I think not. But now to business. At present I have none near me who can successfully accomplish a mission I have in view—or, rather, none who are willing to undertake it—and I was forced to call on your Colonel, who is a gallant officer, and whose judgment I am perfectly willing to risk. You belong to the 15th Mississippi?"

"I do, sir."

"Well, then, I feel justified in trusting to your keeping facts upon which depends the salvation of two armies. I must have no half confidences, Mr. Winston, and you must understand all my plans in regard to this matter, fully and thoroughly. For if you agree to undertake this mission, I can commit nothing to writing."

"I am perfectly willing to undertake any thing, General, for the good of our cause, which is not beyond my capabilities. And I assure you, you need feel no hesitation in intrusting to me all the facts and information which would be indispensable to the successful achievement of the mission, whatever it may be."

"I will not conceal from you, Mr. Winston, that the mission will probably be fraught with great danger. If you should be detected, the consequence would be the loss of your life."

"O, well, General, if that be all, I do not place such a value upon my life that I can not afford to sacrifice it for my country, should it become necessary. If I should fail while in the faithful discharge of my duty, I can ask no greater boon as a soldier."

"You speak like a true patriot, Mr. Winston; but, as time is pressing, do you think that you can make your way into the beleaguered city of Vicksburg?"

"It will be a difficult undertaking," replied Henry; "but, if you wish it, I can try."

"It will be as you say. General Pemberton has got himself into an awful predicament by his disobedience of my orders. I instructed him not to go into Vicksburg, if he should not beat the enemy back to Port Gibson. By some unaccountable blunders he has managed to sustain two defeats in succession. The battle of Baker's Creek is the greatest blunder ever committed on the military chess-board. I fear Pemberton has lost his army by it. However, I want you to go into Vicksburg and learn what General Pemberton is doing, and what he intends to do. Tell him to hold out, if possible, until the 7th day of next month, and I will endeavor to make a demonstration in his favor. The enemy must be attacked in the front and rear, and the army of Pemberton must cut its way out. It is a desperate remedy, but I know of no other way of extricating him from the difficulty. You must attempt to go throughout the Federal army; learn its disposition; in short, find out every thing that can be of any possible benefit. Discover the enemy's weakest points—the points least guarded and defended. I shall then make arrangements in accordance with the report you may bring me. It is hardly necessary to remind you that the utmost secrecy must be preserved."

"Have no fear on that score, General."

"I rely implicitly on your devotion to our cause, Mr. Winston; and I will now acquaint you with some other plans, which it will be necessary to communicate to General Pemberton."

Here Winston was briefly and concisely put in possession of all the facts and plans in relation to the siege of Vicksburg, which may not be interesting to the reader to know.

After the General had completed his instructions to Winston, he said:

"You are certain that you clearly understand me? A mistake on your part may derange all my plans."

"In order that I may commit no blunders, I will, with your permission, repeat the instructions I have received."

"You are right, Mr. Winston. Proceed, sir."

Our hero then related, with remarkable accuracy, the substance of their conversation, besides very shrewdly and modestly asking several questions, which might yet be taken as suggestions, in regard to points upon which the General had not fully expressed himself. The officer listened with profound attention; then his face was seen to brighten.

"I see, Mr. Winston, that you fully comprehend me. You have unintentionally suggested plans concerning some movements upon which I had not entirely made up my mind, but which I had thought of adopting. But, by way of digression, how does it happen that you are only a *private?* A man of your capacity should hold some position in which his talent could be more advantageously employed."

"I have never sought office, General, and I shall hold none until I prove myself worthy of so high a trust. Besides, I think, sir, I can effectually serve my country with a musket in the ranks, where I am more needed."

"Your country, I hope, will reward such patriotism; and if at any time you should need assistance in any laudable effort for military promotion, feel no hesitation in calling on me. But now you must be gone. You must get to Vicksburg as soon as possible. How will you convince General Pemberton that you are a messenger from me?"

"I have the honor of a personal acquaintance with General Pemberton. There will be no difficulty in that respect."

"I am glad to find it so; for General Pemberton can talk the more freely to you in regard to this matter. But I will detain you no longer. You ought to start at once," said General Johnston, extending his hand. "So good-bye, and may God speed you on this dangerous journey." Henry shook the extended hand, and then left the apartment.

Winston immediately returned to camp, made all necessary preparations, and that very night set out for the besieged city. The country through which he traveled had been ravaged by the rude hand of a merciless enemy. On all sides, in every direction, marks of savage devastation presented themselves to the eye. Here lay vast plantations, stripped of all defense against the invasion of animals, with their growing crops choked with weeds and grass. No living animal had been left by the defenders of the Union to pasture on the decaying wheat-fields. Every horse and mule had been driven away; every cow and hog had been butchered. The charred remains of beautiful residences appeared in mournful desolation—the sad monuments of once happy homes. There stood, occasionally, a few dwellings, left accidentally by the Yankees, but deserted by their frightened owners. No smoke ascended curling up from their gloomy looking chimneys; no sound to indicate that the place had ever been tenanted by human beings broke the dead silence. The gates were broken down; the yards were defaced; the fences were burned; in short, every thing bore witness to the savage character of an enemy, who, feeling his inability to cope with Confederate armies in the field, had turned loose the vilest wretches that constitute the connecting link between man and demons to rob and plunder defenseless women and children.

"Surely," thought Winston, as he surveyed these relics of Federal barbarity, "surely God will inflict condign punishment upon a foe who wages war in this manner. For awhile he may lay waste and destroy, but Heaven, in its own good time, will bring the offender to justice, and send upon him a chastisement terrible in severity, and yet scarcely adequate to the atrocity of his crimes. Can it be possible that such an enemy will subjugate and triumph over this down-trodden land?"

The spy, for such Winston had now become, indulging in such reflections as these, by daylight the next morning reached the last Confederate pickets. Having ridden all night, he here halted and rested a short time. When the sun was about one hour high, our spy, leaving his horse with the pickets, and having made inquiries in regard to the position of the Yankee pickets, pursued his journey. He deemed it most prudent, for reasons known to himself, to make the remainder of the journey on foot. In a suit of Federal blue, he looked like any thing else rather than a Confederate soldier. Moving on slowly and cautiously, he met with no living mortal till near the Big Black River. When within a short distance of that stream, he heard, close to the road-side, the military term "Halt!" repeated in a foreign voice. Winston obeyed without hesitation. In a moment a blue-coat stepped into the road. What kind of a soldier he was we will leave the reader to judge from the dialogue, which immediately ensued.

"It was wal, me honey, ye halted whin I tould ye, or else me ould muskit would her stopped ye."

"An shure," said Winston in the same brogue, "it's not a counthryman ye wud be afther shooting is it, an a good souljer to boot, who has bin thramping over the counthry for three days with me eye on the ribil throopers?"

"Show your pass, thin, me friud, and go on."

"May be," said Winston, seeming not to notice the command, and drawing forth from his pocket a well-filled flask, "may be ye wud be afther taking something to drink?"

"Be gor, it's mesilf that will do that same; for, by the howly St. Pathrick, me throat is as dry as me carthridge-box. So pass her over, me darlint."

"She's none o' yer Louisiana rhum," said our spy, returning the half-emptied flask to his pocket, "but the rhaal ould Bourbon, Pat."

"Nather is me name Pat, shure," said the Irishman smacking his lips with great gusto, "but Tim O'Leary, all the way from the ould counthry, in the year forty-nine; and was n't it me that lived in New Yorck, and that jined the Zouaves to fight for the blissid Union? and was n't it me that got three hundred dollars whin I was musthered into service, an sint it to my swate ould mither, to comfort the good ould craythur in her ould age. I say it's Tim O'Leary that's done all that same, an is now fighting aghainst the ribils to set the swate nager fra, poor soul."

"By me sowl, Tim, ye've a big heart to do all that. An now take another dhrink to the memory of swate Ireland an the health of yer ould mither," said Winston, drawing forth the flask. "It's I that loves to threat a counthryman in this ribil land. Dhrink, me frind—dhrink confusion to all the ribils, an a health to Mr. Lincorn."

"Ye're a good, kind sowl, by the howly St. Pathrick! an it's not Tim O'Leary that wud be afther refusin to dhrink with a counthryman and a thrue souljer of the swate Union," said the Irishman, seizing the proffered flask. Taking another swig he returned it. "Be jabbers, counthryman, ye're a souljer afther me own heart," continued Tim O'Leary, now growing in the humor in which our hero desired to see him. "It's not mesilf that would refuse ye a little favor."

"Ye're the thrue grit, Tim; but I must be afther going. But where are the ithers that stand wid ye? Ye are not alone by yersilf, shure?"

"No, indade; the howl company is at the rivher. But where are ye goin?"

"To my command, shure."

"Show yer paphers, counthryman."

"By me sowl, Tim," said Winston, feeling in his pockets, "I hev lost me pass. But ye kin thrust a counthryman, shure?"

"It's mesilf that has orthers to let no one pass from the henemy's counthry; but since I know you are a thrue souljer, ye can go, though you must go rhound the company. So just take that path, me darlint; it will take ye down the rivher, and ye can paddle across in the ould canoe."

"No ither souljers betwane here an Vicksburg?"

"None but sthragglers; but go on quick, me counthryman; yhonder comes the relaife. Go on; they will think you are one of the bhoys of the company."

Winston wanted no second invitation to take his departure, but hastily bidding farewell to his new acquaintance of the Emerald Isle, darted down the narrow path, which had been pointed out, and was soon lost amid the bushes. The path wound along among the thick undergrowth for several hundred yards, and then suddenly turned into the stream, where our spy found the "ould canoe" mentioned by the Irishman. It was but the work of a few moments to disengage it from its fastenings, row across the river, and land on the opposite side. Thinking he might have use for the boat at some future time, and fearing it might be displaced before his return, he dragged it out on the bank, and concealed it from view; after which he continued his journey. Traveling through a country that bore marks of the vindictive nature of the enemy, he met with no adventure or incident worthy of record. Toiling on with indefatigable energy, under a hot, sultry sun, he at length, late in the evening, saw the blue smoke curling up from the Federal camp-fires. He now slackened his speed, and moved slowly but cautiously on. Presently he perceived the Yankee pickets on the road-side. Winston resolved to still play the bold game, march up unconcernedly, and rely solely upon chance, and the story he should trump up to suit the characters on post. So, walking on carelessly, he was soon within hailing distance.

"Halt!" said one of the pickets, when Winston was within ten paces of the post.

"Well, what will you have?" said the spy, carelessly.

"Where are you going?"

"To camp."

"What regiment?"

"108th Illinois," answered the spy, at a venture.

"How came you out of the lines?"

This would have been a difficult question for the spy to answer, but one of the Yankees extricated him from the difficulty unintentionally.

"O, he was detailed with the foragers; let him go."

"Where are the wagons?" asked the first interrogator.

"They are coming," replied our hero.

"Were you detailed?"

"Yes, certainly I was."

"Go ahead then."

And "ahead" our hero went, glad to have gained access to the Yankee army so easily and with so little trouble.

The office of a spy is both disagreeable and dangerous; for detection is certain death, and an ignominious one at that. Besides this, the violence done to the conscience must not be overlooked. The necessary deviation from the strict line of truth which it involves disqualifies a man of conscientious scruples for the position. We think that justice is rarely done to this class of soldiers, who frequently furnish information that insures victory to the party for which they may be acting. Now, Henry Winston was morally and religiously inclined by nature, and when he thought of the capacity in which he was endeavoring to serve his country, it was somewhat revolting to his feelings. But, after a second view of the subject, he relieved the qualms of conscience with the reflection that falsehood and deception were practiced by Washington and other great military men; and, since espionage was recognized by all parties as indispensable, he concluded it would not be wrong to use the means which would insure success. So, dismissing the subject from his mind, he resolved to stroll through the Federal camp, and answer all questions with truth or falsehood, as the emergency should require. Our hero could not be entirely ignorant of the fact that he was possessed of some qualities indispensable to a successful spy—

a total destitution of fear in the presence of danger—a quick perception of the idiosyncrasies of the parties with whom he might be dealing; so that he knew precisely what course to adopt almost as soon as he glanced at his enemy's physiognomy and heard the first intonations of his voice. In other words, he was a good judge of human nature. Add to this great shrewdness and intelligence, and it will be seen that such a man as Henry Winston could not be met with every day.

Our spy walked leisurely through the Yankee encampment without molestation, and listened, with apparent unconcern, to several conversations in regard to the besieged city. Among other things, he heard, with some little surprise, that the Confederates were to surrender the next day. At last, being wearied, he sat down, with the intention of waiting till the approach of darkness should favor his exit from the enemy's camp. He discovered that in front of the city there was a strong line of sentinels, and that it would be an extremely difficult matter to pass them in daylight. He could furthermore see distinctly the Confederate flag, not more than three hundred yards distant, unfurled, as he thought, in proud defiance. His plan was to steal, under cover of night, as close as possible to the Federal sentinels, await a favorable opportunity, then dash straight through before they could recover from their surprise. It was now sundown, and about one hour afterward Winston commenced to execute his purpose. He moved till within fifty yards of the sentinels, whose outlines he could see against the horizon, and who were fifteen or twenty paces apart; then he crawled on his knees till he was within ten paces of one of the guards.

"Who go dar?" said a negro's voice.

Our hero knew that this military interrogation was intended for himself; and, being too far off to make a sudden dash, he slowly rose from his hands and knees. In an instant he decided upon a new plan.

"Who go dar, I say?" exclaimed the negro, in a tone peculiar to that race of animals alone.

"Fren," replied Winston.

"Frens do n't ginerally come a crawlin on dar knees; but vance and gim de sign."

"I fell down, nigger, and hurt myself," replied Winston. "Dis chile am all right;" and he pulled his hat down to shade his face as much as possible, and limped up to the colored sentinel as though he were crippled.

"Now, den, dar, nigger, dat close enuff; gim de sign."

"Gettysburg," said the spy, in a whisper.

"What dat? Say im agin."

"Jackson."

"Uch! O! dat won't do; can't fool dis chile dat way; dat ain't him; guess agin, nigger."

"He! he! he! I jes jokin wid you, nigger; I know it; hold over your head; I giu im right dis time," replied Winston, throwing his hand behind him.

The negro poked out his head over his gun to listen. A glistening bowie-knife whizzed through the air, and poor Sambo fell, with a cloven skull, to rise no more. Our hero waited not to see what effect this maneuver would have on the negro's comrades, who were not far off, but bounded away like a deer. Several guns were discharged at his retreating form, but the balls passed harmlessly over his head. When he had gained the distance of one hundred and fifty yards, or thereabouts, he slackened his speed, well-knowing that the Yankees would not dare to follow, and thinking it dangerous to advance too rapidly on the Confederates. He was right, for in a moment afterward he heard the usual military challenge.

"Who goes there? Halt!"

Winston stopped.

"Who are you?" said he.

"Confederate," was the reply. "Who are you?"

"A friend."

"Advance, friend, and give the countersign."

"I have no countersign," said the spy, going up. "I, therefore, surrender."

"What are you—a deserter?"

"No; but if you are a Confederate, take me at once to the officer in command. I have a communication of importance to make."

The sentinel clapped his hands together twice, and soon afterward a sergeant made his appearance.

"Sergeant," said the sentinel, "here is a prisoner."

"How did you happen to capture him?" asked the sergeant.

"He came up voluntarily and surrendered. He says he has a communication of importance to make."

"And what may that be?" continued the sergeant, addressing himself to Winston.

"I will make it known only to the proper officer; and I ask you to take me, as soon as possible, to an officer."

"I have very little confidence in Yankee 'communications of importance.' But, however, come ahead; I will take you to our Colonel, who is close by."

They accordingly moved but a short distance, when the sergeant said, "That is the Colonel," at the same time pointing to a tree under which reclined an officer dressed in Confederate uniform. Had there been sufficient light, Winston would have beheld a large, tall form, which combined all the elements of a fine-looking soldier. The form was surmounted by a head which phrenologists would place in the first class. A large, mild blue eye beamed under a high, broad forehead, that indicated unusual intelligence. Thin light hair hung almost to the shoulders. Upon the whole, he was, without doubt, the finest-looking officer in Loring's division. It was the brave, magnanimous Colonel Drake, of the 33d Regiment of Mississippi Volunteers. Every soldier in the 33d Mississippi will shed a tear to the memory of the gallant Colonel Drake who fell upon the bloody hills of Georgia, lamented by every soldier in the brigade to which he belonged. He died as firm a soldier, as true a patriot, as perfect a gentleman as ever drew a sword in defense of the unfortunate Confederacy. Rest, brave soldier! rest in peace with the holy martyrs of liberty, whose memories will be hallowed by the tears of fifty, yea, a hundred and fifty generations!

"Colonel," said Winston, approaching, "I wish to see General Pemberton immediately, upon business of importance."

"That is a strange request to bring to me," replied Colonel Drake. "Who are you? and what is your business?"

"You must excuse me, Colonel, I have not time now; neither am I at liberty to make known any part of my business except to General Pemberton in person."

"Well, why do you not go on to General Pemberton? What do you come to me for?"

"I surrendered to your men, sir, and am in arrest."

"Are you a Yankee?"

"No, sir, I am not."

"You talk quite strangely. What are you, anyhow, and where do you come from?"

"I am the bearer of dispatches from General Johnston, and am from Canton."

"How am I to know you are a messenger from General Johnston? This may be some Yankee trick, for all I know."

"You do not know who I am, Colonel, nor have I time to tell you. I only ask you to send me under guard to General Pemberton."

"O, very well; I can do that. Here, Sergeant Cope, send a file of supernumeraries with this courier to General Pemberton's head-quarters."

It was more than a mile to the General's quarters, and our

trio moved on through the beleagured city, which slumbered in silence, darkness, and gloom. After the lapse of three quarters of an hour, they reached the office of General Pemberton. The General was walking up and down the floor, while three or four clerks were busily engaged writing. The spy approached with the familiarity justified by previous acquaintance, but seeing that he was not recognized, it was necessary to make himself known.

"I see, General Pemberton, you have forgotten me."

"Henry Winston, I declare!" exclaimed the officer, after looking closely into his face. "My dear fellow, I am glad to see you. I have inquired after you frequently since the war commenced, but have never been able to find where you were. I expected to hear of you as a distinguished officer in some part of the army. But what in the world are you doing in this garb? You are no Yankee?"

"No, General, very far from it. I assumed this character to make my way through the Yankee army. I am from General Johnston, and as I am in haste to accomplish my mission, if you will see that we are alone for a few moments, I will deliver to you my communication, which is of some importance."

"Come into my private room, then," said General Pemberton, opening an adjoining door, and locking it after entering.

"I fear, Henry," continued General Pemberton, taking a seat, and offering one to the spy, "your communication, if concerning the unfortunate city, is too late, unless it should be something in the form of a miracle."

"Is it true, then, General Pemberton, that the city is about to capitulate? I heard such a report to-night in the Federal camp, but did not consider it reliable; and I have hastened on to lay before you General Johnston's plans for your rescue."

"As I said, Henry," replied the officer, with a mournful smile, "unless the plan of General Johnston should be miraculous, and something which he can accomplish without my aid, or at least with very little assistance on my part, nothing can be done for my relief. To make a long story short, I am compelled, by the force of circumstances, to surrender the whole army to-morrow morning."

"Is it possible? Can you not hold out three or four days longer? On the 7th day of this month General Johnston proposes to make a move for the salvation of your army; and I am instructed to say to you to hold out till then, if possible."

"It is certainly very considerate," said General Pemberton, in a bitter tone of voice; "it is certainly very considerate in General Johnston to postpone this proposition until my noble troops are all half famished; and ten or fifteen thousand of them are languishing on beds of sickness, prostrated by over-exertion, exposure, and want of food. Several weeks ago an effort could have been made, which might not only have relieved this place, but might have entirely defeated the enemy. Our artillery has been booming for days in the very ears of General Johnston, thus giving him to understand that we would hold out to the last. And now, when our commissary is absolutely destitute, and our faithful soldiers are actually reeling in the intrenchments, here comes the extraordinary proposition to hold out till the 7th, when it is utterly impracticable and impossible. What has General Johnston been doing for the last forty-eight days but lying around Canton or Jackson, with an idle army? He ought to have made this proposition at least a month ago. It is too late now."

"I am very sorry, General, you are reduced to the necessity of a capitulation; for, with the aid of General Johnston, in four days your army might cut its way out."

"Further resistance would be a useless effusion of blood, and I do not feel at liberty to sacrifice my wearied men, in their present condition, even if I had the subsistence necessary to the prolongation of the siege. No; there is no help for it; and, as much as I regret it, I am forced to surrender to-morrow morning. Indeed, the articles are already drawn up and signed, and the enemy will take possession to-morrow."

"Such being the case, it is useless to lay before you any of General Johnston's plans, but I trust, General Pemberton, our friendship is still such that I can ask you a question which may be impertinent, considering the difference of our situations, by reason of military rank?"

"Why, my dear fellow, I am surprised at your insinuation. You should, I think, be sufficiently acquainted with me to know that I am not one to be affected in such a manner by mere artificial distinctions of rank. If that were the case, I should have resigned my position long ago; so talk as freely and familiarly to me as you did when I visited at your father's house."

"Well, then, General, what will the country think of this transaction?"

"The natural delicacy of your feelings, Henry, I see, would not permit you to ask a question more to the point. Why did you not ask me what the opinion of the world will be in regard to my *selling* this city? I am aware that such a report has already been whispered about among the troops. Of course it will be generally circulated. I would scorn to notice the vile and absurd slander. I can talk plainly to you, Henry, and I tell you I feel a clear conscience in regard to this matter. I have done all that mortal man could do, and I can not stop to clear up the idle reports which may be circulated concerning me by '*street generals.*' You know it is human nature to err, and I confess I have committed some great mistakes. I have, however, been grievously disappointed in some of my calculations, and one of them was the expected co-operation of General Johnston. As matters have turned out, I suppose I am justly censured for not abandoning this position at first. I could not for a moment imagine that the government would be willing to give up such an important point without a single struggle to hold it. I conceive that I have acted in accordance with the views of the President, for I know he was in favor of defending Vicksburg at all hazards. Now, Henry, I say to you, in confidence though, what I would not say to any other man—the surrender of this city is the downfall of the Confederacy. *Our cause is lost.* You may be surprised, but the Confederacy will be overthrown. I knew the importance of Vicksburg, and therefore I have risked every thing to hold it. Whether our misfortunes resulting from this movement are due to my blunders or General Johnston's *slow motions,* posterity must be the judge. With the army under my command, and another to harass the enemy in the rear, he might have been seriously crippled, if not totally defeated. But nothing of the sort has been attempted. On the contrary, I have been left alone, cooped up within narrow limits, to extricate myself in the best manner I could from my perilous situation. The world will soon know the result. I am aware that I will be censured by the public. Success, with them, is the test of merit. I care not what the qualifications of a man may be, if he meet with unavoidable reverses, he will be condemned by the public. On the other hand, if a commander achieve victories that are the result of accident rather than his own judgment, prudence, and foresight, he will be lauded as a great chieftain. Well, well," continued the General, "this may be all right, and if success is to be the standard, I know I will be blamed by the people. But, if I am to be censured simply because I have been unfortunate in the defense of this city, I will submit to the decision without a murmur. I am satisfied, though, if I had been successful, my name would have been connected with any thing else than the cry of 'traitor,' and all that kind of thing. I should think my loyalty by this time to be beyond all dispute and controversy."

"It affords me pleasure, General Pemberton, to say to you that your devotion to our cause is questioned only by people who are blessed with profound ignorance in relation to military matters."

"I know the public will be disposed to grumble, Henry, and to shift the whole responsibility of this disaster to my shoulders. Well, I can bear it. But one thing is certain; I will no longer hold a high position in the army with the senseless clamor of the public against me. I could not do myself nor our cause justice. I shall resign the position I now occupy, and take any other to which I may be assigned. And if that will not do, I will shoulder a musket and go into the ranks where my country can be effectually served, and myself escape, for awhile at least, the unjust aspersions of an exacting people. I am not one who would feel his dignity lowered by buckling on a knapsack, and marching with my countrymen in the capacity of a private instead of a general. Although I believe our cause is now hopeless, I will stick to it as long as any other man will."

"I hope, General, the public will not be so unjust as you seem disposed to believe."

"All I ask, Henry, is justice. But I know the people too well to suppose that this capitulation will be viewed with any degree of just allowance. I can already see that I will be the only party blamed in this unfortunate affair. I have, however, the consolation to know that I have faithfully discharged my duty. It is nevertheless somewhat mortifying to my feelings to think that my name is coupled with that of Arnold, when I have labored for the preservation of this point with all the energy of my nature. My efforts in procuring subsistence have not been seconded; and it will be found, on investigation, that others beside myself deserve a portion of the people's reproaches. But I will be forced to bear it all. The army, in the eyes of the public, will be a host of martyrs, while their commander will be a Benedict Arnold. The anxiety and the solicitude which have caused me to pass so many sleepless nights will never be taken into the account. While these very people, who are now so lustily crying out 'down with the traitor,' were at home, in peace and quiet, and while they supposed me to be taking my ease, I have been watching, have been reflecting upon the best means for the preservation of the state, till my very nerves trembled with fatigue and weariness. Many and many a night, when our brave soldiers were slumbering in tranquillity, I was lying awake, my mind troubled and perplexed with cares of which no one was even dreaming. And all the reward I receive is the suspicion, and not only the suspicion, but the cry in my very ears of disloyalty to a country upon whose altar I would as willingly sacrifice my life as the best loved and most unsuspected commander in the Confederate army. I will even go into the ranks, but not with the intention of proving my loyalty to this ungrateful people, but from a sense of duty. If I fall, though I have no reason to believe that a single tear will be shed for my fate, yet my blood will not be spilled in vain, and I will reap the true patriot's reward years hence, when another generation can appreciate my motives and my labors. Should I be so fortunate as to survive this cruel conflict, and live to see peace return, I ask no greater privilege than to appear as a private covered with the blood and dust of battles, and receive a discharge from the service of a country for whose independence I am willing to sacrifice all and every thing."

"I am surprised, General, that you are so despondent as to our final success."

"I take a practical view of a plain subject, Henry. I would not talk thus freely to every body. I do not wish to discourage any one. But I say to you, as a friend, it is my candid opinion that before the winter of 1865 the downfall of the Confederacy will be a past event. We will now be gradually driven in on all sides toward Richmond, and the last battle will be fought for the capital. When that falls into the enemy's hands, we can not hold out twenty-four hours longer. It is all sheer nonsense to talk about converting the army into bands of guerrillas. You will see in two years from to-day that my prediction is correct."

General Pemberton then changed the topic, and continued to talk to Winston for half an hour longer, but upon subjects which can be of no interest to the reader. At the expiration of that length of time Henry took his departure. It was with a feeling of sadness that he wended his way to the quarters of a friend along the silent streets of the doomed city.

"Proud city of the hills!" (thought our hero) "nobly hast thou withstood the hurtling missiles of death that have laid low so many of thy brave defenders! Once thy gallant sons, with stout hearts and strong arms, hurled back the wrathful foe from thy defiant forts. Once the loud shouts of blood-bought victory ascended to the skies from the lofty heights of thy cannon-scathed hills. Troy stood ten years with the Greeks thundering under her high battlements. And yet no Trojan horse, concealing lurking enemies, rests amid thy deserted streets. No traitor's foot pollutes thy sacred soil, and desecrates the spot crimsoned with the blood of thy fallen heroes. Thy soldiers are true, thy general is true, but still relentless fate has decreed that thou shalt be ravaged and torn by the vandal hand. Starvation walks lean and gaunt amid the faithful vindicators of thy honor, and soon the hated foe will clamber up thy steep hills, and his huzza will echo among thy sorrowful dwellings. Though such is thy inevitable doom, yet the heroic deeds achieved in thy defense will equal the proud and time-honored glories of ancient Rome!"

CHAPTER X.

"Onward they march embattled, to the sound
Of martial harmony; fifes, cornets, drums,
That rouse the sleepy soul to arms, and bold
Heroic deeds."

THE following morning a brilliant sun peered above the high hills of Vicksburg, driving away the straggling remains of the previous night that loitered in the train of the sable goddess. It was a day rendered sacred and illustrious in the annals of American history by the associations with which it is connected. Looking far back into the dim mists of the past, the "mind's eye" can see a small band of patriot heroes that declared a nation free and independent. Ever since the eventful period of '76, this day has been an epoch in our history. With feelings of glowing patriotism the people have celebrated it with religious fervor, pouring out libations in honor of the canonized heroes who have handed down to them the rich legacy of civil and religious liberty. For nearly a century, men, women, and children, dressed in their best suits, have assembled annually on this sacred anniversary, under the wide-spreading boughs of oaks, venerable with age, to rejoice over the great boon of freedom, purchased with the gore of a seven years' conflict. Long will be remembered the many interesting scenes which have transpired on this never-to-be-forgotten day of jubilee—the foot-races, the fights, and other innocent amusements characteristic of the American people.

The day bid fair to be clear and sultry. The Federals commenced early in the morning to make preparations for entering the fallen city in triumph. Officers, bedecked in the gay trappings of Yankee uniform, went dashing on spirited chargers, that pawed the earth in the pride of their strength. Regiment after regiment was drawn up, with gleaming arms, that reflected the rays of the morning sun in the eyes of the gloomy Confederates. The Mississippi River teemed with dark-looking gun-boats, from whose ugly tops thousands of flags, displaying the "stars and stripes," floated in the summer breeze. Soon the vast column on land was put in motion, and marched into the city with banners streaming in the wind, with drums and fifes playing "Yankee Doodle," and other airs peculiar to the Yankee nation. The Confederate soldiers looked on this exhibition with mingled emotions of silent rage and sorrow. No one viewed it with more profound feelings of regret and vexation than Henry Winston. As soon as the head of the column had appeared within the streets, he stepped out, fully armed and equipped as a Yankee soldier, and moved along in the reverse direction to that which the jubilant enemy was going, without exciting any suspicion. He had not moved a great distance, however, before he recognized a personage whose acquaintance he did not care to acknowledge on the present occasion. He furthermore saw a movement of this personage which he did not exactly approve; so he suddenly turned from the road, and was in a moment hidden among the high hills of Vicksburg. When he had reached what he thought was a safe distance, he at length paused on the top of a lofty height that commanded a view of the enemy's movements for some distance, along a straight sloping piece of road. He seated himself upon a cannon, which had been abandoned, owing apparently to derangement of some of its machinery, and leisurely surveyed the moving body that wound among the hills like a long, black snake. Presently a deafening peal of artillery rent the air, shook the earth, and then rolled down the river.

"Vile rabble!" exclaimed Winston, starting up, "to rejoice over what you should consider disgrace! Ye desecrate the

4th of July by refusing others the rights our forefathers won through a successful rebellion. Ye are now celebrating a day upon which was declared the very principle this fallen city was attempting to defend. Your proud flags stream not, as ye think, over the tottering hydra of rebellion, but over the lacerated form of departing liberty. Inconsistent crew! an evil fate now permits you to triumph over a down-trodden foe; but, if there be justice in heaven, you will sooner or later receive your merited deserts. Move on, savage herd! your punishment will probably come like a thief in the night, when you least expect it."

Another earth-shaking boom reverberated from hill to hill, followed by a loud cheer ascending from thousands of Yankee throats.

"I would," continued the spy, somewhat enraged, "this good piece were charged with grape or canister; I would fire a salute that some of you would long remember. It may be that some ammunition has been left with this abandoned gun," he said, dismounting and going to a caisson which had also been injured. "Thanks be to heaven! here are three or four charges in this box; and now I will make my first experiment in artillery practice. If this piece will work, I doubt not the Yankees will have reason to curse this untimely display of my marksmanship. As good luck will have it, the gun can be used, and I will proceed to load it in the most approved style with a shell," said he, ramming down a twenty-four pound missile of that description. "One good thing is," continued the spy, deliberately directing the piece, "I have a large target and can scarcely miss the whole mark. Just so I give my gun sufficient elevation, it will be so unceremonious as to lay somebody in the dust. Now, then, I think that will do. May God have mercy on all whom this shot may send into his presence!" At that moment another peal burst from the Federal artillery, followed by cheers. "Now, my Yankee friends, here is the response from Dixie. In the name of God and liberty, *fire!*" he exclaimed, and jerked the string attached to the fuse.

The spectators in the distance, whose eyes happened to be turned in that direction, saw a huge volume of smoke roll up from the top of the hill on which Winston was performing this fool-hardy exploit. In an instant afterward something was heard howling and whizzing through the air, making a noise similar somewhat to the tones of a hollow top. On and on it went, with unerring certainty, straight to the slowly-moving column, which, striking about middle ways, it burst with an explosion and a power that it at once checked the astonished enemy's progress. Winston, standing upon his gun, saw this; he knew that the shot had taken effect, and he was satisfied with his performance. He discovered, furthermore, a small detachment of Federals from the main body making their way rapidly to his position. Waving his hat, and with daring recklessness giving three cheers for the young Confederacy, he darted down the hill in the opposite direction, and was in a moment lost from view.

The reader's attention must now be called to a conversation which was going on in the Federal column, half an hour previous to the tragical exploit of Henry Winston. A colonel rode leisurely at the head of his regiment, and by his side was another officer of inferior grade. These two, with even this brief description, our reader has already recognized as Colonel James Burrell and Captain Walter Hallam.

"Colonel," said the latter individual, "I had occasion this morning to be at the head of the column when it entered the city, and I'll bet you a treat you can not guess whom I saw."

"Done, sir, done!" replied Colonel Burrell.

"Who, then?"

"Why, Yankees, of course," was the laughing response.

"True; but I saw more rebels than Yankees—and especially

one who is a rebel indeed—one whom I have met before, under aggravating circumstances—and one who has given cause of offense to us both; for it was no other than that d—d villain and traitor, Winston."

"Well, there is nothing remarkable in that fact; you would be as liable to see him as any other rebel."

"No, it is not wonderful that I should see him, but it is a little strange that I should see him armed and dressed in Federal uniform, and moving along the line of our march in a contrary direction with perfect freedom."

"Why did n't you have him arrested, Captain?"

"I°was on the point of doing that very thing, when the d—d rascal dodged in a turn of the road and could be seen no more. I make no doubt that this d—d rebel is and has been a spy in our army."

"The evidences of his guilt are not so palpable to me as they appear to you, Captain Hallam. The probability is, the man has dressed himself in our uniform, and has thus made his escape. I have not the same cause, perhaps, for prejudice, Walter, that you have, which induces you to place the most uncharitable construction possible upon all his actions."

"Do not call it prejudice, Colonel; you may call it hate, if it so please you. I look upon him as a *murderer*, and the murderer of my own sister at that. I have never explained this to you, but some time, when we have leisure, I will show you the proof. You will then see whether I have just cause for 'prejudice,' as you call it."

"Something of this have I heard from Emily, but I could find no sufficient grounds to justify the grave accusation of murder. His face, I am sure, is indicative of any thing else rather than such a character. Say what you may, he is undoubtedly a brave man. By the gods! he faced you and your squad gallantly on the field of Corinth, when you had him bound, and your primed guns pointing at his breast. I never saw a finer exhibition of cool bravery in my life. By G—d, Hallam, it makes me mad, even now, to think you would have murdered such a man in cold blood, without giving him a single chance for his life."

"I had good reason for so doing, Colonel. I once intended to challenge the fellow to fight a duel, but he proved himself to be any thing but a gentleman, and after the repetition of the offense at the battle of Corinth, I did not consider him worthy of such a privilege."

"What offense was that, pray?"

"Why, he struck me as he did at Corinth, but did not stay to face consequences. He took to his heels, giving me no opportunity to resent the insult."

"I never knew before that you had had a difficulty with Winston previously to the battle of Corinth."

"We never had much of a difficulty. Your brave man acted the coward as completely as you ever saw."

"When did that happen?"

"The day before he ingloriously fled from Kentucky. I saw him returning from your father's with the speed of a madman, and I thought it a suitable occasion to ask an explanation of his conduct in regard to my sister. But, sir, instead of returning a civil reply to my question, he struck me unexpectedly, as I told you, and then fled. That night, you know, he left for 'parts unknown.'"

"His conduct, in some respects, I own, is incomprehensible; but I am not disposed to condemn him without hearing his statement concerning the matter. He may have had very good grounds for acting as he did."

"I do not care now any thing about his statement, when I have proof positive of his villainy; and I should think, Colonel, when you consider how he trifled with cousin Emily"——

"Hold, Captain Hallam!" cried Colonel Burrell. "we will

waive that subject, if you please. I care not for my sister's name to be mixed up with your quarrels. The man is nothing to me or my sister either. Emily, I trust, has forgotten this school-girl's affair to which you allude. Though at present I can not reconcile his actions with General Winston's statement, I am nevertheless disposed to believe his nephew was laboring under a mistake of some character. Whether he was or not, it is a matter of indifference to me and to my sister. Even if he were guilty of faithlessness, I could not consider it a sufficient crime to justify me in taking his life in cold blood."

"I think, Colonel, you are disposed to be rather severe on me. I had reasons, which I see you can not or will not appreciate, but which I considered a sufficient justification of my conduct. Under similar circumstances, I think I should act just as I did at Corinth."

"By the eternal G—d! if I should see you at it, I would be tempted to blow your brains out."

"It appears to me, sir," said Walter, somewhat nettled, "you are wonderfully taken with this d—d rebel."

"No more so than with any other brave man. I never could and never will see a brave man imposed on, even though he be a rebel and an enemy. If there is any quality I admire, it is true bravery, and this fellow Winston seems to possess it in an eminent degree. I never saw a more god-like look in mortal man than at Corinth, when he stood surrounded by enemies bent upon taking his life. By G—d, Walter, if you had murdered him, I believe I would have involuntarily chopped your head off."

"I declare, sir," replied Hallam, with a smile, "you are complimentary. I venture to say, though, the man who performs the exploit you have mentioned would do well to see that his own cranium is set firm to his shoulders. There are very few men who would, without some little resistance, part with the important member which you can so easily sever from the body."

It was at this moment the shell sent by Henry Winston exploded in the midst of the regiment commanded by Colonel Burrell. It fell not ten feet from the Colonel himself, and one piece carried away his right foot. Hallam escaped unhurt, but a Dutchman behind him was killed instantly. It was the man who had taken the spy's watch! Thus it will be seen that even in this world God frequently metes out just punishment for crime.

> "Aye, justice, who evades her?
> Her scales reach every heart;
> The action and the motive,
> She weigheth each apart;
> And who swerve from right or truth
> Can 'scape her penalty!"

When Walter Hallam picked up his hat which had been knocked off, he saw lying by it the watch which had been jarred from the Dutchman's pocket. On examining it, he discovered engraved in plain letters on the case the name of *Henry S. Winston.*

"That d—d rebel's fate seems strangely connected with mine," thought Walter. "I will keep the watch, however, in spite of h—ll. I would not be at all surprised if he fired the cannon which threw this shell." Happening at that moment to look in the direction whence the missile had come, he descried a man, mounted on a gun, waving his hat in triumph. "I 'll bet that is the d—d rascal now. Boys!" cried Hallam, pointing to the hill upon which Winston was stationed, "bring that man here, dead or alive."

But Winston, as we have already seen, saw the movement, and thinking "discretion the better part of valor," beat a hasty but orderly retreat. Leaving the Yankees inconsistently rejoicing over the two events, *the* RISE *and the* FALL *of liberty,* and thanking God, in their foolish hearts, that the temple of freedom was erected that they might have the exquisite pleasure of tearing it down, we will follow the motions of our spy.

Winston made his way out with very little difficulty, as the enemy was careless and good-humored after the surrender of the city. Proceeding leisurely, he reached, late that evening, the Confederate pickets with whom he had left his horse. With these our hero remained during the greater part of the night, and early the next morning set out for the village of Canton, to report the result of his mission to General Johnston. In the afternoon he discovered clouds of dust rising high in the air. In the course of half an hour he met Major-General Loring, who was in command of the troops, and was then moving near to the Big Black, ready to make a demonstration for the relief of Vicksburg when General Johnston should give the order. Winston, who was still in the garb of a Yankee, was of course halted.

"Where are you going?" asked General Loring.

"I am on my way to Canton, to report to General Johnston."

General—H—ll! what has a Yankee to do with General Johnston?"

"I am no Yankee, sir."

"What are you, then?"

"I am a Confederate soldier, sir, and belong to the 15th Mississippi."

"Robertson," said General Loring, "ride back and tell Colonel Farrell to come to the front. "Where are you from now?" asked General Loring.

"Directly from General Pemberton, sir."

"Been into Vicksburg, have you?"

"Yes, sir."

"When?"

"I left yesterday morning."

"What is Pemberton doing?"

"Not to detain you unnecessarily, I will answer briefly. He surrendered yesterday morning, and the enemy was entering the city when I left."

"The h—ll he did! On the 4th of July?"

"Yes, sir; it could not be avoided, I suppose."

By this time Colonel Farrell had made his appearance.

"Colonel Farrell," asked General Loring, "do you know this man?"

"Yes, sir; he belongs to my regiment."

"What he says may be believed?"

"Yes, sir; I would as soon doubt the Gospel as Winston's word."

"Is he under orders from General Johnston?"

"He is, sir."

"Well, then," said General Loring, turning to the spy, "you had better report to General Johnston as soon as possible. Tell him I will halt the troops until I receive further orders."

The spy was then permitted to pursue his journey without molestation. By hard riding, he reached Canton that night at ten o'clock. He found General Johnston alone in his office, almost in the same position in which he had left him. Henry again had to make the officer aware of his presence.

"I am ready to report, General Johnston."

"Ah, Mr. Winston," said the General, after a moment, "I am indeed glad to see you. I hope you have plenty of news?"

"Yes, sir; such as it is."

"I hope you were successful, and have seen Pemberton?"

"I have, sir, but he was a prisoner in twelve hours afterward?"

"What! You do not mean that he has surrendered?"

"It is unfortunately the case."

"When did this take place?"

"Yesterday, the 4th."

"On the 4th! I am sorry for that."

"It is to be regretted, but General Pemberton did not think he could hold out another hour. I saw him on the night of the 3d, but the articles of capitulation were already signed."

"He ought never to have gone into the place. I gave him plain orders, which he could not misunderstand, not to let the enemy get him hemmed in. He is guilty of a willful disobedience of orders, and ought to be cashiered."

"General Pemberton is very much mortified at the result of his effort to discharge what he thought was his duty. As he is a particular friend of mine, I am sorry to see that his superiors have found room for censure. His feelings are also very much hurt at a report, circulated in Vicksburg, that he had *sold* the city for two millions of dollars."

"That is all nonsense," replied General Johnston. "Pemberton is as true to the cause as I or any other man can be. No thinking man will believe any such report. But I must blame him for disobedience of positive orders."

"General Pemberton," answered the spy, "intends to resign as soon as he can, and I hope, therefore, the people will not bear down too hard upon a true patriot, who is already deeply mortified by his ill success."

"I do not know what will be done; but changing the subject, I must compliment you for the handsome manner in which you have acquitted yourself. Few men could have done what you have. You must have had considerable difficulty in going into and coming out of the city?"

Winston here briefly related all the circumstances of his journey, with which the General was highly entertained.

"I have a notion, Mr. Winston," said the General, after the spy's summary narrative was concluded, "to detail you as a regular spy. I need a good spy very much now, and I think you are the very man. What say you?"

"It is a dangerous and unpleasant office, General; but, nevertheless, I always try to do what my officers require. If you think I can serve my country best in that capacity, I will undertake it."

"Very well; I will write out your detail myself. I want you to start as soon as you can."

The General then wrote the necessary paper, and gave it to the spy.

"What instructions, General?"

"I do not wish to trammel your actions with instructions. I leave all to your judgment. Report to no one but me."

Henry, after some further conversation in regard to his new duties, took his leave.

General Johnston could not, as will be seen, have selected a more suitable person for the office.

CHAPTER XI.

> "Oft what seems
> A trifle, a mere nothing by itself,
> In some nice situation turns the scale
> Of fate, and rules the most important actions."

LEAVING the village of Canton, Henry Winston passed through Panola County, Mississippi, *en route* for Memphis, Tenn. For very obvious reasons, he could not use a pass from the Confederate authorities, in order to get beyond the "lines." He chose, therefore, to go in the character of a deserter. It would have been rather dangerous for our spy to have made himself and his object known to Confederate soldiers, even on post, who might probably, in less than twenty-four hours, become deserters themselves. To meet such persons afterward, in the city of Memphis, would have subjected him to extreme inconvenience, if not danger. He easily avoided the Confederate pickets by the directions of those known under the name of *blockaders*. All of the counties within fifty or sixty miles of Memphis were guilty of a violation of the Confederate law against "running the blockade." Having been abandoned pretty much to the tender mercies of the Yankees, many of our citizens were forced to trade with the enemy for the necessaries of life. Cotton was smuggled through the lines by these blockaders, who, eschewing the highway, knew all the by-ways and hog-paths between Panola and Memphis. This contraband trade was conducted mostly by women—delicate ladies, who, although trained to ride in carriages and buggies, did not now mind mounting a cotton bale on an ox-wagon, and traveling by night through lonesome swamps, and camping out by day in wild thickets infested with robbers, until they could reach the great metropolis of southern degradation. Excuse them, kind reader, for all these risks and dangers were undergone for *husbands, brothers,* or *fathers* in the Confederate army, who were barefoot and hatless. It may be an interesting question to decide who did the most injury, these innocent women, impelled by pure love and patriotism, or the large majority of the men detailed by the Confederate Government to put down the trade—men who would assist the blockaders for five dollars in Federal money. But we will waive the discussion of the subject, and return to our spy, who, occasionally traveling with the blockaders, was soon within the military jurisdiction of the United States.

Did you ever think, reader, upon what trivial circumstances, considered within themselves, great events in human life frequently depend, or how one event affects another, with which it seems to have no apparent connection? How one single moment of time can change the whole course of a man's destiny; and how this change affects others, with whom his relations are distant and slight?

> "There is a tide in the affairs of men,
> Which, taken at the flood, leads on to fortune;
> Omitted, all the voyage of their life
> Is bound in shallows and miseries."

Probably all the great and prominent events in an individual's life depend upon the gaining or losing of but a few seconds. If the origin of all the accidents which happen in this sublunary world were traced out, they would be found to turn upon "a trifle, a mere nothing by itself."

We have thrown out these disconnected, rambling thoughts, reader, as a sort of an explanatory preliminary to a circumstance which, without a preface, may appear to be an irrelevant incident. It, however, had an influence over the life of more persons than one, as will be seen in the progress of this history.

One evening, when within a short distance of Memphis, as Winston was slowly pursuing his journey along a path which was about half a mile from the public road, he heard a confused muttering of voices. His first conclusion was that the path he was traveling led to the head-quarters of a gang of robbers, or a nest of deserters. Before proceeding further, he thought it would be the best plan to find who the party was, and what it was doing. He was in the middle of a creek bottom, dense with trees and bushes. Turning aside, he crawled cautiously amid the undergrowth till he discovered an opening. In the center of this open space he beheld two Yankee soldiers, and an officer of the same nation. Being within a few steps of the party, he could distinctly see and hear their whole proceedings without exposing himself to view. The two men were binding the officer fast to a tree. Winston saw that the officer's face was deathly pale, and he guessed the wretches were about to commit a foul murder. He kept his position, however, anxious to see the result of this strange maneuver.

"Say your prayers, Captain," remarked one of the men, when the officer was firmly bound. "I give you only ten minutes to live. If you have any account to settle with heaven, you had better be at it. Your time has come."

"Men," said the officer, with a countenance as ashy as death, "I beseech you, in God's name, not to murder me. I have done only what I conceived to be my duty. You will gain nothing by this monstrous crime. Release me; I will pay you any amount, and swear to you I will never reveal this circumstance."

"We 've gone too far with it, Captain. We would be pretty d—d fools to turn you loose now, to have the woods scoured until you could find us, and have us shot."

"I swear, before God, I will never mention it."

"It's no use talking about it. I have sworn to have your

life, and you need n't beg. I tell you, as sure as there is a God above us, or a devil below us, you shall die. The deep disgrace you put on me can be washed out only with blood."

"That's what I say," chimed in the accomplice.

"If you have any thing to say to old Master," continued the first speaker, "you'd better be at it. You can spend the time in any manner you please, though."

"How shall we kill him, Jim? Shoot him?"

"No, by G—d; do you want to let the whole world know what we are about? I shall cut his throat."

The poor Federal officer seemed to give himself up for lost. He spoke not a word for two minutes, but gazed at the two ruffians in silent despair.

"Can nothing induce you to avoid this crime?" asked the officer, in a voice of extreme agony. "I ask you, in the name of mercy, to spare me. I will pay you till you are satisfied."

"You did n't spare me, Captain. You ought to have thought of this when you were disgracing me by using your little authority. It is my time now. 'Every dog has his day,' you know. Your time is nearly out," continued the wretch, drawing a long bowie-knife. "You have half a minute only."

"O God! save me from these wretches," cried the poor officer, in a tone of despair that aroused every instinct of humanity in the spy's heart. Winston could endure it no longer.

"God answers the prayer!" cried the spy, bounding like a tiger from where he stood, with a cocked pistol in either hand. The surprise was so sudden that the two soldiers stood stock-still, as if petrified. "Raise but a finger, move but a muscle, and I will shoot you where you stand," said the spy, leveling a pistol at the breast of each. "Drop your weapons where you are, or else you will be dead men in less time than you gave your victim."

"And who are you?" asked one of the men, recovering from his surprise, but without daring to move.

"Drop your weapon, sir, or I will shoot you through the heart. Drop it instantly."

The two crest-fallen wretches saw the fire flashing from the blue eye, and they knew this person was not to be trifled with; so they let their knives fall to the ground."

"Now, then, undo your belts, and lay down your pistols. If I discover the least sign of resistance I will send you both into eternity without a moment's warning."

"Before I do that thing," said one, "I want to know what for?"

"Do as I bid you, if you want to live," replied the spy.

The wretches obeyed; and as soon as they were disarmed, the spy ordered them to untie the rope with which they had bound the officer. When this was done the spy said:

"Now, gentlemen, I would like to have an explanation of this extraordinary occurrence. I am a stranger to all parties concerned, but I love fair play. Captain, what does this mean?"

"These two wretches," replied the officer, "were some time since detected in the commission of a very disgraceful crime, for which I had them severely punished. There lives in the neighborhood of this place a nice family, in which I was deeply interested. But because they were rebels in principle"——

The sentence was not finished; for the two men suddenly and simultaneously jerked out each a pocket Derringer. Three reports, following each other in quick succession, were heard. But only one of the men had fired; for Winston, who had kept his eye on them, perceiving their intentions, leveled his pistol as quick as thought, and one of the soldiers dropped dead in his tracks, with his undischarged weapon in his hand. The flash was scarcely seen from the weapon of the other before a ball from Winston's unerring repeater had penetrated his brain. The two men were lying corpses, side by side.

"Are you hurt, Captain?" asked the spy.

"No, not at all," was the reply.

"Then, *farewell!*" exclaimed Winston, springing into the bushes, and leaving the astonished officer alone with the dead. He heard the Federal Captain calling after him, but, for reasons known only to himself, he returned no answer.

* * * * * * *

CHAPTER XII

"That face of his the hungry cannibals
Would not have touched, would not have stain'd with blood;
But you are more inhuman, more inexorable,—
O, ten times more than tigers of Hyrcania."

WHEN the spy had been in Memphis a day or two, there was considerable excitement in regard to a grand raid which was to be made into the State of Mississippi. These movements were extensively inaugurated by the Yankees as one means of starving out the rebels—a system of policy which, it was thought at one time, would put an end to the revolution. Wherever they went, desolation, misery, and suffering were sure to follow in their wake. With even worse than savage barbarity, they would seize the last morsel of food from a poor widow, whose husband had fallen on the battle-field, and wantonly destroy it before her face. They have been known to take bread from a child and throw it to the dogs, despite the piteous cries of the helpless and starving infant. Dwelling houses were burned to the ground at the dead hour of midnight, and women and children were turned out without a single change of clothing—sometimes in a state of almost entire nudity—to shiver in the wintry winds. In some instances, old gray-headed men were murdered simply because they had the audacity to give burial to a Confederate guerrilla, killed in lawful combat. In short, the records of antiquity may be searched, the histories of the most cruel wars of ancient times may be ransacked, and nothing can be found equal in hellish atrocity to the acts committed by the Unionists of 1861. Let the reader compare the following directions of Abu-Bekr, issued more than twelve hundred years ago, with the savage events to be described in this chapter, and he will conclude the Yankees have relapsed into barbarism.

"If you conquer," said this heathen commander to his generals, "spare the aged, the infirm, the women, and the children. Cut down no palm-trees; destroy no fields of corn; spare all the fruit-trees; slay no cattle, but such as are wanted for food."

If the Yankees in the war of 1861 did not violate each and all of these directions, then the testimony of a million of witnesses goes for naught.

At the time Winston entered the city of Memphis, there was a colonel making preparations for one of these raids, designed for the collection of booty and for the commission of general outrages. We will not insult the reader by mentioning the name of one who is marked in the black book that contains the roll of those who violate God's holy laws. It is recorded in the infernal regions, and there let it rest till the owner shall answer to it, when he goes down to the dark spot where there shall be "wailing and gnashing of teeth." For the sake of its appropriateness, we will call him by the expressive and significant *sobriquet* of Nero. The spy, in order to become better acquainted with the enemy's purposes and his mode of warfare, attached himself to the body-guard of this doughty officer. When the force was sufficient and all ready for the expedition, Colonel Nero marched forth from the city, with the black flag streaming in the breeze. The troops had scarcely reached the suburbs of Memphis before the work of robbery and plunder commenced. Squads of five or six together broke off from the main body, and completely ravaged the country for miles on either side of the road; and wherever they made their appearance the inhabitants were left in a totally destitute condition. Huge volumes of black smoke rolled up to the clouds, showing plainly in what direction the enemy was going and in what he was engaged. Mothers with their frightened infants fled to the woods; old silver-haired men hobbled to the forests. They did not dare to meet an enemy who would rob them of even their last garment. The Yankees, finding dwellings thus abandoned, destroyed every thing which could be of any possible use, and then fired the houses; and when the frightened owners returned, they saw their once happy homes a heap of ashes. Many a sufferer will remember, with a sorrowful heart, this first day's march of Colonel Nero. Winston was compelled to witness many scenes of heart-rending outrage at which his feelings revolted, but which he was powerless to prevent. The next day he took occasion to remonstrate with the commander of the expedition.

"Colonel Nero," said the spy, in a mild tone, "I observe some of our men committing outrages which I think you will not approve, and that are certainly contrary to all the recognized modes of warfare. I take the liberty of mentioning this to you, thinking you are unaware of it, and that your sense of justice and right would prompt you to take measures for the prevention of unnecessary severity."

"Who the h—ll are you?" asked Colonel Nero, with an expression of sternness, but at the same time of interest, or at least with something akin to curiosity.

The hero had spoken in a tone that marked him as a man of education and intelligence; and the Yankee officer seemed extremely surprised to find a person in his horde of cutthroats of so much refinement of feeling. Therefore, notwithstanding the uncouth language he had used, he did not appear averse to a closer acquaintance with Winston.

"I volunteered, sir," was the response to Colonel Nero's question, "in the city of Memphis, to participate in this expedition; and, as a loyal citizen of the United States, and one who wishes to restore peace to this distracted country, I feel in duty bound to report to you the outrages committed by our soldiers, which I venture to say are unauthorized by the government, and are done without your knowledge and consent."

"And what outrages have my soldiers been guilty of?"

"I have observed some of them insult defenseless females; I have seen others tear up, in mere wantonness, the wearing apparel of women and children; and, worse than that, I have seen them destroy the last morsel of food belonging to a poor destitute widow. I can not believe, sir, that such unnecessary deeds will meet with your approbation."

Colonel Nero seemed a little amused. "And these you call outrages?" said he, laughing. "Well, if you see no worse than what you have mentioned, the rebs will fare d—d light. I guess before we get back you will not be quite so squeamish."

"Do I understand you to mean, Colonel Nero, that all the proceedings I have witnessed are authorized by you?"

"Whether they are or not, I don't care a d—n. Why, what does war mean? Isn't it right to forage on the subsistence of your enemy? Isn't it right to do him all the harm in your power? I thought all nations had recognized such a principle."

"But still, Colonel, it is not necessary that the horrors of war should extend to women and children. A state of warfare in any country is to be deplored, but it becomes doubly and trebly so when those become subject to its ravages who are in no way responsible for its inauguration. In a country like ours, where we profess to be fighting for the restoration of the Union, and that alone, it appears to me that the more leniently the people are treated, the more easily will our object be accomplished. We should not, in my humble opinion, interfere with any property except that which the rebel government claims. How must the Confederates feel toward us, who wantonly destroy the food necessary to the maintenance of their families? Why, by so doing, we will drive men into the ranks of the rebels to fight, not for the Confederacy, but merely for revenge. We should treat the southern people as erring children, and thus prove to them that our only object is to re-establish the government which they, in their blindness and folly, have overthrown. Thus all, seeing that our intentions are to preserve the country and defend her honor, will flock with their former reverence and devotion to the time-honored 'stars and stripes,' wherever they may be unfurled. But it appears to me that if we persist in the adoption of a different line of policy, we will defeat the object we have in view, and widen the unfortunate breach we are now attempting to repair."

"Well, by G—d!" exclaimed Colonel Nero, "I must say you would do better as a preacher than a soldier. If I had a vacancy in my command I would appoint you chaplain. But may be you will not be so tender-hearted when you soldier it awhile. You will find that your line of policy will not do for these d—d Mississippi rebels. Why, they would laugh at us for contemptible fools if we passed through the country without laying it waste, and curse us for imbecile dotards, afraid to draw down upon our heads the vengeance of fire-eating secessionists. No, by G—d! we must destroy as we go, and make this d—d people *feel* the power of our government. The State of Mississippi is a damnable 'secesh' hole, and her citizens richly merit all the punishment it is in our power to inflict; and they shall be handled without gloves wherever I go."

"I greatly fear, then, Colonel, our efforts will never be crowned with success. This people will be inspired with hatred of us and our cause, and will look upon us as little better than savages."

"They may look upon us in any way they please," replied Colonel Nero. 'I believe the whole race of whites in the South will have to be entirely exterminated. Indeed, this is the avowed policy of the government. This country must be repeopled with a loyal race, and the sooner they are killed off the better. Once having agreed that extermination is the true doctrine, and that it furnishes the true solution of the problem of the war, we may as well commence to put it in practice. But if we protect women and their rebel brats, the d—d traitors will increase like—like the children of Israel under Egyptian task-masters."

"Let our government," replied Winston, in a solemn voice, "take care that the southerners do not, indeed, become the children of Israel, and ourselves their cruel oppressors; and that we do not meet with a retribution similar, in severity at least, to that which overtook Pharaoh and his followers. For our cruelty to this people, God might send upon us troubles more destructive than the plagues of Egypt. Already many of the first-born in our country have been slain; lamentation is heard in nearly every dwelling; around nearly every fireside there is a vacant seat; our whole country may soon be enveloped in gloom, and we may curse the day that witnessed the beginning of this cruel and savage conflict."

"You remind me very much," answered Colonel Nero, "of a dialogue I used to act when a boy. You recollect what Lochiel said to the wizard? May be it will do you good.

> "'Go preach to the coward, thou death-telling seer!
> Or, if gory Culloden so dreadful appear,
> Draw, dotard, around thy old wand'ring sight
> This mantle to cover the phantoms of fright.'"

"And, Colonel, I also recollect what the wizard said to Lochiel. His words may not be inapplicable.

> "'Ha! laugh'st thou, Lochiel, my vision to scorn?
> Proud bird of the mountains, thy plume shall be torn!
> Say, rush the bold eagle exultingly forth
> From his home in the dark-rolling clouds of the North?

Lo! the death-shot of foemen out-speeding, he rode,
Companionless, bearing destruction abroad;
But down let him stoop from his havoc on high—
Ah! home let him speed—for the spoiler is nigh.'"

"Ah, well, never mind now," said Colonel Nero, interrupting. "I did not wish to get into an argument on this subject. You will see before we return what kind of arguments are necessary to convince rebels; and I doubt not you will make a good soldier; but, changing the subject, what state are you from?"

"I am from Ohio."

"You do not belong to the regular army?"

"No sir; I attached myself temporarily to your body-guard."

"If you would enter the regular service, I think I could easily procure you a commission. Will you accept it?"

"I desire no position, Colonel, at present. Perhaps in time to come I might take your advice; but just now it would not suit my purposes to adopt your suggestion."

At this moment a courier came galloping up with the intelligence that a strong force of guerrillas was ahead. The reports of several guns had already been heard, apparently about a mile in advance of the main body. On this, the second day of the enemy's march, they had been considerably annoyed by this species of warfare, and more than one had been seen to fall from his horse while passing by dense thickets, or other positions favorable to the concealment of ambuscades. This mode of combat was particularly disagreeable to the Yankees, who dreaded nothing more than the Confederate horseman, flying from hill to hill, and pouring the contents of his deadly rifle into their moving ranks. Consequently, whenever a guerrilla was so unfortunate as to be captured, he was treated with unusual severity. So bitter was the hatred of the Federals against this class of warriors, that all who showed the least favor to, or manifested the least sympathy for, a Confederate rover of the woods, were subjected to punishment of the most cruel and vigorous character. The rage of the Yankees, in this respect, bore a striking resemblance to that of a school-boy, who vents his spleen upon the unconscious obstacle that checks his locomotion by resisting the momentum of his feet. With similar feelings, the Federals would set fire to houses behind which their Confederate foes had sheltered themselves, or they would apply the lash to defenceless females and crying babes who were in any way connected with the rebel guerrilla. Sometimes deeds of bloodshed were committed which will darken the page of history on which they are recorded, and tinge with the blackness of infamy what little military glory our "northern brethren" have otherwise acquired during the progress of the war. Such a scene Henry Winston was now doomed to witness. For when Colonel Nero reached the spot at which the fire of the Confederate guerrillas had been unusually destructive, and saw a large number of corpses dressed in blue stretched upon the earth, his rage knew no bounds. He cursed and swore in his wrath that "the whole d—d race of the South should be wiped out; d—d cowardly assassins, to skulk in the bushes and behind trees to shoot down brave soldiers! By G—d, the inhabitants of the country should suffer for it, and rue the day in which they had offered encouragement to d—d outlaws and robbers, who called themselves Confederate guerrillas; that they should, by G—d, or his name was not Nero!"

While thus raging and foaming, his attention was directed to several persons standing in front of a small, neat cottage, that was situated not a great distance from the road-side. The party consisted of an old lady, her daughter, and a little boy, apparently fourteen or fifteen years of age. He was the old lady's son. A pale, sickly young man, in almost the last stages of consumption, was lying bleeding upon the ground, severely wounded in the side. He proved to be the youthful husband of the young woman who was bending over him with frantic affection. Colonel Nero approached.

"By G—d," said he, "here is one of the d—d rascals now. Here, men, take the infernal guerrilla and swing him to yonder tree by the road. It will be a good lesson to the d—d rebels."

"O, sir!" exclaimed the young wife, terrified by the approach of several soldiers, who were preparing to execute the command of their officer, "O, sir, my husband is no guerrilla. He never was in the army in his life. He had nothing to do with the fight, but was standing in the yard when he was shot from the road by your men. O, for the love of heaven, spare my poor husband! I will get on my knees to you!" cried the distracted wife, suiting the action to the word, and wringing her hands in unutterable anguish. The scene would have aroused the pity of even a brute, but it made no impression on the *mustard-seed* heart of Colonel Nero.

"Do as I bade you, men!" bawled Colonel Nero, paying no attention to the pitiable entreaties of the kneeling woman.

During all this time little attention was paid to the boy, who stood with his hands working in his pockets, his dark eyes wide open with astonishment and horror. His frame shook and shivered under the influence of feelings which can not be described, but may be imagined. The little fellow looked on for a moment; then, when he fully comprehended the proceeding, he suddenly seized a gun lying on the ground, and before the Yankees were aware of his intentions, fired into the midst of those who were binding his wounded brother-in-law. Two of the wretches dropped dead, and the others shrank back with exclamations of surprise and rage.

"Thank God!" exclaimed the old lady, scarcely aware of what she was saying, and of the full import of her words.

"D—d old hag!" fairly roared Colonel Nero. "I will teach you to thank God! The little viper shall hang by the side of the guerrilla, and both shall dangle in the air, and their rotten carcasses be devoured by buzzards."

The boy, as soon as he saw what he had done, was attempting to make his escape, but was quickly overtaken and bound hand and foot. The poor child screamed and called upon his mother in the heart-rending language of infantile fright.

"O, my poor, my poor boy!" cried the mother, throwing herself by his side in fearful agony. Colonel Nero seemed to hesitate. It was, however, only for a moment, and not from any feeling of sympathy. The heartless desperado was dead to any emotions of that character. He was merely studying what disposition to make of the two females. It did not require the diabolical wretch long to make up his mind.

"Here, men, seize these two hell-cats, tie them with their backs to that tree, and let them witness the death-struggles of this little devil and this d—d guerrilla; then we will leave them all to perish together. Be quick."

The cruel and never-before-heard-of command was literally obeyed, and the two females were fastened to the oak to which Colonel Nero had pointed, and in the manner he had directed. Two ropes were then adjusted around the necks of the boy and his brother-in-law, and thrown over a limb that projected immediately over the heads of the mother and daughter. Winston now reached the spot upon which this tragedy was enacting. His first impulse was to draw his weapons and shoot the merciless officer, who was giving directions with a heartlessness surprising even to his own followers. When the spy beheld the two women bound, the wounded citizen and the boy with ropes about their necks, his hand involuntarily grasped the butt of his pistol, but in a second afterward the folly of executing the thought that prompted the act was apparent and obvious, and would be attended with extreme danger, if not certain death, to himself, without alleviating the distress of the sufferers. So, curbing his feelings, he approached Colonel Nero, and addressed him:

"In God's name, Colonel Nero, I beg you to remember who you are. As the commander of this expedition, it becomes you to put a stop to this foul proceeding. The United States Government does not"——

"Take care, young man, take care," exclaimed Colonel Nero, in a stern voice. "I want none of your preaching now. Don't preach to me, sir."

"Colonel," said the undaunted hero, in a solemn tone, "as you hope for God's mercy yourself, I beg you, I entreat you, in the name of all that is sacred, to desist from your purpose. The crime you propose to commit will demand the sternest retaliation on the part of the rebel government, and you will thus cause double misery. I beg you not to load your conscience with the guilt of murder, and not to disgrace our government by the execution of a wounded non-combatant and a child."

"Hush, sir, or, by G—d, I will put you in their company. Swing them up, men—swing them up!"

Winston drew back with feelings of horror when he saw that Colonel Nero was determined to execute his bloody purpose. The two victims felt the ropes tighten about their necks, and in an instant they were dangling and struggling in the air. The mother and daughter cast one look of ineffable agony and despair upon the bodies that were swaying to and fro; and then, after two or three loud, heart-piercing shrieks, kind nature applied the remedy demanded by overwrought feeling, and they were ignorant of passing events. The husband's blood, which was now started afresh by his violent struggles, streamed down upon the unconscious wife. The bells were ringing in "the lower world" for joy, because a deed had been done which swelled the "black list," and placed many Yankee souls beyond the reach of human repentance and God's mercy.

Colonel Nero looked on this tragical scene, probably the most horrible and revolting to the human heart that ever was recorded upon the history of a civilized nation, with apparent enjoyment. After surveying it awhile, he suddenly started.

"Mount, men—mount and away!" he exclaimed.

And the whole command was soon passing near the little boy and the unoffending citizen, from whom life was rapidly ebbing away. Satan himself, could he have been standing by, would have loudly rejoiced at the depravity of soul and heart, and the destitution of feeling, evinced in the various remarks made by different soldiers of the moving army.

"Grin on, my larkies," exclaimed one, as he looked up at the uncovered faces of the gasping bodies—"grin on; you'll soon get your discharges."

"Jim," cried another to his comrade, "don't they whirl and dance with a vim; how they 'cut the pigeon-wing!'"

"I guess," replied the individual addressed, "you would dance, too, if you were standing on nothing and pulling hemp."

"Look at the little devil," said a third, "kicking at his mamma. The old woman never learned him any manners."

With such heartless exclamations as these, the whole army passed by; and in a short time the helpless victims of Yankee barbarity and malignity were left to themselves—two to die, their last struggles unseen by human eyes, and two to recover from their swoon, only to behold the ghastly spectacle of all they loved dangling from the bough of the tree to which they themselves were securely bound.

Acts similar to the above, be it recorded to the eternal disgrace of the whole northern race, were committed all the way to Oxford, Mississippi. When the Yankees reached this pleasant little village, the location of the State University, their treatment of the unfortunate and helpless citizens is not equaled in cruel vindictiveness in the world's history from the creation of man. The citizens, including delicate and refined females, were grossly and brutally insulted; their dwellings were closely searched; their yards were dug up, under the supposition that treasures or valuables of some character might have been buried in the earth. No nook nor corner escaped the inquisitive glance of these argus-eyed vandals. Sometimes a ham or a jar of preserves, which a fond mother had concealed for her darling babes, would be drawn forth, amid the brutish laughter of the *restorers of the Union*, who declared that the "southern soil is the richest in the world to grow preserves in the ground."

No living animal was left in the town, and when the enemy decamped, the inhabitants were actually on the point of starvation; and for several days afterward they were forced to the necessity of subsisting upon decaying hog's heads, and other debris, which the Yankees had thrown away. Many parents, who were living in Oxford at the time, will recollect with shuddering horror how their famishing children cried for bread, and even begged food of a thrice-cursed enemy. All this, however, might have been borne with patience, as the unavoidable sacrifices of a people battling for liberty and independence, had the robbery of the Yankees been confined to the living. But the sanctity of the graveyard was invaded, and the wretched Oxonians were doomed to see the skeletons of departed friends, who had been dead and slumbering peacefully for years, disinterred, and their resting-places disturbed in the search for gold. The mother saw her beloved infant's little bones rudely trampled on the ground. One saw the ashes of an aged father poured on the surface of the earth; another saw the coffin of a dear wife burst asunder with an ax, and her fleshless fingers rigidly examined for *rings!* And, to crown this unheard-of proceeding, Colonel Nero had the skeleton of a prominent citizen sent back to Memphis to a friend, who was a physician. In a word, the proceedings of the Yankees at Oxford are without a parallel in the history of man.

One more exploit of the redoubtable Colonel Nero must be recorded—an exploit Winston had the mortification to witness. It was as much as our hero could do to restrain himself from shooting the brute; but he knew it would be worse than folly, and would only furnish the Yankees with an excuse for committing still more horrible outrages. He, therefore, choked down his anger as well as he could, and looked on in sorrow and disgust. Colonel Nero entered the residence of a gentleman who had an accomplished daughter, a young lady of refined manners and cultivated mind and heart. Going into the parlor, where the lady happened to be seated, Colonel Nero addressed her with a most unjustifiable and impertinent familiarity.

"My sweet creature," said he, "I am so glad to meet you; you look so much like an angel compared with the rebel girls. I hope, my dear, my entrance will not be regarded in the light of an intrusion."

"I have not," replied the young lady, trembling, "been in the habit of receiving strangers without an introduction. We are, however, at your mercy, and I bespeak that protection due to my sex."

"Fear nothing, my darling girl; I merely called for some music. I see you are a musician. Now, my little angel, take this guitar," said he, rising and handing it to her, "and favor me with one or two airs; then we will part good friends."

The frightened girl, thinking to rid herself of the presence of the brute by a compliance with his request, received the instrument.

"What shall I play, sir?"

"The Star-spangled Banner, to begin with, if you please."

The air was sung without any spirit and in a tremulous voice.

"That did very well, Miss. You sing like an angel. Now we will sing that good old national air, Yankee Doodle, together. I hope you are still sufficiently patriotic to appreciate it."

"You must excuse me for not complying with your request, as I am not in the habit of singing that, and never have been."

"I hope, Miss, you are not one of the d—d rebels, too; therefore, I insist."

"If you are a gentleman, you will excuse me when I tell you it is disagreeable to my feelings."

"Disagreeable! ll—ll! what makes it disagreeable? You can sing it; and I insist upon my request being granted. I can inform you that I profess to be a gentleman, too."

"Your present conduct proves you to be any thing else, sir," replied the young lady, with considerable spirit; "and I fear I have already compromised my dignity by remaining in your presence this long. I did hope, however, that the commander of the Federal forces—for such I understand you to be—might have some respect for defenseless females. I did hope that he at least was a gentleman."

"I tell you, Miss, I *am* a gentleman; but you must sing Yankee Doodle."

"Then I tell you, sir, I will not do it."

"By G—d, Miss, there is a way to make stubborn people grant small favors."

"I understand you, sir; but you will find there are some who can not be forced into disgraceful measures," replied the young lady, whose fear was now all gone, and who was fully aroused; "and I do not hesitate to say you can not intimidate me by your threats. You may kill me if you wish."

"I'll be d—d," said Colonel Nero, in a rage, taking the guitar, "if I do n't try your powers of endurance. Now play

Yankee Doodle, or I will break the instrument in pieces, and over your head, too, if you provoke me."

"Break it, monster—break it! Such an act will be in keeping with your character."

The instrument was slowly raised aloft, but the girl, now wrought to a point of heroism that would have defied human power, looked at the brute without flinching. Winston would at this moment have interfered, but the young lady was one with whom he had been acquainted, and recognition would have placed him in a very embarrassing situation. Besides, he did not think Colonel Nero would carry his threat into execution. He was, however, mistaken, for the instrument descended upon the young lady's head with sufficient force to burst it wide open. She fell to the floor momentarily stunned, but almost immediately recovered. She arose and left the parlor. Colonel Nero followed, and entered her own room, and in the young lady's presence kissed the chamber-maid.

"If you were not a brute," said the young lady, "I would ask you to retire."

"You are still impertinent; take care, Miss, or I will carry you off as Ulysses did Chryseis. That would be quite interesting and romantic, would n't it? Ha! ha! ha! But lend me the key to your wardrobe. I want to see what you have to wear, if I should carry you off."

"You can get no key from me, sir."

"O, very well, Miss Stubborn, I can easily break it open. Girl," said he to the chamber-maid, "bring me an ax. Go quick, my love, and I will make you a present."

The maid, who was extremely frightened, obeyed, and soon appeared with the desired implement. Colonel Nero took it and with one blow burst open the lady's wardrobe. Taking out a very fine silk dress, he turned to the chamber-maid.

"Here, beauty, this is very pretty; I promised you something; take it, and wear it for my sake."

"O, marster, I don't want it. It belongs to Miss L——."

"Now come, don't you be a d—d fool, too. Here, take it, and try it on. I want to see how it fits."

"O, marster, I don't want to. I can't."

"By G—d, you shall! Now do as I tell you, or I will split your head open with this ax. I'll be d—d if I don't."

And the Colonel raised up the ax as if he were in earnest. The maid was thus forced to comply with the officer's wishes, and arrayed herself in her mistress' apparel.

"I declare!" exclaimed Colonel Nero, with a hoarse laugh, "you look really handsome. Go with me, and you shall be married to some of my officers. You deserve a good husband."

"I don't want to be married; I'd rather stay with Miss L——."

"You would, eh? Well, stay with Miss L——, and I want you to teach Miss L—— some manners. Now, Miss L——, the next time I call, I hope you will be in a better humor. Good morning, ladies."

Henry Winston was sick at heart, and completely disgusted with Yankee proceedings. Seeing that he could accomplish no good by remaining longer, he resolved to desert his present command. So, after conveying information to the Confederate authorities, by means which need not be mentioned, as to the intentions of the enemy, his numbers, and so on, he set out that very night in the direction of Memphis. The next day he reached the spot which was the scene of one of the most disgraceful and horrible deeds that ever tarnished the fame of any civilized nation under the wide canopy of heaven. The two women were still bound to the tree, nearly famished. They were, however, soon released by our hero, who then proceeded to take down the bodies of the little boy and the citizen. The poor wife laid her hands on her husband's face; then, looking up vacantly, she uttered a wild, piercing scream, the mad shriek of a raving maniac, and rushed to the woods. She was never seen again. But months afterward a skeleton was discovered in a deep ravine, several miles from the scene of this tragical occurrence, and was supposed to be that of the unfortunate citizen's wife. Winston, after seeing that the corpses were properly interred, and assisting the poor old woman to a relative's house, where all her wants could be supplied, journeyed on, and in due course of time arrived in the city of Memphis. But he made only a short halt. Taking a boat, he was soon sailing on the bosom of the great "Father of Waters."

CHAPTER XIII.

"I know I love in vain, strive against hope,
Yet, in this captious and intenable sieve,
I still pour in the waters of my love,
And lack not to lose still; thus, Indian-like,
Religious in mine error, I adore
The sun that looks upon his worshiper,
But knows him no more."

WE must now return to Emily Burrell. Those who have been so unfortunate as to feel the pangs of disappointed love can, without any difficulty, imagine what she suffered. No human misery is so acute and exquisite as pure love sustained only by slight hope. Time can assuage the grief occasioned by the death of friends, but when the arrow of Cupid pierces deep in the heart, the wound it inflicts is eternal; and the victim of unrequited passion pines away, like Narcissus grieving for a shadow. The wheel of Ixion, the stone of Sisyphus, the thirst of Tantalus, are but feeble types to express the agonies of slighted love. In vain the suffering soul strives and struggles to forget; the coveted plunge into Lethe can not be made. Earth loses all her charms; the mind's appetite is gone; the vale of Tempe, Mount Parnassus and Helicon, Hippocrene and Castalia, can no longer furnish pleasure to the sick, craving soul. In vain Euterpe's strains come swelling on the gale; in vain Phœbus strikes the lyre, and Calliope recites the song; wherever the disappointed lover may fly, he feels the anguish of Prometheus pinned to the rock, with vultures gnawing at his self-restoring heart; until, at last, he is ready to exclaim, in the accents of despair, as did Satan when expelled from the glories of Paradise:

> "Me miserable! which way shall I fly
> Infinite wrath and infinite despair?
> Which way I fly is hell; myself am hell;
> And, in the lowest deep, a lower deep
> Still threatening to devour me opens wide,
> To which the hell I suffer seems a heaven."

Poor woman, stricken with hopeless love, indeed suffers the tortures of Tartarus. With man the case is different. Amid the exciting scenes and intoxicating pleasures of the world he finds some alleviation of his torments. As Byron expresses it—

> "Man's love is of man's life a thing apart—
> 'T is woman's whole existence; man may range
> The court, camp, church, the vessel, and the mart,
> Sword, gown, gain, glory, offer in exchange
> Pride, fame, ambition to fill up his heart."

The affection of woman is naturally stronger than that of the "rougher sex," and when she yields up the rich treasures of her heart, her happiness or misery is eternally sealed. No substitute can supersede the cherished idol she worships. Like the deep, calm waters of a placid stream that glides on, undried by the summer's sun, her love flows constant and true, till death stills her blood and chills her heart.

With such undying affection did Emily cherish the unfading image of Henry Winston. The intensity of her deep feeling was evidenced by the pale cheek, the sunken eye, the slow step, and the vacant look, which showed plainly to the observer that her thoughts were far from the objects at which she gazed. Winston was in her thoughts by day, and in her dreams by night. Every thing around her father's dwelling spoke of him. If she rode out, she passed by the old oak under which she first saw him lying as dead. If she visited her bower, she blushed at the recollection of the thrilling words which had fallen upon her ears like music from an angel's harp. And then when she reflected that he whose voice had stirred such wild emotions in her heaving breast was gone, and probably gone forever, her heart sank within her, the paleness of death would overspread her countenance, and she would clasp her hands in mute, silent despair. She would wander into the room in which he had suffered, in which she had read to him, and in which her young love had burst forth, when she was ignorant even of its very nature. Then the recollection of her utter desolation of heart would rush to her mind, like the dim shadow of a frightful ghost, and she would attempt to flee from her own wretchedness. Sometimes she could not but weep in the bitterness of her disappointment.

> "O, those are tears of bitterness,
> Wrung from the breaking heart,
> When two, blest in their tenderness,
> Must learn to live apart!"

To add to her troubles, Major Burrell had died, and she was now indeed alone. Emily would have sunk under the weight of her severe trials had not the hope of eventually meeting Henry Winston sustained her. This conviction, or rather presentiment, fastened upon her mind, and frequently dispelled the clouds of darkness. Sometimes bright visions of future happiness would dance before her upon the murky bosom of the slough of despondency. She had not heard one word from him since his abrupt departure from Kentucky. Months had dragged slowly by, and had lengthened into years, but still no tidings of the absent lover had gladdened her aching heart. Somehow, though she could not tell why, she felt that her brother would meet with Henry, and write to her concerning the fact. Yet she had received frequent letters from James, and the beloved name of Winston had never been mentioned, though she was looking for it in every line. Then she would partly abandon this idea, and would hope that when the difficulties which distracted the country should pass away, the rash lover would return to her side and fully atone for his folly. She still believed him true, although she could not reconcile all his actions. And in this state of suspense, of doubt and of fear, she lived on from day to day, in the alternations of hope and despair, in wretchedness and misery.

Immediately after the fall of Vicksburg, Emily received a letter from Colonel Burrell, stating the accident which had happened to him on the 4th of July, and requesting her presence until he would be able to travel. She at once complied, glad of an opportunity to fly from her lonesomeness. She soon joined her brother, and they were staying at a private house in the city. Faithfully and affectionately she attended to the wants of the wounded officer, until now he was almost healed. As yet she had not breathed a word of her sorrow, though she had no secrets from her brother. One morning they were sitting together in the parlor, when the Colonel said:

"I have just received two months' leave of absence, Emily, and I have an idea of setting out to-night for Washington City. I am going to get my papers of retirement from active service. Would you like to accompany me?"

"I will go anywhere you wish, brother. I have no desire to return home. I find only misery there. To be with you is now the only pleasure I have on this earth. I will go anywhere you say."

"I do not understand why you should be so wretched," said Colonel Burrell, fingering her glossy curls, "and yet I see something distresses you. I notice a great change in your appearance, too, my dear sister. You look pale and sickly; but probably you have paid too much attention to me, to the neglect of your own health."

"No, no; I experience no physical suffering. There are some ills," she said, leaning her head on his breast, "which the 'healing art' can not relieve. They rankle in the heart, and such are *mine*."

"I hope my suspicions are incorrect, and that I misunderstand you; but, for fear I may mortify your feelings by a guess, tell me what are the ills to which you allude."

"If you would think of the past, it seems to me you could be at no loss. The events of my monotonous life have not been so many that you might not select one which would cause distress."

"Is it our father's death you take so hard?"

"That is one, but there is yet another."

"Emily," said the Colonel, with a troubled expression, "is this man Winston, this rebel, connected with your distress?"

It was the first time she had heard the name mentioned for months. It sent the warm blood to her countenance. Starting up, she eagerly looked the officer in the face.

"Rebel, brother, rebel! How do you know he is a rebel?"

"I should think I have very good reason to know, when I saw him myself; and not only that, but saved his life."

The crimson tide curdled to her heart, and a deathly pallor overspread her beautiful features, as she thought that Winston might be dead. She could not speak, but gazed at her brother with an inquiring, anxious look, which was pitiable to behold. The Colonel noticed the sudden change, and seemed troubled.

"My poor sister," said he, taking her trembling hand in his, "is it possible you are still interested in the fate of this faithless man?"

"Does he *live?*" she cried, with a sudden start. "O, tell me, for heaven's sake!"

"He does, for aught I know to the contrary. He was seen in this city the day of the surrender. I saw him myself some time before this." And here Colonel Burrell gave Emily a full account of the circumstance which took place at the battle of Corinth.

"And you saved his life? God will bless you, brother James, and I thank you a thousand and a thousand times."

"Emily, I am astonished at this emotion. Can you love a rebel, now in arms against his country?"

"Rebel!" cried she wildly, springing to the floor. "O, heaven! I believe I would love him if he were a highway robber! Don't frown, brother James, don't frown; I can not help it. Would to God I could! O, James, sometimes I want to lie down and die; I want death to release me from my miseries." And she took her seat by her brother's side and wept bitterly.

"My poor, unhappy sister, I sympathize with you deeply; but I did hope you would not waste your affection upon a rebel."

"I, too, am a rebel," she said, drying her tears. "I never was in favor of this aggressive war on the South, and I have always been sorry that you took sides against your native country."

"Why, Emily, my rash-talking sister, this is treasonable, and I would not have any one else hear you talk so for the world."

"If it is treason, I can't help it. My sympathies have always been with the Confederates—or rebels, as you choose to call them; and I hope and believe they will meet with ultimate success. I have never said this much to any one before, but it was on your account. I regret that you did not deem it your duty to take up arms in defense of our native state, instead of assisting the tyrant to plant his foot on her neck."

"My God! I take up arms in favor of this accursed rebellion! Why, you must be crazy. You know not what you say."

"I know, brother, you think us poor women ignorant in

regard to politics; but I have read more on this subject than you are aware of; at least I have read enough to form an opinion, which is now unalterable. I tell you candidly I see nothing dishonorable in being a rebel. Indeed, I can not call this movement a common rebellion. It is a grand revolution—the reclamation by the southern people of rights to which they are entitled under the Constitution, and by the very nature of the government itself."

"You are stark mad, Emily, and guilty of high treason, too."

"If this is treason—the mere expression of my opposition to the prosecution of this unjust warfare, and the persecution of the southern people—it only shows that our boasted freedom of thought and speech is gone, and that our republican government has assumed the character of a despotism. The sooner, then, it falls to pieces the better. I do not know much about politics, it is true; but I know it is galling to my spirit to see Kentucky, 'the dark and bloody ground,' overrun by hired minions."

"You do not call me a hired minion, I hope?"

"No, James, no; but you are affiliating with them. You are helping to rivet chains upon the country which gave you birth."

"I take quite a different view from that. I look upon it as a great and patriotic work to put down rebellion. I do my state service when I help to whip her back under the protection of the best government the world ever saw."

"But then, brother, fifty-eight counties were represented in the convention which declared Kentucky again free and independent. The majority rules, you know."

"I do not concede to Kentucky nor any other state the right to secede from the Union, and thus subvert the government. It is but a poor and weak government that recognizes the abominable principle of secession, and allows its member to withdraw whenever they see proper."

"You speak of things as they should be, brother, or rather as they might be. I speak of them as they actually exist. I do not take upon myself to determine whether secession, as a principle, is right or wrong. I leave that for wiser heads than mine. But it seems very clear to me that, from the nature of the government, and the manner it was organized, its component members, the several states, have a perfect right to withdraw whenever they think themselves aggrieved. The several states made the General Government, and delegated to it certain powers; but still reserving to themselves the right to reclaim those granted powers when the Union should cease to accomplish the objects for which it was intended and established."

"And where did you learn all this?"

"I have been reading the history of the adoption of the Constitution. I recollect very clearly that the convention of Virginia, which ratified the constitution for that state, stated distinctly and forcibly, in resolutions, the character of the political contract into which the states were about entering. I suppose you have read them, brother?"

"No, I have not."

"Well, I can easily find them." And going to the library, she returned with a book, and read as follows:

"'We, the delegates of the people of Virginia, duly elected in pursuance of a recommendation from the General Assembly, and now met in convention, and being prepared, as well as the most mature deliberation hath enabled us, to decide thereon, do, in the name and in behalf of the people of Virginia, declare and make known that the powers granted under the Constitution, being derived from the people of the United States, may be *resumed* by them whensoever the same shall be perverted to their injury or oppression; and that every power not granted thereby remains with them and at their will,' etc.

"Now then," continued Emily, laying the book aside,

"these resolutions were at the time taken as the true exposition of the principles constituting the basis of the government. No objection whatever was raised to Virginia's construction, and upon it the Constitution was adopted. Accordingly Kentucky and all the other states, in their sovereign capacities, had a right to secede from the Union."

"General Jackson," replied Colonel Burrell, "did not think so when he was about to chastise South Carolina for rebellious conduct."

"South Carolina, brother, if I am correctly informed, did not attempt to secede; she simply declared her right to remain in the Union and nullify a law of Congress. She did no more than what every state in the North, with the exception of Illinois and New Jersey, has done. For when the fugitive slave law was passed, in 1850, the northern states not only nullified it, but resisted it by combinations of armed men, and thus were guilty of the very thing for which South Carolina was so loudly condemned. The northern states have nullified *two* acts of Congress, and a clause of the Constitution besides. But even if South Carolina had seceded, General Jackson's action or opinion can not alter facts. If the southern states should be forced back into the Union (and I for one should deplore such an event, because this republic could not then be any thing but an oppressive monarchy or despotism), the fact still stares you in the face that they created the government; they made it and are, in consequence, superior to it. Their subjugation will only prove that brute force can sometimes triumph over right and justice. In the event they are subdued, it seems to me the conquerors will be at a loss to reconcile their victory with the principle that constitutes the corner-stone of all republics. How can a government deriving its powers from the consent of the governed, consistently hold in subjection states that would be admitted into the Union upon the footing of equals? These conquered provinces—for they could be called nothing else—would exercise the functions of sovereignty only by the permission of those who, from the very terms of the political contract, could lay no just claim to superiority. That will be a strange position for a sovereign state to occupy."

"Your arguments are mere quibbles, sister; for the grounds diametrically opposite to those you take appear to me as plain as daylight. Secession is an abominable principle, and one which, if it be acknowledged as a feature in government, the very foundations of society would be overthrown. Such a government would be next to anarchy, and would contain within itself the elements of destruction. No one would have any guarantee of security in a commercial point of view. The right of property would stand upon such uncertain grounds that free trade would necessarily be shackled and restricted. There could be but little confidence between the citizens of different states. For instance, how could I own real estate here in Mississippi when she possesses the right to withdraw from the Union at any time, and to make laws which would place me on the footing of a foreigner, and probably render my title insecure? Besides, what inducement would there be for the General Government to extend its boundaries if new states, admitted to all the rights and privileges which the others enjoy, can secede as soon as they emerge from the condition of a territory, and leave her companions to pay the purchase money? You see your doctrine will not do, and I am sorry you have formed such erroneous opinions."

"I do not see it from any thing you have said," replied Emily, with a faint smile. "You seem to me to avoid the main question. I can admit every word you have said, for you have made no attack upon the position I took in the outset. You are discussing general principles rather than the particular question at issue. As I told you before, I do not say that secession, as an abstract principle, is right or is wrong. I am not enough of a politician for that. But this I do know, that when the Constitution was adopted the rights and powers of all the states were distinctly defined, and among these was the right of secession. If it has not operated in accordance with expectation, we must abide by the consequences. It is certainly too late now to say that the states did not possess this right, simply because it was inconvenient to New England to lose the wealth wrung from the South, in the shape of high tariffs, etc. This power, it was explicitly declared, is reserved to the states. If such were not the case, I would agree with you that this is a rebellion on the part of the South. As it is now, the war is nothing but a grand conflict against truth and justice."

"O, well, sister, I do not care about arguing the question. If your views are correct, we have discovered our error, and are going to reorganize the government. We will not, as you say, hold the southern states as conquered provinces; for the rebels will be exterminated and replaced by loyal citizens, who will cheerfully discharge those duties which traitors have the audacity to contemn."

"O, brother," said Emily, with solemnity, "do not speak so lightly of 'exterminating the rebels.' It is a most fearful undertaking to blot out a whole nation from the face of the earth—one you should be certain God sanctions and approves. O, James, be not of the party engaged in this unholy work. Think of poor, down-trodden Poland, that all the civilized world saw torn to pieces, limb by limb, and her lands divided among her rapacious conquerors. What if this should be the fate of the South? What pleasure could it afford you to see the proud State of Mississippi, now stained with the blood of her noble sons, subdued and humbled to the dust, and her high-spirited people driven, like the poor Indians, to the wilderness. You, a Kentuckian and a southron, and your heart not sicken at the very thought! I hope and trust in God you will never see a southern state reduced to such an humbled condition. I tell you, brother, heaven will not suffer it. God will raise up armies to fight for this people, as he did in the days of Washington. Do you not recollect what our fathers suffered in the revolution of '76? They were driven from every stronghold, and a British guard was stationed at nearly every door; yet they were not conquered. The half-clad followers of Washington fled to the forest; barefooted they marched over ice and snow, and the blood streamed from their feet as they walked; with no covering to protect their shivering bodies from the howling blast, they rested their weary limbs upon the cold, damp bosom of the earth; dark, gloomy clouds gathered over them at the hour of midnight, and the pitiless rain beat upon their defenseless heads; gaunt hunger pinched their famished bodies; and yet, in spite of all this, they faltered not. The consequence was, God crowned their heroic efforts with success. In like manner will the southern people be successful. Their country may be overrun for awhile; Richmond, Atlanta, Charleston, and all other cities may fall; their armies may be dejected and discouraged; but they will finally be triumphant. Virginia, Mississippi, Louisiana may now groan beneath the iron tread of the oppressor, but they will yet shake off their fetters in proud defiance. Kentucky, our native state, that now lies bleeding at every pore, will spring up from the dust, full panoplied in the armor of war, and strike down the invader whose foot pollutes her soil. I know I appear to you as a Cassandra, but I feel what I say, and you will see that my predictions will be literally fulfilled. The day is not far distant when all this will be accomplished. Proud, then, will be the humblest soldier that shouldered a musket in defense of the South; and happy will be even the mother, the blood of whose son has been washed from southern soil by the rains of heaven."

"And how do you know all this?" asked the officer, who seemed deeply interested in and entertained by the impassioned eloquence of his sister.

"I pretend not to be inspired nor to be blessed with the gift of penetrating the future more than other mortals. But if I know it not, then the experience of all history is in vain. I know it because I can not believe that God will suffer the crimes committed by the Federals to go unpunished. Such a people can never carry out the infamous policy proposed by the United States Government. No; but, instead, Nemesis will hurl back, with tenfold vengeance, upon the instigators of this cruel war, the afflictions they intend for the South. Too many dark deeds have been perpetrated. It would be too great a triumph of vice over suffering virtue and innocence for the North to succeed in her efforts."

"For God's sake, sister, do not let any one else hear you talk so. You would be sent to prison."

"And if I should, I would only be one among a thousand sufferers. Their treatment of citizens in this respect is scandalous and disgraceful in the extreme. I have not yet told you of the fate of our kind neighbor, General Winston."

"No; what of him?"

"One cold, winter night, the poor old man was dragged from his bed and taken before a Federal officer. The General promptly refused to take the oath of allegiance. He was then sent to Alton, Illinois, and all his property confiscated. A few weeks ago we received tidings of his death, brought about by exposure and starvation. But he is only one among hundreds who have been treated in the same inhuman manner. Some of the most revolting crimes have been committed in our neighborhood that ever harrowed the feelings of the human heart. You recollect the Waldrop family? Well, poor old Mr. Waldrop was shot before his wife's face; and when this horrible tragedy was ended, the murderers told Mrs. Waldrop and her two daughters to get what clothing they wanted out of the house. As soon as they had done this, the wretches set fire to the building, and while it was burning they took the clothing the ladies had gotten out and threw it in the flames. The poor creatures were then left, half-clad, to shift for themselves. The widow Warren, who lives about ten miles from our house, they beat with a leather strap until the old lady was nearly dead. She was confined to her bed for several months afterward. They told her they wanted her to see how her servants felt when she chastised them with the strap. Your old friends, the Johnsons, the Tremewheres, the Waltons, and the Lindsays, have all been sent beyond the Federal lines, simply because they would not take the oath of allegiance. Just to think, then, that all these disgraceful deeds, in one neighborhood, constitute only a single link in the long series of cruelties practiced over the whole territory of the South, is enough to nerve the arm of the veriest coward to fight in the defense of helpless women and children."

"The rebels would treat the Unionists just as bad should they invade our country."

"The rebels, as you call them, are making no attempt to invade the territory of the United States. They are fighting exclusively on the defensive. They simply ask you to go home, and let them alone in peace. You have no right to treat them cruelly, and contrary to all the established usages of warfare, merely because you *suppose* they would act as the Federals do should they become the invading party. The Confederates have not acted in this infamous manner in the few instances in which they have gone beyond their own lines. And even if they should act like the Federals, they would be justified by the *lex talionis* in any deed they could possibly commit."

"If you uttered such sentiments, how did you escape banishment with the other rebel sympathizers? or do you hold your peace in Kentucky?"

"It is wise, brother, to be silent sometimes. I have not gone from home since the commencement of the war. As I told you, I have never talked upon this subject before, not even to our father. You know I have always been a sort of a recluse. Henceforth I expect to live in entire retirement. I can not enjoy society. I can truly say, in the language of Margaret Davidson:

> "'A shade hath passed
> Athwart my brightest visions here;
> A cloud of darkest gloom hath wrapped
> The remnant of my brief career;
> No song, no echo can I win—
> The sparkling fount hath dried within.'"

"Emily," said the brother, sorrowfully, "it pains and grieves me to see you give way to such feelings of melancholy. I do not think, in this instance, you display your usual good sense. If this man Winston has proved false, it seems to me the best thing you can do is to forget him as soon as possible. Come, cheer up. The whole bright world is before you. You are young, beautiful, and accomplished; and it is worse than madness to throw your affections away, and waste your youthful bloom in useless sorrow. We are going to Washington City, where all is bright, gay, and happy. You must there go into society. Amid the festivities and gayeties of the place you will forget this little unhappy incident, which, I doubt not, in the course of time, you will laugh at as one of the childish follies of youth."

"When do you say we start?" asked Emily, making no reply to this last insinuation against her constancy.

"I think we would better go to-night, on the gun-boat ——, for safety. It would be dangerous to go any other way now, as guerrillas are numerous along the banks of the Mississippi. I am compelled to go by the way of Memphis. By the way, our cousin Walter has received an appointment in Washington, and will accompany us."

"Brother," said Emily, with a look which seemed to somewhat surprise the officer, and appeared rather foreign to his sister, "do not say *us;* at least do not include *me.* Walter Hallam can no longer possess even my friendship. I have lost my respect for him, and he will be no company for me. Of course I shall say nothing against his going on the boat, but I wish to see as little of him as possible. The very sight of him will make me miserable."

"Well, well, sister," said the officer, with an appearance of some little vexation, "do as you please; but go now and make the necessary arrangements for our departure."

Emily obeyed without another word, and the officer was left alone to his own cogitations.

CHAPTER XIV.

*"To-night you, pilot, shall not sleep,
Who trims his narrow'd sail;
To-night you, frigate, scarce shall keep
Her broad breast to the gale."*

That night the splendid gun-boat —— steamed slowly out from the city and up the river, with her complement of men and arms. A lady, attended by two gentlemen, one of whom hobbled on a crutch, was observed to get aboard by several bystanders, who were watching the boat's departure. It was Emily, Walter, and Colonel Burrell. For several days the dark monster, looking like an immense turtle, moved slowly up the broad stream of the Mississippi. Emily had rather a lonesome time of it. She avoided Walter Hallam, and repelled all his advances with a coldness which deeply wounded his feelings. Seeing that his attentions were so palpably disagreeable, and ignorant of the fact that Emily had been made acquainted with his exploit on the battle-field of Corinth, he resolved to demand an explanation of the sudden and, to him, unaccountable change which had taken place in his cousin's feelings. He had never mentioned the circumstance himself, and was in hopes she never would hear of it, at least until her partiality for Winston should be obliterated by the progress of time.

One evening, a little before sunset, when the boat was within twenty or thirty miles of Memphis, he again sought Emily, whom he found gazing with a pensive air on the glories of the sinking sun.

"May I join you?" asked Walter, approaching, "or do you still prefer to be alone?"

"Alone, if you please," replied Emily, without turning her head.

"Before I leave you, Emily," said Walter, "I want you to tell me why you have avoided me and treated me with such rudeness on this trip. Have I offended you in any way of late?"

"I do not always feel like talking," she slowly replied. "Sometimes I like to be by myself, and enjoy the pleasure of my own thoughts."

"Yes; but I have observed for several days that you have avoided me as if I were a monster instead of your relative. You have not spoken half a dozen words to me since we left Vicksburg. You surely have some reason for such strange conduct. Now I, for one, despise all little petty deceptions. If I do not like a man, I tell him so, and tell him why, too. If I have made you mad, I want you to let me know it, and do not always be pouting when I come near you. Emily, I have loved you—I love you *now*. Often I have thought of you, even when the balls of the rebels were whizzing around my head."

"Are you sure," cried she quickly, and looking him straight in the face, "that your actions upon battle-fields, 'when the balls of the rebels were whizzing around your head,' did credit to your heart, and would add luster to the character of a *brave* man? Answer me that, I pray you."

"By the powers of heaven, Emily, if you were not a woman, I would hurl you into the water below. Do you accuse me of cowardice? Is this what you mean?"

"I did not accuse you of any thing. I only asked you a question."

"From the peculiar manner in which you looked at me, and your tone of voice, you meant something, and I should like to know what it is."

"Why, does the cap fit?"

"Cap—what cap? I wish you would talk common sense, Emily. What am I to understand by your question?"

"Do you think all of your exploits are worthy of a *brave* man? I think you might understand that question."

"When you can point to one of my actions which I would blush to own, then you can ask me such a question."

"I think I could mention one which a *brave* man would blush to own."

"By the eternal gods, Emily, do not call me a coward, or I may forget your sex, and treat you as a man. No *man*, Miss, could have said with impunity what you have. I would lay him to the earth, even should he be President Lincoln. Name any action of mine that I would be ashamed of."

"I can mention one I would be ashamed of were I a man."

"What is that?" said Walter, who was now beginning to guess to what Emily alluded.

"Do you think," asked Emily, looking him steadily in the eye, "do you think it characteristic of true bravery to bind a wounded prisoner, though he should be an enemy, and take his life in cold blood?"

"Ah, that is it, is it? So you have heard of my difficulty with Winston? If it had been any other person in whom you were less interested, you would think differently. You now take altogether a one-sided view of the matter. But you need not think I am ashamed of it."

"You ought to be, if you are not. I would not treat even a cur in such a manner."

"And that is why you have so scrupulously avoided me for the last week or two?" said Hallam, thoughtfully.

"If such a supposition will prevent your asking further questions on that point, you can take it as a reason."

"If it were any body besides yourself, Emily, I could make a satisfactory explanation. But you are so wrapped up in this traitorous rebel, or at least you seem so to be, that you can not listen to reason. If any man ever was justifiable, I certainly was. I am sorry I did not accomplish my purpose every time I think of my innocent sister, who fell a victim to a premature grave on account of this man's rascality. You are acquainted with the circumstance; and, since you are, it does appear strange and incomprehensible to me that you will insult your friends for the sake of a vile wretch who has evidently sacrificed your feelings for the gratification of his pride and vanity. Here, for the last two or three weeks, you have treated me shamefully—me, who would not injure a hair of your head, you have scarcely spoken to, and when you did speak it was in monosyllables, and with an indifference that was chilling to my heart. And for what, Emily, I ask you—for what? For a man who scorns the love you lavish upon him; who has treated you with contempt; who has played with you, as a child sports with a toy, for an hour, and then throws it aside for some other more interesting; and who, if you grieve for him till you sink to the tomb, will boast that you died for him."

Poor Emily could make no reply. She was puzzled, sorry, troubled, and vexed. At one time she was ready to interrupt Walter, and overwhelm him with a torrent of indignation. Then again she thought she had probably treated him with unjustifiable rudeness. And she had no assurance that Henry loved her now. He had threatened to forget her, and he may have done so. It might be, as Walter said, that he would now hold her in contempt. So, amid all these conflicting emotions and thoughts, she could not but listen. Walter continued:

"You think this man loves you, Emily. I tell you he does not. Why will you not take a common-sense view of the matter? Why do you cling to the idea that he adores you, when, in fact, you have no grounds for such a belief? I am acquainted with the whole affair. You need not ask me how I obtained my information; but you engaged yourself to this fellow, and on very slight acquaintance, too. You knew nothing whatever of his character; nevertheless, you were engaged to be married; and he told you, on a certain evening he would ask your father's consent to the union. Did he come? You did not see him on that day, but it seems he was lurking around the house; nobody knows for what purpose. That night he left the country without speaking to you, without seeing you, without making any explanation even to his uncle; and still you think he loves you. Is this what you call love—to be deserted in contempt?"

"O, Walter, Walter! you are *killing me.*"

"My dear cousin, I know it is an unpalatable truth; but you ought to look the truth square in the face. Now, hear the whole truth. The fellow wrote you a letter; I am aware of its contents. Does he explain his conduct? He makes you the party to blame. He tells you that you have *deceived him.* He does not say how or in what; but he takes care to make himself appear as the injured one, whose feelings have been bruised. There is an air of mystification about the whole document. He then writes a note to his uncle, and tells the same tale. He lied, Emily! he lied in his foul throat. He knew you made no attempt to deceive him, though I say it to my own sorrow. If he thought you deceived him, why did he not demand an explanation, in broad, open daylight, like an honest man? Why did he not explain himself to General Winston? He merely made this a pretext to cast you off in derision and contempt. He was ashamed to see you, because he knew you were true—yes, too *true* to such a black-hearted villain, who would now rejoice over the distress which he has caused you."

"General Winston," said Emily, in painful confusion, "thought his nephew was laboring under a mistake."

"A mistake! Yes, no doubt a very convenient mistake.

Why did he not give you an opportunity of clearing it up, then? Even if there was any mistake, he did not want an explanation. It seems that he feared you would hold him to the contract of marriage, and he left before you could explain your conduct, if it appeared inconsistent to him. He left at the dead hour of night, and the next thing we hear of him he turns up in the rebel army, and the next thing after that he is seen in the Federal army."

"What!" cried Emily, "in the Yankee army?"

"Yes; in the 'Yankee army,' as you call it, but not as a Union soldier. I believe he was after no good. A few weeks since I saw him with my own eyes in the uniform of a Federal soldier. I was going to have him arrested, but he sneaked off, just like he did in Kentucky."

"And would you have *murdered* him had he been apprehended?" asked Emily, with a return of the same feeling she had manifested at the beginning of this interview.

"No; I would not. He would have been delivered over to the authorities, and no doubt would have been hanged as a spy, as he deserved to be."

"But you would have been instrumental in having him put to death? You would have been a witness?"

"And why should I not have been? It was clearly my duty, and I would have been false to my country not to have appeared against him. I would be a witness against any spy. The fellow ought to have been killed long ago. Had it not been for the interference of your brother, he would certainly have received his just deserts at Corinth."

"I am glad somebody had a more feeling heart than you did. I have thought less of you ever since I heard of that disgraceful transaction of yours."

"Emily," said Walter, sorrowfully, "I have borne your abuse long enough. Now, I want to know in what relation we are to stand hereafter. I have loved you; I have humbled myself to you; I have never said a word to hurt your feelings, and I have patiently borne your insults. I am tired of it, and I will no longer tolerate it. If you hate me, say so, and I will never trouble you again with my presence. I I shall not again beg your friendship. But now I want it distinctly understood upon what footing we meet henceforth."

But Emily did not make any reply. She could not determine between her clashing emotions. When she heard Walter's sorrowful tone of voice, the first impulse of her heart inclined her to forgiveness. Then Winston would rise up in her imagination, bound and bleeding, and Walter pointing a gun at his defenseless breast. She knew not what to say.

"Will you answer me or not, Emily?"

"Give me time," said she; "I can not analyze my own feelings just now. To-morrow or some other day I will talk to you. Please leave me now; I want to be alone. I do not feel like conversing with any one."

Hallam gazed at her for an instant without speaking; then, turning slowly, left her to the solitude of her own reflections. Emily buried her face in her hands and thought:

"Did Henry Winston, indeed, love her? Had he really been trifling with her, as Walter had said? Had he ever loved Carrie Hallam? Was it not strange that Winston had never even alluded to that young lady? He could so easily have explained it all. May be Walter was right, after all, and Henry had caused his sister to die of a broken heart. Why did not Winston see her before he left, and ask an explanation, if he thought he was deceived? Why could he not have explained himself to General Winston? It did seem strange. He certainly did not love her. But, then, why should he have uttered such falsehoods? There was no use of that. Should she ever see him again, and have all these mysteries cleared up? Walter said he was a spy. No telling, then, where he might be now. It would not be impossible for him to be on the boat at this very moment. Would it not be strange if he were?"

As this last thought flashed over Emily's mind, she did not really believe that Winston was within a few yards of her; but, nevertheless, it is true. He was on top of the boat as a *sentinel*. Not far from him stood another soldier in the same capacity. The night was dark, and the weather was rather cool for the season, and one of the sentinels would occasionally shiver under the influence of the casual breezes that swept without resistance over the bosom of the Mississippi; but the other seemed not to feel any inconvenience from the inclemency of the weather. Could his countenance have been seen, it would have indicated that his mind was so deeply occupied with some project or thought that his physical organization was for the time insensible to the sensations of ordinary heat or cold. He was, however, presently interrupted in his thoughts, whatever they may have been; for the other sentinel, becoming tired of the silence, intimated his desire to break it.

"Jones," said he, addressing himself to Winston, who seems to have given that as his name, "I'll be darned if I like to stand out here this cold night. There's no sense in it, neither. You couldn't see a man five steps, and there's no danger of the rebs firing on the boat such a night as this."

"Well, never mind," replied Winston, "our time will be up presently, and we will be relieved."

"Jones," said the other, changing the topic, "how long have you been in the service—the naval service?"

"Not a great while," was the response.

"Neither have I, and I don't like it, either. Be darned if I don't quit it the first good chance I git. It don't suit me at all. There's no chance to plunder the rebs on one of these darned iron-clads. I'd rather belong to cavalry. We used to have jolly times when I was a cavalryman. I did love to go on a raid; I always got so much plunder from the secesh; and then I used to hug and kiss them rebel gals that pretended they did n't like it, and ran away screaming, jest as if we was a set of devils."

"The very thing you were, every one of you. Were you not ashamed of yourself to insult females?"

"Ashamed! No; they were rebels."

"Could you be a good soldier and be guilty of such conduct?"

"I a good soldier, Jones? No, siree. I never pretended to be. I am not such a fool as that. Darn the war; I never did like it, and I did n't want to have any thing to do with it; but they forced me into it, and I must have my pay somehow. So I take it out o' the rebs. I take care never to git hurt, either. I haint been into a fight yit; and, more than that, I never expect to be in one. I've no fancy for that kind of work. I always play out, and leave the game of balls to them that likes it."

"I am afraid you are rather a coward, Williams."

"No, Jones, I'm not a coward by nater; but what the h—ll do I want to be killed for? It makes no difference to me whether the nigger is free or not, and that's what all this fuss is about I would n't give my life for all the black rascals in the rebel states, nor spill a drop of blood to free the whole darned set. These secesh have never done me any harm. I used to be sorter seceshy myself—kinder Democrat, you know. Why, then, should I throw my life away? What good 'll it do me if the Union is restored, and all the d—d niggers free, if I've got a dozen bullet-holes through my body? No, sir. I'm a-goin' to take care of this carcass. When peace is made, I want to be thar to drink whisky and bust fire-crackers as well as any body else. Nobody'll give me credit for gittin' killed. Then, by hoky, I'm not a-goin' to set my carcass up for the rebs to shoot at. I won't be benefited neither one way nor t'other, if the rebs are whipped or not whipped. It makes no difference with me."

"I think you have very little patriotism, Williams," said Winston, who was listening intently to all the fellow said.

"Not a darned bit of it, Jones. I'd as soon live in one country as another. I am selfish, and I know it. But darn me if I care about sheddin' my blood for the Union, when some general gits all the credit and honor, and all the pay, too. When the war ends, all these officers will run their fists into the public crib, and 'll live like lions. But nary nubbin will I git. No, by jingo, if I should ask any little favor of the people, no matter how hard I might have fit, they'd kick me, and send me to the devil for all any body'd care. Then, by dads, the best thing I can do is to take care of A No. 1, and I intend to do it, too. I'll live as long as any other soldier of my age, unless I'm tuk off by a lawful spell of sickness. Darn me if I don't."

"You will have no chance to avoid a fight if one occurs while you are on this boat. You will have to take your chances with the rest. You can not play out then."

"No, by hokey, I can't; and that's what uneasies me. But I don't expect to be in the service long."

"Indeed! how will you get out of it?"

"There's more ways to kill a dog besides hanging him. I can desert, if there's no other way."

"Are you not afraid I will report you? You have laid yourself liable."

"No, I'm not afraid of you, Jones. I know who I'm talkin' to. I've been watchin' you, Jones, ever since you've been on this boat; I ken see you don't like the service any better than I do."

"Why, do I not discharge my duties?"

"Yes, but you go at it like you was thinking of something else all the time. Sometimes, Jones, do you know, I suspicion you of bein' a reb yourself. I aint often mistaken in my opinion of a man, neither. Now, talkin' of reportin', I might report you, too. Tit for tat, you know."

"I have not said any thing, I am sure, that would lead any one to believe I am not a good soldier."

"Now, Jones, you need not be afraid of me. There's no danger of my betrayin' you. It's true, you've said nothin', but you've *done* somethin'," said the man, in a whisper. "I've been watchin' you, Jones, when you did n't know any body was lookin' at you. Do n't be frightened, old fellow, nobody knows it but me."

"Knows what? What are you talking about?"

"I'm mighty hard to fool, Jones; especially when I smell danger ahead to Jack Williams. But I tell you, you need n't be afraid of me. I could a had you put in irons long ago; and if I'd a bin a good soldier, I'd a done it, too. But blast me if ever I cared which side whipped. I've got nothin' agin the rebs. If I was on neutral grounds it would make little odds with me whether Lincoln or Davis was President. But now, Jones, to show that I keep my eyes skinned, and that all the confidence may n't be on one side, let me ask you a question."

"Very well, go ahead."

"*What's all them pins and that auger fur?*" was whispered.

The Yankee would have started back with fright and fear could he have seen the countenance of the spy at the moment this whispered question was propounded. The hand of Winston grasped the handle of a bowie-knife, and drew the dangerous weapon half-way from its scabbard. It would have been but the work of a moment to silence the babbling Yankee forever. But another thought seemed to strike him—if the fellow had any intention of betraying him, he could have accomplished his purpose long ago. So the instrument was quickly thrust back into its sheath.

"Do you know," said the spy, slowly, "that if I were a suspicious character, and were bent on doing mischief, and were afraid of your rattling tongue, I could, a dozen times to-night, have given your body to the fishes and alligators for food?"

"I told you, Jones," said the man, drawing back a pace or two, "you need n't be afraid of me. I did n't know exactly what you was after. But I thought it looked kinder suspicious like. I meant no harm. But you see it would n't be safe to tell tales on me."

"What kind of tales could I tell on you?"

"You're a shrewd boy, Jones, to pump me in that way. But I aint afraid to tell you about my desertin'."

"Are you going to do that?"

"I am, Jones, and I believe you are, too."

"Well, Williams, you have guessed right for once. I have been studying about it for several days. But the difficulty is, we will be liable to be apprehended as deserters as long as this boat is on the river. We would be advertised at once, you know."

"That's so; and so you're a-goin' to sink her?" said the Yankee.

"I did not say so," quickly answered the spy, who did not care to reveal too much at once. "But would you sink her, if you could do so with safety, if by that means you could secure your exemption from military service?"

"I do n't understand you exactly, Jones. I mout escape from this boat if she was sunk. But then I would be drafted agin. So that would be jumpin' out o' the fryin'-pan into the fire."

"Why did you ever enter the army, Williams? and why have you not deserted before now?"

"I told you, man, I was drafted. I did n't have three hundred dollars to buy my way out. I have stayed this long because I was tryin' to confiscate enough from the rebs to pay my way out, and live decently on the balance."

"And have you got enough for this purpose?"

"Not now I haven't. I did have; but the officers took it from me. The rule is to divide with them for allowing us to plunder; but they always take the lion's share. So I have concluded to dissolve partnership. I would have left some time ago, but I did not have money enough to buy a breakfast."

"Now, Williams, if this boat were sunk, and you had five hundred dollars, what would you do?"

"Well, I would travel on North till I was drafted agin. Then I'd fork over my three hundred, git my papers, go on to Canada, and thar I'd stay till the war ends."

"Would you sink the boat for that amount?"

"Well, I don't know; but if I did, who'd give it to me?"

"That is not the question. Would you sink the boat for five hundred dollars?"

"If I could and save my own bacon, I would."

"Now, Williams, do it, and you shall have the money. You shall have it in advance."

"Look here," cried Williams, "aint you one o' them fellers as is hired by the rebs to travel the river and burn boats?"

"No; I am not. But mind how you talk, Williams. I will tell you a thing or two to make you a little cautious. You may suppose that you have 'pumped' me, as you say, very nicely. If you do, you are mistaken. You are completely in my power. Not in the way you think, though. You do not know what danger you are in at this very moment."

"You are not a-goin' to murder me, I hope?" said the man, in alarm.

"Not if you are wise, and will hold your tongue. For your own good, I will tell you that if you merely cheap, if I discover the least sign of the traitor about you, I can blow this boat to atoms in a second. It was well, Williams, you kept silent in regard to what you saw. Had any attempt been made to arrest me, you would ere this have taken a trip in the direction of the moon."

"And whar would *you* have bin?" asked Williams, with a shudder.

"I have made preparations for my own safety. Besides, I am not such a coward as you are. I know you, Williams, to the very bottom—every inch of you. You are afraid of me, and you had better be; for if you make any attempt to betray me, it will be the last act of your life. I will touch off the magazine, and if I can not make my escape, we will all go up or down, as the case may be, together. I am not afraid to die, like you are. You understand me, Williams?"

"I guess I do; but there is no use o' blowin' the darn thing up. I'd ruther not try that. So give me the five hundred and tell me how, and I'll sink her. That's what I've bin watchin' you for. I was afraid you had some sich notion. I'm mighty glad you told me, because I never did like to drink water in my sleep."

"It is well you agree; I knew you would. I will give you the money as soon as we are relieved. But now I will give you the plan. We will go to the hull of the boat; there is only one sentinel there, and he is a negro. I will relieve him. You must take the auger and those pins which you saw; bore half a dozen holes through the bottom of the boat and stop them with the pins. When all is ready, we will let the water in and then make our escape. Do you understand?"

"I do; but what will become of the other soldiers?"

"They can swim ashore, I suppose. If they can not, they may get out of the difficulty in any way they think best. It will be every man's business to take care of himself."

"There is a woman aboard, Jones. What will become of her?"

"That is a strange question for a man of your avowed selfishness to ask. What do you care for soldiers or women if you can save yourself? But I will see to the lady, if there is one on the boat. If no way offers for her to escape, I will swim ashore with her. I am well provided with swimming apparatus, and can easily save one life besides my own."

"Jones, I want to know if you aint one o' the rebs?"

"Yes, I am; but if you dare to reveal it, you are a *dead* man the instant the deed is done. I have got you completely in my power, Williams, and I intend to keep my eye on you. I could kill you now if I wished to; but you are in no danger if you will only do what I tell you. I will watch the engineer and fireman while you are at work. If you are discovered, away goes the boat into the air, and Williams along with it. So you must be very cautious."

"Great God!" cried Williams, in terror, "do n't blow it up while I 'm on it."

"You need not fear if you do your part. I will attend to the engineer and fireman. The others will all be asleep."

"But the pumps, Jones—the pumps. The water can all be pumped out; then we will be discovered."

"You would make a good spy, Williams. But I have considered the case of the pumps. As a general thing, I perform any thing I undertake thoroughly. I could not be such a fool as to overlook things of that sort. I have seen the pumps, and I do not think you could get a drop of water out with them in their present condition. My impression is they will not work well to-night. So if you show no signs of fear, but do your part like a brave man, you will be in no danger. You can swim, can you not?"

"O, yes, a day at a time. I do n't fear on that score."

"Well, then, you need have no fears on the subject. Do as

I tell you, and I will pay you five hundred dollars. Now you understand me clearly. If you know what is best for you, you will not hesitate nor falter. But keep silent; I hear the relief coming now."

Accordingly in a few moments Winston and his companion were relieved. They descended into the hull, and found, as the spy had said, only a solitary negro sentinel. Winston easily persuaded the negro to let him stand guard in his place. Cuff was no exception to the general law of drowsiness to which his whole race is subject, and he gladly consented to the proposed arrangement without any inquiry. All the rest of the soldiers were buried in deep and profound slumber. Winston's part of the contract with Williams was now fulfilled, and he signaled to the Yankee, according to previous agreement, to proceed. The spy watched narrowly the motions of the engineer and fireman, but he discovered no signs that they were aware of any thing unusual. Williams worked rapidly but still cautiously; and in a short time he announced to the spy, in a whisper, that the work was completed. In a low breath he was ordered to let the water in. This the Yankee quickly did, and moved away to the upper deck, with the auger still in his hand. In spite of all his precautions he had been observed by the engineer, who did not, however, suspect any thing at the time. Our hero abandoned his post, and marched leisurely up to the engine, and halted. It was not long before the bottom of the boat was covered with water.

"Boys, where is all this water coming from?" cried the engineer, looking down in surprise. The water rose rapidly.

"Wake up the crew!" bawled the engineer, in alarm, as he heard the water hissing around the engine. "To the pumps, boys! to the pumps! My God! the boat is sinking!"

The alarm was now soon given, and the wildest confusion prevailed in all quarters. Winston hastened away to look after the lady mentioned by his accomplice. It did not require much time to find Emily, who was standing in a conspicuous place, with a light in her hand. When within ten steps of her Winston came to a dead halt. The impressions of years were crowded into the space of a single moment. For a few seconds a deathly pallor overspread the features of the spy, and a keen pang shot through his heart. But Emily was looking for her brother, and saw not her former lover. Winston had little time for reflection, and with a sigh fell back to a darker spot, as he saw Walter Hallam come dashing along, followed by Colonel Burrell, who moved as fast as his condition would allow. They approached Emily, and some words were uttered, in a quick, hurried tone, which did not reach our hero's ears. However, the trio ascended to the top of the boat, and Winston followed at a sufficient distance to prevent recognition. Above was another scene of confusion and disorder. Not a single skiff nor canoe could be found that was not perforated in the bottom with auger-holes, and damaged in other ways. Men were betaking themselves to the water, and swimming in the direction of the Arkansas shore. They followed each other like a gang of frightened sheep, and aimed for the further bank. The boat was steadily going down, and it was evident that in a short time she would rest on the bottom of the river. Colonel Burrell and Hallam were standing a few paces from Emily conversing rapidly, but the majority of the words were lost amid the din and bustle. Winston heard Hallam say only, "I can barely swim myself, Colonel. With my life-preserver, I can probably save myself, and that is the utmost I can do. In the name of heaven, what will we do?" Colonel Burrell did not hesitate long. In a loud, trembling, husky voice, that showed he was nearly beside himself, he exclaimed: "Five thousand dollars to the man who will take this lady ashore!" Emily almost fainted when she thus suddenly discovered in what a terrible condition she was placed, and in breathless anxiety the trio listened for some one to accept the proposition. But no one seemed to regard it. Life was more valuable than gold, and the men continued to strike out for *terra firma*, until they were all gone but three or four, who were making preparations to commit themselves to the waves. Colonel Burrell repeated the proposition, and then doubled the amount. No one appeared to hear it.

"God of heaven!" cried Emily, in a voice of despair, "save me from the waters!"

The Colonel and Walter seemed petrified. They stood stone-still. It was at this critical juncture that Winston stepped up, with his back to the light. He spoke in a disguised voice.

"Trust to me, lady," he said—"trust to me; I will save you though I should perish. Fear nothing, but do as I tell you."

"Thank God," cried Colonel Burrell, "there is one brave man on the boat. Take her to the shore, my fine fellow, and I will reward you till you are satisfied. Which side are you going?"

"To the Mississippi shore; it is nearer."

Without more ado, Winston hastily instructed Emily in the part she was to perform, and they were soon buffeting the waves of the Mississippi. Colonel Burrell and Hallam were not far behind. They could without much difficulty, both being provided with artificial helps, keep within speaking distance, as Winston was burdened with the weight of Emily. However, not a word was spoken, and nothing was heard save the sullen roar of the waves and the occasional leap of some inhabitant of the watery element, that would rise to the surface in pursuit of its prey; then fall back with a heavy plunge, as if frightened by the thought of its own audacity. Slowly and steadily the swimmers approached the shore. Winston's thoughts were in rather a tumult while battling against the waves, with Emily clinging to him with wild energy, occasioned by the terrible perils of her situation. His mind was carried back to the day when, with seemingly undisguised sincerity, she had promised him her hand and heart; and the thought caused his bosom to heave with a thrilling emotion that almost raised him from the water. Then he recalled the last scene in the bower, when he heard the astonishing declaration that *he was not loved;* and his body seemed inclined to sink beneath the dark wave. For whom was he now saving this fair burden? Another question presented itself. Should he reveal himself or not when the shore was reached? This question he could not decide; but it soon demanded a decision, for in a few minutes after it had crossed his mind the twentieth time he was seen standing upon firm ground. Emily was shivering with cold. Pulling out a water-proof match-box, Winston struck a light and in a short time had a bright fire blazing in the gloomy swamp of the Mississippi. Colonel Burrell, with the assistance of Hallam, had managed to reach the fire after emerging from the river. The two men commenced donning their vests in order to dry themselves. Winston, with a heavy heart, was on the point of leaving without claiming his reward or awaiting the thanks of Emily, when his eye fell upon a watch which Hallam drew from his vest pocket and hung to a bush. He thought the instrument similar to his own.

"Thank God," exclaimed Colonel Burrell, "we are all safe! I owe much to you, my friend, for the preservation of this lady," he said, turning to Winston, "and you shall have your reward as soon as we can get to Memphis. It will be impossible for me to redeem my promise here in the swamp."

"I ask nothing for saving a fellow-creature's life," replied the spy, in the same disguised voice he had assumed on the boat. "I have done only my duty. Will you allow me," he continued, addressing Hallam, and taking the watch from the bush—"will you allow me to see what the hour is?"

"Certainly," said Hallam—"certainly, sir."

"And your name, then, is Winston?" asked the spy, looking at the name engraved on the case.

"No, sir," replied Hallam, casting a glance at Emily, who drew nearer in surprise at hearing the name of Winston— "no, sir; that watch was captured from a rebel, and fell into my hands by a mere accident."

"I suspect you are telling an infamous falsehood," said Winston, in a cool tone, that caused the three other personages to start in astonishment at such an unexpected turn of events.

"Look here, friend," said Walter, in perfect amazement, "what mean you by using such language to a stranger?"

"I mean, sir, that this is stolen property. And to prove it," continued Winston, in his natural voice, "the owner stands before you. Do you recognize him?"

The hat was taken off, and a strange expression, which it is impossible to describe, played over the features of the spy— an expression which made an impression on all the parties present. Reader, Emily did not faint nor scream. The ashy hue of death was depicted on her face, and she stood still, as if her feet were rooted to the soil. The power of utterance was momentarily gone, and she looked on this strange scene in mute amazement and perplexity. For a moment the spy stood with uncovered head, and not a word was spoken. At last Winston replaced his hat and broke the death-like silence.

"I presume, Mr. Hallam, you will urge no objections to the lawful owner claiming his property. *Captured*, was it? You know under what circumstances it was captured. To steal. Mr. Hallam—to rob a wounded man—you call to capture. That, sir, is a very convenient term for a man who would act as cowardly as you did. You formed a league with the very lowest of the human species to rob defenseless prisoners. I believe you capable of any crime, sir."

"I can stand such language no longer," exclaimed Hallam, springing at the spy. He made but a step or two, however, before he lay at his full length, felled by a powerful blow from a stout arm.

"But you *shall* stand it, though, Mr. Hallam. Now, sir, lay still where you are. If you attempt to rise, I will frail you with a stick like I would a dog. Nay, sir," he continued, seeing Hallam making an effort to draw a weapon, "keep quiet. If you show a weapon I will crack your skull with this cudgel. I would scorn to exhibit a weapon to such a fallen pickpocket as you are. Lay still, sir, or I will chastise you, even in the presence of this lady. You probably recollect the treatment you extended to me on the field of Corinth. You would have murdered me had it not been for the timely interference of this gentleman. You robbed me; you abused and insulted me; you called me coward when I had no chance to defend myself. Now, sir, we will see who is the coward. I would not imbrue my hands in your foul blood without giving you, villainous dastard as you are, a showing for your life. Now, rise, sir. I have a couple of pistols; you can take your choice; or, if pistols suit you not, select your own weapons. The place and time, though, must be here and now."

"I object to the time, as the challenged party," said Hallam, sulkily, and rising from the ground. "Duels do not usually take place in the dark. Wait till daylight, sir."

"Detestable thief!" cried Winston, showing a couple of pistols, "take your choice. You have as fair a chance as I have. Take your choice; or will you stand here before this lady and this gentleman as the most pusillanimous wretch on earth?"

"Great heaven! gentlemen," cried Emily, now recovering from her surprise and confusion, and rushing between the two men with uplifted arms, "do not, for heaven's sake, commit murder. Put up your weapons. I entreat you, Mr. Winston, for the sake of what once passed between us"——

"In God's name, Emily," exclaimed Colonel Burrell, "do not disgrace yourself. Hush, and let me settle this difficulty."

Emily, thus rebuked, retired, with a blushing face, to her former position.

"Now, Mr. Winston," continued the Colonel, "we have met before, as you have said, and under unpleasant circumstances. You acknowledge that I rendered you an important service. Well, if I did, and you think it really deserving of gratitude, I ask you to drop this matter. You have, though, sir, already overpaid me in saving the life of one I hold dearer than my own." The spy felt a keen pain in his breast. "It seems, then, that we are both under mutual obligations; or, at least, have been. Will you not then oblige me still further by giving up this purpose of fighting a duel at such a time, and in such a place, and under such circumstances? No one here doubts your courage. You have shown yourself more than once a brave man, and I respect you for it. Now, crown your bravery with the God-like virtues of forgiveness and forbearance. Put up your weapons, and let this difficulty rest where it is; or, at least, postpone it until a more suitable time. The impropriety of it will appear obvious, if you will reflect that there is no surgeon here, in the event that either of you should fall dangerously wounded. In short, considering every thing, it would be a duel very much out of place."

"Perhaps you are right, sir," said Winston; "be it as you say. At your request I desist. But I can not do it if I remain here. I am under obligations to you, and I now return you my heart-felt thanks. You appear to be a gentleman, and I hope you and this lady may be happy together. It may not be a secret to you that I once loved her myself;

but I am glad she has found a husband worthy of her beauty and her heart. May God bless you both!"

It may appear surprising to the reader that Emily or Colonel Burrell, or both, did not interrupt Winston in the midst of these last rapidly uttered remarks, and explain the evident mistake under which he was laboring. But neither spoke. The supposition appeared so absurd to the Colonel, that the first thought which flashed through his mind was, how any sensible man could ever have committed such a blunder. Emily comprehended it all, and the mystery of Winston's abrupt flight from Kentucky was now unraveled. A thrill of wild joy at the thought that she was still loved prevented her from speaking. She was waiting for her brother to make some reply. Our spy was one of those strange characters whose intentions can not be divined until they are accomplished. He thought and acted almost with the quickness of lightning. So, while the Colonel and his sister were casting at each other glances of surprise, and each asking the other, in the language of the eye, if Winston's words were understood aright, during that interval of only a few seconds the spy had turned and was gone. He had vanished almost like a shadow. When the Colonel and Emily looked toward the spot where Winston had been standing, he could not be seen. A second surprise at his sudden disappearance prevented either from speaking for the space of half a minute, and during all this time Winston was moving rapidly away.

"O, my God!" cried Emily in a wild tone; "he is gone—he is gone, without even speaking to me!"

"Come, Emily," said Colonel Burrell, with a stern look, "you will render yourself contemptible to every body. Hush! the man can not be far off."

"O, brother, for heaven's sake, call him back—call him back! Let me thank him for the preservation of my life."

"You are mad, Emily, mad! Hush, if you have any self-respect left. If he sees proper to depart in this manner, let him go. But do n't, for my sake, disgrace yourself."

"I say let him go, too," cried Hallam in a voice of rage, examining a pistol, "for, by the living God, if he again makes his appearance here, he shall die—so help me heaven!"

"Do not talk *now*, Walter," said Emily, with a glance of withering scorn and contempt. "If I were you, I do not think I would ever open my mouth again."

"Emily," said the brother, in a stern and peremptory tone, "I *command* you to keep silent. Hold your tongue."

"By heaven!" said Walter, "I will have revenge if it takes me a lifetime. The d—d devil is a spy; I will bet my salvation on it he sunk the boat to-night. By all that is holy, I will hunt him down, and he shall hang by the neck till he is dead—dead—dead! I will do it, if I lose my life in the attempt. I swear it, by the bones of my sister."

"Why did you not avenge yourself just now, when you had such a chance?" exclaimed Emily, forgetting her own interference in the affair."

"My God!" said Colonel Burrell, "I believe the girl is crazy—stark mad—a perfect maniac!"

"You may scoff, Emily; but I will have his blood, if I have to wade through forty thousand h—lls to find him! Witness the oath, men, devils, and angels!"

CHAPTER XV.

"A prison is . . . . . .
A touchstone true to try a friend."

THE next day the four personages last mentioned in the previous chapter were all in the city of Memphis. It might naturally be supposed that the spy, after the exploit of sinking the gun-boat, would not venture near the vicinity where the deed was performed, at least until the remembrance of it had partially faded from the public mind. But Winston, as we have already said, was a strange and rare character. He was one who had very vague ideas of the nature of fear, and had never felt it in his life. If he desired to visit a place, he went without further reflection, regardless of consequences. Whenever danger to himself was the question, he gave it not a single thought. This feature in the composition of Winston's intellectual machinery made him one of the most useful and successful spies in the Confederacy, although the assertion may be somewhat paradoxical. Let a man move among his fellow-creatures like he courts suspicion and deserves it, like he feels himself in a dangerous position, and he is almost sure to meet with detection. On the other hand, let him play the bold game without shrinking, let him look around with an air of indifference, and an appearance of candor, innocence, and honesty, and there are ten chances in favor of to one against success. Such a character will accomplish his purpose in situations of danger without any difficulty, where a more timid man would not dare to venture. If there is any one quality indispensable to an efficient spy. it is boldness. And this is one attribute which stood out prominently in the character of Henry Winston. For the achievement of his object he would go into the presence of Abraham Lincoln with an undaunted front, and with the same appearance of loyalty that he would attend a summons from the commander of the southern armies. He was rather an eccentric character, difficult to comprehend. One of his most remarkable powers was, he could make you read thoughts and emotions in his face which really had no existence in his heart; or, if they did, were assumed, and yet were seemingly felt as if they were actually genuine. He won upon your confidence the moment you cast your eye on his face. Nature appeared to have stamped upon his brow the words—this man can be trusted. This power, however, would have been comparatively useless in the capacity of a spy had it not been associated with another which has already been mentioned; he could read your mind apparently at a single glance. He seemed to know by intuition how far he could go with, and how much he could say to, his enemies without exciting their wrath or suspicion. In some instances he may have appeared to the reader to act with rashness, when, in fact, the action was but the result of cool judgment, formed almost in an instant, founded upon a just appreciation of the character and motives of the party with whom he was dealing. Being such a man, it is not a matter of surprise that he should be found in the city of Memphis a few hours after the destruction of one of the finest gun-boats the enemy had in his possession.

Colonel Burrell, Emily, and Hallam had reached Memphis with very little trouble; for about the time the sun was casting his first golden rays on the gloomy swamp a skiff appeared in sight, going up the river. The owner was hailed, and in a short time our trio was seated in the light craft. In three or four hours they were registered on the books of the Gayoso, in the city of Memphis. Almost as soon as they arrived, Walter Hallam, who was still smarting under the indignity he had sustained, reported the transaction of the preceding night to the military authorities. He gave Winston as the author of the disaster, and stated his belief that the spy was lurking somewhere near, if not within, the city itself. After giving an accurate description of Winston, he took his departure, and went back in the direction of the Gayoso. While this was going on, the spy, now transformed into a citizen, was leisurely strolling up and down Main Street in apparent unconcern. And while thus engaged, he was rather surprised to see Williams coming up the same street, under guard. Stepping into a store, he waited until the guard had passed, and then followed on to discover for what his accomplice had been arrested. The prisoner was carried to the office of the provost marshal. Winston approached near a window, and could easily hear what was going on inside of the office.

"This is the man," said the engineer, whose voice the spy recognized, "who I believe had a hand in sinking the boat. I observed him dodging about in the boat a short time before it was sunk, though I did not think any thing of it at the time. Several of the crew besides myself saw him with an auger in his hand. I even picked up the auger after he dropped it, and found it just fitted the holes in the bottoms of our skiffs, which were all too badly damaged to be used. When we got to land, I thought this circumstance sufficient to justify his arrest. We found upon his person five hundred dollars, when it was known that that very day he did not have five cents. I am under the impression that he robbed somebody, and then sunk the boat to avoid discovery."

"What have you to say to this?" said another voice, which Winston thought he had heard before.

"I say it's not so," was the response. "I came by the money honestly. I'd like to know who there was on the boat that had so much money to lose."

"Did any person miss that amount?" said the Provost to the engineer. "Was there any money at all missed?"

"We can not tell now, sir. I had more than that amount, so did the captain, and several others; but our trunks were lost, and we did not have time to see what was missing."

"If you did not know, Mr. Williams," said the Provost, "of any one on the boat who had that much to lose, how did you get your five hundred dollars?"

"I did n't say I got it on the boat. It was on shore."

"That's a lie, Williams; you have had no chance to get that much unless you stole it. Some of the soldiers can swear you did not have a single cent yesterday."

"They can swear a darn lie, then. I do n't tell every fool what I have got; I do n't have to account to you for my money."

"What were you doing with the auger, Mr. Williams?" asked the Provost Marshal.

At this question Williams was observed to slightly wince and shrug his shoulders. However, he replied:

"I stumped my foot against it on top of the boat, and I picked it up to see what it was."

"But, Williams, I saw you with it before you reached the top of the boat."

Williams was now evidently confused, and made no response.

"Do you think," said the Provost to the engineer, "that Williams had an accomplice in the affair?"

"There was a man with him by the name of Jones. I saw them both go down into the hull together; and, since I think about it, I recollect Jones was standing near the engine when I first discovered the water. It is strange he said nothing about it, though he must have seen the water before I did."

"And where is he now?"

"No one knows; he has not been seen since last night, while he was on the boat."

"He must be found, if possible," said the Provost Marshal. "This affair must be investigated. You had better take three or four men," he continued, to the engineer, "and hunt him up."

Winston heard this last remark distinctly, and he thought it high time to take measures for his own personal safety. For that purpose he was turning to leave, when he was accosted by a file of Yankee soldiers, who happened to pass at that moment, and who thought Winston's movement rather suspicious. It was one of those unlucky accidents which sometimes happen in this lower world, despite all human precaution.

"Faith, an what are ye doin' here?" asked one of the soldiers.

"I suppose, sir, I am at liberty to go where I please?"

"By blazes, Pat," said the other soldier, who was eyeing Winston's face intently, "I believe this is the very man; his face suits."

"An sure it is, be Jasus! Come jist into our hand."

"There's no harm in trying; so I arrest you. You are my prisoner. Come into the office."

"By what authority?" asked Winston, who saw the folly of resistance; "and for what am I arrested?"

"The Provost Marshal has ordered us to arrest a man whose description suits your face exactly; for what purpose we know no more than you do. If you are not the man, you will soon be released. There's no harm done."

By another strange but unfortunate coincidence, Walter Hallam happened to step up at this juncture. He heard the last remark of the guard, and cast a glance at Winston.

"Well, by heaven! this is lucky," exclaimed Hallam. "Arrest him, men, arrest him. I know the d—d scoundrel. You've changed your garb, Mr. Winston, but you can't fool me. I know you, sir. You look very innocent indeed; but you will soon see what you have been arrested for. By G—d, do you expect to travel all over the United States and destroy public property with impunity. No, sir; you are fairly caught, and the evidence against you is ample; my own will hang you. Revenge is sweet, Winston—revenge is sweet. You have not forgotten the scene of last night, have you? Now, by heaven, my time has come. I would take pleasure in tying the rope around your neck; for you will be hanged as sure as h—ll; and all I regret is, that I can not see it done. Bring him on, men, bring him on."

Winston did not reply to Hallam; but, casting upon him a look of scorn, he yielded without a word to what seemed the decrees of inevitable fate. They made but a few steps before they were in the office of the Provost Marshal.

"Ah, here is Jones now," said the engineer.

"Jones—h—ll!" exclaimed Walter; " he is no more Jones than I am. I have known him for several years; his name is Winston; and a more d—d villain walks not unhung. He can," speaking to the Provost, "be convicted of being a spy, if the testimony of two witnesses is any thing."

The Provost Marshal and Winston were looking at each other in mutual surprise. They both recollected where they had met first and met last; but neither betrayed any sign. The bystanders did not observe the mute indications of reciprocal recognition, concerning which, we may observe, *apropos*, that a single glance of the eye often conveys as much meaning and intelligence as could be enforced by a volume of words.

"You must prefer written charges," at last said the Provost to Hallam, "and to-morrow this affair will be investigated." Turning to the guard, he said: "Take these two men to prison, and confine them in separate rooms."

"This man Winston, sir," said Hallam, "should be put in

irons and closely guarded. He is as slippery as an eel, and if he has half a chance will make his escape."

"I need no instructions in regard to my duties," was the response. "He will be properly attended to."

Accordingly Williams and Winston were conducted to prison; and Hallam, as nothing more could be done at present, returned to his hotel. Walter's eye glistened with joy when he thought of his success. O, how he would make his proud, scoffing cousin beg and entreat on her knees, and wring her hands in anguish of soul; and his bosom glowed with malicious pleasure. It was his time now; his star was in the ascendant; he would use his advantage. As such thoughts as these were passing in his mind, his steps were light and buoyant, and he arrived at the Gayoso, before he was scarcely aware of it. He could not keep the good news longer to himself, but hastened immediately to Emily's room. She was alone, engaged in reading.

"To what purpose am I indebted for the honor of this visit?" said Emily, in a tone of slight sarcasm, and laying aside her book after Walter had deliberately seated himself. She felt vexed at his impudent intrusion.

"You can talk coldly enough now, Emily. I see you are disposed to treat me as a stranger. Well, be it so. I guess though, I could move your proud, stubborn heart—I could bring tears to your eyes, if I were so disposed."

Emily looked him full in the face, to discover, if possible, his meaning. She observed his twinkling eye, and knew it boded no good to her. She felt the blood creep, cold and sluggish and chilling, through her veins.

"If you have any thing to say that concerns me, be at it at once. If you have not, I can consider this visit but as an intrusion on my privacy."

"Intrusion, is it? That word shows very plainly to my mind that you no longer regard me as a friend. Well, if it so

18

please you, I have no objection. But I have a little bit of news which you may think concerns you. Indeed, I have no doubt you would feel deeply interested in it; and I rather think it would be extremely unkind in me not to tell you of it. Shall I communicate it or not?"

"You can do as you please, sir."

"If you are so indifferent in regard to the matter, I do not know that I shall enlighten you at all. I know you would be glad to hear it, though. No, I think, may be, you would be sorry. The case reminds me a little of what Ben Franklin says about marriage—'If you do marry, you will regret it; if you do not, you will be sorry for it; if you do either, you will repent it.' So, if I do or do not tell you, you will be sorry; and if you do not repent, you will no doubt exhibit one of the indications of true repentance. You know what that is."

"I do not know what you are talking about, sir?"

"I suppose not; but it would be painful to my feelings to be more explicit. The sight of grief always did affect me unpleasantly. I never did like to see a woman—especially a young woman—in tears. I do not know of a more heart-rending spectacle than to see a beautiful maiden wring her hands and look up to the skies, with the big, glistening drops rolling down her cheeks. Then, sometimes, they will scream, and fall in a swoon; or be converted from rational beings into howling lunatics, and become at once fit subjects for the madhouse. I have frequently heard of instances of the like; but I have never seen a case yet, and I hope I never may. But still," he continued, looking Emily straight in the face, "it may be my lot to behold a well authenticated case of intellectual derangement—not exactly intellectual, either, but a disease of the heart—yes, what they call *broken-heart*. I have never seen a case of that illness, disease, or complaint, or whatever it may be called, yet. But, according to the general law of nature, I may live many years yet, and I may be an eye-witness. The time may not be far off, when I will see a maiden of disordered mind. I hope not, though. Is it not a painful thing to see the human mind in ruins; or did you ever see a case of insanity?"

"I think, sir, if you do not furnish an example of it yourself, I know not where to find one. With your permission, I will ring for assistance, and have you sent to the lunatic asylum."

"Nay, nay, sweet cousin; keep your seat until you hear the latest news. Then you can send me to the mad-house if you choose; and if I do go, the probability is you will bear me company. But when you hear the news, you, being a true patriot, will be disposed to recommend my promotion for signal devotion to the glorious cause of the Union, instead of having me put in straight-jackets as a madman."

"Walter Hallam, if you have any thing to say to me, out with it, and then leave me to myself. I am tired of your incoherent strain."

"Nay, good, kind cousin, do not be impatient. You will hear it soon enough. The truth is, I do not like to assume the responsibility of breaking the news. What was it one of your poets—Shakespeare, I believe—said about the 'bearer of ill-tidings?' I sometimes remember a few snatches of poetry. 'Hath but a losing office,'—something to that amount. Can you recollect it? You read the poets."

"Tell me, for pity's sake, what do you mean? Has any thing happened to—to—to brother James?"

"No, indeed. But do not become so excited, my worthy cousin," continued Walter, with an ill-disguised feeling of pleasure. "I thought you could be moved to show feeling of some sort—I thought you could be induced to lay aside your highly becoming *nonchalance* and your freezing indifference."

"If that is your object, monster, you shall be disappointed. If you have intruded upon me to frighten me by groundless hints and inuendoes, for the sole purpose of beholding distress, you shall, for once, be denied that pleasure. I presume you have no communication to make; so leave me, if you please."

"You are presuming a little too much, my cousin. I do know something in which you would be deeply interested. But if you commence to call me hard names, I do not know but that I will leave you to find it out the best way you can. If you still insist on it, I will go."

Emily would not have been a woman had she been destitute of curiosity; so she did not insist upon his departure.

"Well, then, if you have any thing to tell, why do you not tell it? Why are you trying to keep me in suspense? It is useless, for I am determined not to be frightened by your hints."

"Be patient, generous cousin. I will be more kind to you than you have been to me. I will have more respect for your feelings than you have ever had for mine. I would not communicate this news at all, but I know you will hear of it; and it might be you would not hear of it until the catastrophe had become a recorded fact; and then the consequence would be, somebody's nerves would be considerably shocked."

Emily made a slight start, in despite of her resolution, as a sudden thought flashed like lightning through her mind. Walter observed it; but, seeming not to notice it, went on:

"I have observed that the wife does not faint often upon the corpse of the husband if she attends him in sickness, and witnesses his struggles against man's last enemy. She is then prepared for his death. But only let him, in the bloom of health, leave her some day, and then let his bloody corpse be sent to her, and her agonies are insupportable. Thus, when we hear of the sudden death of any of our friends, the impression it makes is more stunning in its effect than when we anticipate such an event. If we know our friends are bound to die before a great while, when the event does take place, we are prepared with the necessary fortitude to meet it."

"And what has all this moralizing, these philosophical reflections, to do with me or my friends?"

"It may have something to do with you, unless you have obtained a special exemption from the distresses incidental to humanity. If you have done this, then these philosophical reflections, as you please to call them, are not worthy of your consideration. Last night, at least, you were subject to the common emotions of mortality."

"I think, sir, the scene of last night has rendered you *non compos mentis*—deprived you of your reason."

"It did, eh? Well, we will see. But I will now come to the point. Answer me one question first. Are you a true patriot?"

"I do not see proper to answer questions so digressive."

"Digressive, indeed! You will see presently that it is closely connected with the subject which is now the topic of our conversation. I am surprised that you do not see its applicability at once. But never mind; I can explain it. True patriotism in these times requires many grievous and painful sacrifices. The mother sends her darling boy to the tented field, and never beholds him more; the sister sees her brother depart for the wars, with ambitious hopes swelling in his breast, and the next news she hears his bones are bleaching on the southern hills; the distracted wife clings to her husband on the door-step, but he tears loose and rushes to the conflict; her prattling babes often gather around her, and ask questions concerning the absent father, which cause the sorrowing wife to wipe the unbidden tear from her eye; but after awhile the sad news comes that the husband's body molders beneath Virginia soil, and the wail of anguish arises from the widow's cottage as she clasps her children to her breaking heart, and tells them their father is dead."

"Jesus Christ, have mercy on this unfeeling wretch!" cried Emily, with the tears rushing to her eyes.

Hers was a sensitive mind; and she could see all these pictures, which Walter had drawn in simple, pithy language, as plainly as if the realities had been before her. The exclamation, however, was not the result of any apprehension of similar evils falling to her lot. But the tone of voice in which Hallam was speaking, and the language he used, were so at variance, were so antagonistic, that she shuddered with horror at his brutality, while she wept at the thought of the stern realities which were now occurring all over the southern land. The contrast was somewhat similar to boisterous laughter in the house of mourning, or mockery in the face of a corpse. The feeling of amazement at her cousin's want of sensibility was predominant, and under its influence she uttered the above exclamation. Walter appeared to enjoy her emotion for a moment, and then proceeded:

"But, my fair cousin, if you interrupt me at this particular point, you will not clearly see the unity of my ideas on this subject. With your permission, I will continue. These are all the necessary sacrifices of true patriotism; but there is one other which I was going to mention when you interrupted me, which, if last, may not be least. The maiden, in these dark days of blood, bids adieu to her fond lover, who girds on the armor of battle and hies away to the field of carnage and strife. A while after he is gone she reads in the papers the adored name connected with some deed of valor achieved in the face of mighty dangers, and her bosom heaves with joy and pleasure. She longs for the absent one to return with his laurels budding upon his brow. But what are her feelings of agony when she reads the list of casualties, and finds that her faithful betrothed has crossed the river that divides the living from the dead? Yet she is sustained by the fact that her beloved one fell with his feet to the foe, and she submits to the terrible bereavement as one of the sacrifices of true patriotism. But now tell me, Emily, what will be the emotions of that maid whose lover dies, not with his country's flag waving over him, but who, instead, takes a leap from the gibbet, struggles for a few seconds till the last gasp is over, and is then ignominiously buried, with his head to the north and his feet to the south? What consolation will such a maid have in this dread hour of trial? Do you think you are able to inform me?"

"I tell you I will not answer your senseless questions," said Emily, seeing that Hallam paused, as if waiting for a reply. She spoke in a trembling voice, evincing a feeling of uneasiness she could not conceal.

"I might go on to illustrate my position more at large," continued Hallam, "and prepare your mind for the reception of the news."

"We can dispense with further illustrations," interrupted Emily. "You might proceed in this strain for hours, and I would be no better prepared; so you may just as well waive the remainder of your gibberish, and tell me to what all this is the prelude."

"Well, then, you are fully prepared to meet the shock? I am glad of it. So, then, I will enlighten you without any more ado." He fastened his eyes on Emily's face. "You recollect how you mocked and scoffed at me last night? You also recollect the vow I registered in heaven? Providence has answered my prayers. I have hunted this man Winston down; I have found him; *I* arrested him; *I* will make out the charges against him; *I* will furnish all the testimony in his case—I, yes, even *I*, will do it all! Success will crown my wishes; and, as sure as we now breathe, your rebel lover shall hang by the neck, as a spy, till he is *dead—dead—dead!*"

Walter uttered these last expressions with as impressive an

air as he could possibly assume, with the hope that it would have the "desired effect." It was with deep interest that he watched the varying hues that played over Emily's countenance. Judging from his previous conversation, he expected some tremendous outburst of grief and agony. When he repeated the three last words with solemn emphasis, he saw Emily's bloodless lips slightly quiver, and an ashy color overspread her face. But in a moment the expression changed, as her thoughts were transferred from the danger of Winston to the malignity of Hallam. She saw it all now. Hallam had, indeed, hunted down her lover—had entrapped him—and was now glorying in his success; and then he had come to her, and had been cruelly tantalizing and teasing her for the last half hour, and was enjoying her confusion and distress. The defects of his character were now made plain and patent; so she did not faint, as Walter expected, but she slowly rose from her seat and stood directly in front of him. The blood returned, and the veins swelled on her forehead; the dark eye fairly glowed, and, in appearance, emitted sparks from the raging fire within. It was like the first symptoms of a volcanic eruption. The slender form dilated, and the thin nostrils expanded. Walter looked upon this unexpected transformation with a species of fascination similar to that which causes the charmed bird to flutter briefly around the serpent's head and then plunge into the very jaws of death. He could not but think of what he had read in Grecian mythology of the Erinnys, and he thought he saw before him the living embodiment of Tisiphone and Megara, and he absolutely quailed before the terrible expression which seemed to combine all the attributes of rage, hate, revenge, and wrath. And thus she stood, without speaking a word, for at least the space of half a minute.

"Fiendish monster!" said she, in a voice not "loud but deep." "Spirit of Satan! Incarnation of malice! O, that

I could find one single term in the English language that would embrace all the epithets that villains deserve! For this act of dogging a man's steps—a man before whom you cringed and whined like a whipped cur—a man whose generosity spared your worse than worthless life—a man whom you would not *dare* to meet alone—a man from whom you would shrink and hide like a quaking poltroon—for your ungentlemanly, cruel, and dastardly attempt to trample upon and crush the bleeding bosom of a *woman*—yes, a woman— for you have not the courage, it is not in your nature, to tantalize any but a feeble woman or a helpless child—for all this may you suffer torments which I shudder to mention! May your own conscience lash and sting you till remorse loses its power only in the last convulsions of death, and you sink down in disgrace to the silent darkness of the tomb! May God forgive you, if a merciful heaven can overlook the enormity of your wickedness; but ask not me, a frail, weak creature of the dust. I *hate* you! O God! I despise the very soil your foot desecrates! You are no relation of mine from this time henceforth. O, if I thought one single drop of your vile blood flowed in my veins, I would sever all the arteries of life to let it out. I disown you *forever!* Never more come within my presence; never let me see your face again. Go, monster, go!" she pointed to the door. "Go, hide yourself, and repent in sackcloth and ashes. Leave me—leave me *forever and forever!*" She paused.

Walter Hallam thought it best not to tamper with the fury of the tempest he had unexpectedly raised. He did not venture a word in reply, but rose with a look which evinced that the fearful imprecation of his cousin had not been totally thrown away. He left, and Emily stood alone. The unnatural excitement died away, and she threw herself upon a bed, weakened and prostrated by the subsiding of overwrought feeling. If the reader be disposed to think that

Emily compromised her dignity and modesty by the utterance of the preceding anathema, we will not attempt to combat his position. It may have been rather unfeminine; but all mortals are sometimes thrown off their guard, no matter how thoroughly their tempers may be disciplined. Emily had temporarily lost control of herself, and she spoke the execration in the exact words we have recorded. We have only this apology to make for this violent outburst of virtuous indignation: she was a woman of very enthusiastic, strong, and powerful emotion; therefore, some allowance must be made for the ebullition of her feelings, whether they be unlady-like or not.

She lay motionless on the bed for nearly half an hour, then arose. Taking a seat, she kept perfectly still for several minutes. Her mind was deeply absorbed in thought. Suddenly arising, as if her decision were made, she rang the bell and sent for her brother. Colonel Burrell soon made his appearance, and Emily closed the door behind him and locked it. Drawing a chair close to her brother's side, she spoke, but in such a low tone that her words reached only the Colonel's ears. He started, and a shade of displeasure and vexation rested on his face.

"I am surprised at you, Emily," he said. "You appear to me to have lost your wits and all sense of propriety. Why, it is impossible for me to do what you ask—absolutely impossible. I would lose my reputation as a loyal soldier, and be false to my oath of allegiance."

"Then, brother, I will do it myself. I owe no allegiance to this wicked government, and I never will. If I am ever forced to swear fealty to any government, it is due to the Southern Confederacy, and I will cast my lot with the rebels."

"Hush, sister, hush!" said the Colonel, in a whisper. "You know not who may be listening to you; and, if you are reported to the authorities, you will take up lodgings in the

Irving Block in spite of all I can do. I could not prevent it. You must beware how you talk. Do you not know that there are detectives all over the town?"

"If it were not for your sake, James, and I had the power, I would thunder forth my sentiments all over this continent, till every vale should ring and every hill should shake with the words of defiance. Even at Washington's capitol trumpet-tongued treason should stand, with a brazen front, in the presence of Abraham Lincoln and all his host. I would shriek it in the ears of the hated old tyrant till his head would ache with the sound."

"If you will not hush, I will leave you. You will draw suspicion upon us both if you continue to talk thus." And he arose.

"Stay, brother, stay!" she cried, holding his arm. "I will hush—I will say no more about this; nor will I again ask you to do any thing which you think you ought not. But I will make one proposition which does not require you to act."

She lowered her voice to a whisper. The Colonel listened, and then put his hand to his forehead and studied for a moment. He saw that she was fully determined, and that she would attempt to accomplish her purpose alone if she could not persuade him to accompany her. He believed that she was essaying an impossibility, and that she would soon discover it. So he reluctantly agreed to what she proposed, and soon afterward left the apartment, with the promise of an early return.

CHAPTER XVI.

"A murderous guilt shows not itself more soon
Than love that would seem hid."

WHEN the shades of night had fully settled upon the earth, a lady, closely vailed, and a gentleman, were observed to leave the Gayoso in a carriage. It was Colonel Burrell and his sister. Not a word was spoken by either, but a profound silence was maintained until they arrived at the quarters of the Provost Marshal. Alighting, they rapped at the door, and fortunately found the officer at home. According to previous agreement, the Colonel was to say nothing, but was to leave Emily to manage her own affairs as she thought best.. When they were seated, the Provost spoke:

"Can I serve you in any way, sir?"

"This lady wishes to see you," replied Colonel Burrell, "on business of her own. I have simply escorted her to your quarters. She informed me that she desired a private interview with the Provost Marshal."

"I would say the hour for business has passed. You should have come to my office before night.

"I am aware of that," replied Emily, "but my business is of such a character that I must see you alone. I could not do so conveniently during your office hours. Besides, it is in regard to an affair which does not come within the scope of your ordinary duties."

"As you are a lady, I will for once violate my rules. I would not do it, though, for the transaction of ordinary business. If you will walk into the next room," addressing the Colonel, "the lady's interview can be private, as she wishes."

The Colonel accordingly did so, and Emily was left alone with the officer. She felt rather awkward from the strangeness of her present position, but it was now too late to falter. She knew not how to make a beginning; so she sat still until the Provost, seeing her embarrassment, encouraged her to proceed.

"What business," said he, "has procured me the honor of this call? In what way may I be of service?"

"My mission is rather an extraordinary one, sir; and I hardly know how to broach the subject that weighs on my mind. But before I reveal the affair which brought me here, I must exact a promise of you that any thing I say will not be repeated to a third party, or made use of to my injury."

"I give you my honor," said the Provost, "that nothing you may say shall ever go beyond the door, unless you choose to divulge it yourself."

"I demand no other pledge. But I must further request you not to take offense at any thing I may say in my present agitation and distress, or at least perplexity."

"If that be all, lady, proceed. I would indeed be an ill-bred clown should I presume to manifest any feeling of displeasure in the presence of so much beauty and intelligence."

"Well, then," replied Emily, not noticing the compliment, "these preliminaries being settled, I am now forced to the necessity of stating my business here to-night, and why I have requested this interview." She made a short pause, and then continued. "You have a prisoner confined"—— A deep blush of shame mantled her cheek, which, however, the officer did not observe, as she turned her head.

"If I had not more than one," replied the Provost, with a good-humored smile, "my duties would be extremely light. I am so unfortunate as to be responsible for several hundred. So, if Madam, or Miss—I have not yet learned to whom I have the pleasure of speaking?"

"It matters not. My name or my condition would throw no light on the business that brought me here."

"Excuse me, lady, for asking a question which I, perhaps, had no right to propound. I must say, though, it is sometimes pleasant to know the names of those with whom we are conversing. But just as you please. I do not insist upon an answer if the question is improper or irrelevant. But you were speaking of a prisoner."

"Yes, sir; of a prisoner who was apprehended to-day." She paused.

"I would suggest, lady, that if you are not more explicit, it will be impossible for me to form any idea, or even make a guess at the prisoner's name, to whom you allude."

"His name is—is Winston," she said, in painful embarrassment.

"Ah, yes; Winston, *alias* Jones; he seems to be known by more names than one. But what of him? Is he a relative of yours? and do you wish to see him?"

"I came not here to make such a request; and I almost fear to tell you why I have come."

"Fear nothing, lady, but tell me at once the nature of your business. You must excuse me, if I inform you my time is not my own."

"Then, as your time is precious, I will be brief. O, sir, if you only knew what it costs me to speak, you would bear with my frailties and my woman's weakness. But," checking her rising emotions, "I will not encroach further upon your time by apologies for and explanations of feelings you are supposed to know nothing about. I came here, then, to procure this man's release, if possible."

"Indeed; and how do you propose to do that?"

"I came here to find out that from you. He is in your power."

"You do not wish him to stand a trial, then?"

"No, sir—not if it can be prevented. I do not know what the charges against him are; but I want him released before the trial takes place."

"You must think the evidence is strong against him, then? Is the man your husband, or brother, that you take such a deep interest in his welfare?"

"He is neither the one nor the other; nor am I married at all, if your curiosity must be gratified."

"I beg your pardon, young lady. I did not mean to be rude or impudent; and if you will excuse me, I will ask no more questions concerning yourself. What is your proposition in regard to this man's release? Am I to understand that you wish me to shoulder the responsibility of releasing him without the consent of other parties?"

"Yes, sir; and I will offer you any inducement—I will pay the gold till you are satisfied—I will"——

"Tempt me no more, lady," quickly interrupted the Provost, "or you might make me forget my promise. I see how it is: you have come here to bribe me. So, to save multiplication of words on that subject, I will tell you now that that can not be done. If I could, without violence to my conscience and duty, set him free at all, I would do it without pay. My own friendship for the very person of whom we are now speaking would be a greater inducement to me to forget what is due to my government than all the gold it is possible for you to lay before me. It is useless, therefore, to speak of bribery."

"Is he, indeed, a friend of yours?" asked Emily, in trembling surprise, as she thought that if such were the case, the Provost might know more concerning her history than she expected.

"He is one to whom I am under lasting obligations."

"If such be the case, will you make no effort to liquidate your obligations, when you have the opportunity?"

"Now, lady, it is my time to be vexed." replied the Provost, laughing, "for you are inquiring into my affairs. But I did not say that I would make no effort. I scarcely know what to do at present. No charges have been yet preferred, and I do not know exactly what evidence may be against him. His trial is to take place to-morrow or next day; but there is *one* way it can be prevented; and as you know more about the man than I do, and the parties opposed to him, you or your friends can try that, and it will relieve me of the necessity of making the effort you so much desire."

The Provost arose, and going to a desk opened a book and handed it to Emily, at the same time pointing with his finger to a certain passage.

"You will see from that," continued the officer, "that you or your friends can probably do more than I can."

"I do not clearly comprehend it," said she, reading the passage.

The Provost explained it to her satisfaction.

"At what hour was he confined?" asked Emily.

"About eleven o'clock."

"And you say in twenty-four hours?"

"Yes, to-morrow, at twelve, say."

With this information Emily took her departure. As she and her brother were on their way back, the same silence was preserved, with the exception of a few remarks which may serve to show the workings of Emily's mind.

"Brother James," said she, "I have one single request to make of you, and I do not want you to ask me why I make it."

"Well, let us hear it."

"I want you to detain Walter Hallam at the hotel to-morrow morning until nine o'clock. Allow him to leave under no pretense whatever. Will you do this small favor for me?"

"For what purpose should I do this?"

"I told you, brother, I did not wish you to ask me any questions or any reasons."

"Yes, I know you did; but you are always asking me to do things which my position will not allow."

"You need not fear; you can do this consistently."

"Very well; I will try, if it is any accommodation to you. I care not what may be your motive. Probably it would be best for me not to know."

"Thank you, brother; it will be a kindness which will place me under additional obligations to you."

Not another word was exchanged until they arrived at the hotel; soon after which the Colonel and his sister separated until the next morning; but they were not the only parties interested in the spy's destiny, who were busy under cover of darkness; for, while Emily was engaged with the Provost Marshal, Walter Hallam was walking in the direction of the building in which the prisoners were confined. Going to the officer in charge, he exhibited his pass, granting permission to visit the Yankee, Williams. The fellow was asleep when Hallam entered, but he was soon aroused.

"I am told your name is Williams?" said Hallam.

"An' s'pose it is; what of that?" answered Williams, sulkily.

"If that is your name, you are in a perilous situation, Mr. Williams. I have heard the evidence in your case, and I make bold to say to you, you will hardly escape conviction."

"What do you tell me this fur? I do n't want any ov your Job's comfortin'. If you 're a priest, and can't offer no better consolation than that, I 'd rather you 'd a let me sleep on."

"I am no priest, Williams; but I have come to befriend you. I have learned that you are without friends, and, if you will allow it, I will be your friend. I can advise you in such a manner that you can easily rid yourself of this difficulty."

"You 're one o' them darned lawyers, then—fellers as would take the last shirt off yer back, promise to save yer neck, and then 'll have you hung to git your breeches. No, siree, Mr. Lawyer—can't come that game over this chicken; nary copper will you git out o' me. I 'd like to know what 'd make you take sich an interest in me if you did n't expect to git the tin for it? You 're no friend o' mine; I do n't know you; an', more 'n that, I do n't care to know you. I can git plenty of lawyers when I need 'em; I do n't like one that is so pushed fur business that he must come ov nights, and wake up honest men to have 'em hung or shot. They 're the little pettifoggers."

"You are very unjust, Williams, in your supposition. I am neither priest nor lawyer. You say I am no friend of yours. Well, now, I do n't care a d—n. I would as lief you would be hanged as any body. If it were not for another fellow, whom I want punished, you might go to the devil for all I care, since you are so very suspicious."

"Now you begin to talk to the pint. But what have I got to do with this other fellow? What do you come to me fur?"

"You have a good deal to do with him, sir; for you or this other fellow must be hanged. It remains with you to say which. You can take your choice."

"Darned if I would n't like to know what you mean."

"You know very well, Williams, what I mean. You know what you are guilty of. Do not try to deceive me."

"Look here, friend, you need n't try to trap me in that way; you can't do it. Not a word 'll I say till I know what you are talking about. No, siree."

"I can be plain enough, if you wish it. Well, then, to the point. You are confined here on a charge of sinking the boat last night. That you will not deny. Now the testimony is strong against you. I have investigated your case thoroughly, and when your trial comes on, you will find that more evidence will be brought against you than you suspect. It will be sufficient to condemn and to hang you. There is a witness against you, Williams, that you do not dream of; and that very witness is doubtless more guilty than yourself."

"Who is that?" said Williams, quickly. "Is it Jones?"

"Ah, well, I am glad to see you take a sensible view of the subject, and are willing to confess."

"No, but I haven't confessed nothin', though," replied Williams, in some confusion. "Not a single word."

"If you have not, you soon will, when I tell you what this man is going to do. You and Jones sunk the boat last night; you can not deny it."

"But I ken, though, and I do deny it."

"If you swear to such a thing, you will be guilty of perjury. Now listen to me. You and Jones sunk the boat. This can be proved by very strong circumstantial evidence. I know all about this man Jones, and he has imposed on you. He is in the employ of the rebel government, and he bribed you in what you did."

"How do you know he did?" asked Williams.

"Jones has confessed it all, but in such a way as to throw all the guilt on you. As matters stand now, he will be cleared, and you will be hanged or shot."

"Jones has betrayed me, has he?"

"Yes, he has; but you can save yourself yet, and I have come here to tell you how to do it."

"An' to git all ov my money fur it, too."

"No, d—n your money. I wouldn't have a cent of it. This Jones is an enemy of mine, and I want him hanged in your place. You understand that, do you not?"

"Yes; but how is it to be managed?" asked the frightened Yankee.

"The easiest thing in the world. All you will have to do is to confess it to-night, and to appear as a witness against

Jones, who is the principal in this affair. If you will do this, you will get rid of this ugly scrape at once, and Jones will be made to suffer in your stead."

"How do you know this?" asked the hesitating Yankee.

"Do I not know what the law is? If you care any thing for your personal safety, you will do as I tell you. If you wait till to-morrow, you will be hanged as sure as you are now alive; because Jones will appear against you. So, if you want to save yourself, the best thing you can do is to take my advice. I have not put myself to all this trouble because I have any particular friendship for you, but because I hate Jones. Were it otherwise, it would make no difference with me if you both should suffer the extreme penalty of the law."

"Let me see Jones by himself first," said Williams.

"You are a d—d fool, Williams. What do you wish to see Jones for? It is just as I tell you. It is impossible for you to see Jones; and, besides, you have already confessed it all to me."

"I'll be darned if I have confessed any thing."

"I will be d—d if you have not, though, and I will swear it before the court-martial; then both of you will go up together. But I will not bandy words with you if you will not let me befriend you. You have said enough to convict yourself and Jones too. Just so he suffers, I would as soon as not you should bear him company:" and Walter turned as if he were about to leave.

"Come back—come back," cried Williams.

"Well, what do you want?" said Walter. "I have no time to trifle with you. Say what you want, quick."

"What is it you want me to do? How am I to save myself?"

"You will have to make a written confession here to-night, in the presence of witnesses. That is all."

"You can't make a feller a witness against himself?"

"No, I do not want you to criminate yourself. Tell merely what part Jones had in the affair."

"Will that clear me? Are you sure?"

"If you do it," said Hallam, "I swear on the Bible you will be free as soon as the trial comes on."

"Fix up the document, then," said Williams, after a moment's hesitation.

This Walter soon did. He took down Williams's statement in the presence of two witnesses, read it aloud, and the Yankee attached his signature. Hallam then carefully put the manuscript in his pocket and returned to his hotel.

"I have him now," said he to himself, on the way. "There is no possible chance for him to escape. If he gets rid of the first charge, which I think quite a difficult matter, the destruction of the boat will do the work for him. I will risk the elegant maledictions of my furious cousin, who disowns me in such a graceful manner." And he chuckled as he wended his way along the streets.

Walter had not more than fairly gained the street before the Provost Marshal entered the building Hallam had just left. This officer was in the habit of visiting the prison very frequently at night, and his entrance, therefore, excited no surprise in the minds of the guard. As soon as he was within doors, he went to the apartment in which Henry Winston was confined, and found the spy pacing up and down the floor.

"I think we have met before, Mr. Winston, or Jones, or whatever your name may be," said the Provost.

"The occasion upon which we met was probably calculated to make a deeper impression upon your mind than mine. I, however, recollect your face perfectly, though I know not your name."

"You left so suddenly that I had no time to tell my name,

nor even to thank you for your timely interference in my behalf. You are now aware that I am provost marshal of this city. I knew your face the moment I cast my eyes on you. I have frequently wondered why you left me so abruptly after shooting the two villains who were on the point of murdering me. Gratitude demands that I should make you a suitable return. I am sorry that I find you in a situation where you will need the assistance of a friend, though I presume, from certain indications, you are not totally without friends."

"I know not," said Winston, in surprise, "what indications can form the basis of such a presumption; for if I have a single friend in this city, I am not aware of it."

"Indeed! I am surprised at that; for there is one who seems to be deeply interested in your fate; in truth, she is so greatly concerned that she would unhesitatingly sacrifice her allegiance to the government for your salvation. But I speak too fast, for I do not know that she regards her homage as due to the government I have the honor to serve."

"She!" said the spy, with a brightening face. "I am to understand, then, that it was a lady? Will you be so kind as to tell me the name of this unknown well-wisher?"

"That I am not able to do. She refused to reveal her name, from motives of delicacy, perhaps, for she told me that she was unmarried. But you should call her something more than a well-wisher. She is a *doer;* and left my office a short time since, intending to act upon a suggestion of mine, which may set you at liberty without a trial. I hope she may be successful; but if she should not be," continued the Provost, closely scrutinizing the features of the spy, "how can I repay a portion of my debt of gratitude, without violence to my duties as a military officer?"

Winston cast upon the officer one of those proud looks—a look "that laughed the petty attributes of rank to scorn"—and then slowly replied:

"I understand the hint perfectly, Captain. This precaution would have been entirely unnecessary had you been better acquainted with the person to whom you are now talking. Take me not, sir, for one of those timid, weak-hearted creatures who would tarnish the honor of all his friends rather than bear the burden of his own actions. I consider you under no obligations. And if I were on the brink of a precipice, with certain death staring me in the face, I would die, sir, before I would beg your assistance, merely because I had done you a little favor, and remind you of obligations which the golden rule annuls. I have always endeavored to do unto my fellow-creatures as I would have them do to me, leaving it to heaven to reward the action. So I have no favor whatever to ask. Your debt of gratitude, as you please to call it, is already discharged. Do whatever you may consider to be your duty. If you are disposed to feel grateful for the preservation of your life, at the time to which you allude, return your thanks to God, in whose hands I was only an instrument. I assure you I claim nothing at your hands. So, do your whole duty; and if I fall a victim to the vengeance of military law, God, I trust—I know—will reward all deeds of mine which Holy Writ declares to be meritorious."

The Provost Marshal was moved with mixed feelings of sorrow and admiration. The spy had made a deeper impression on the mind of his auditor by thus disclaiming all merit for a former service, than he could possibly have done by demanding from the officer a return of the favor as a meed justly due.

"I am sorry to hear you talk thus," replied the officer. "You speak as if you were guilty of some crime which the law severely punishes. I hope such is not the case. But upon this point it would be ungenerous in me to ask you questions. I seek to know no more at present. But if I can do you any little favor in your unpleasant position, do not hesitate to ask it. I must leave you now. Good night." And the Provost warmly grasped his hand, and then retired.

"I can not imagine," thought the spy, as soon as the officer had gone, "who this lady is. It can not be Emily, for she is married; or if she be not, I can not account for the fact of her traveling alone with such a man as Hallam and—is it not strange that I have never discovered the name of this other gentleman? Well, no matter; it can make but little difference with me. She is lost to me. And if she is interesting herself in my case, it is merely the recompense of a grateful heart. It may be, too, some warm lady friend of the South, who is attempting thus to serve her country." And with this last thought, he dismissed the subject from his mind, and laid himself down upon his couch, where he slept till the sunbeams of next morning were struggling to enter his narrow prison-cell.

CHAPTER XVII.

"He that hath nature in him must be grateful;
'T is the Creator's primary great law
That links the chain of beings to each other."

Colonel Burrell, in accordance with his promise to his sister, detained Walter Hallam at the hotel the next morning. He had no difficult task to perform, however, for Walter appeared in no way uneasy, and evinced no disposition whatever to change his locality. The Colonel was not acquainted with any of his sister's plans or arrangements; so he did not attempt to watch the motions or proceedings of Hallam, and only considered himself bound to detain Walter at the hotel until the hour of nine arrived. Hallam had early that morning written a letter, as the Colonel supposed, about the contents of which he did not make a single inquiry. After this document was dispatched, he made no objection to any disposition of the time the Colonel proposed.

"May I ask, Walter," said Colonel Burrell, in the course of the morning, "what your intentions are in regard to this man Winston? I understand he is in arrest."

"Certainly, sir; there is no secret about it. All I intend to do is to prefer the charges against him, and then let him take the consequences of the law. The penalty can not be any thing short of death. There is too much proof of his guilt. He it was who sunk the gun-boat; this will be proved beyond all dispute. You yourself saw him on the battle-field of Corinth; therefore, you know he is a rebel; and you will, doubtless, be summoned as a witness to establish this fact."

"If I am," said the Colonel, showing symptoms of rising anger, "I shall not obey the summons."

"You will not? And why, pray?"

"Because, sir, I feel myself under some obligations to this man, whatever may be his crime."

"Suppose you should, have you not also a duty to perform to your country? You see what he has already done. If he is suffered to run at large in that style, there is no accounting for the damage he may do. I think, sir, your duty to your country should overrule all considerations of a private nature."

The Colonel, as the reader has already discovered, was a man who, when once his opinion was made up, did not particularly care to investigate the grounds of his belief. Mingled, also, with his rather profane feelings were some redeeming qualities. Among these was a nice sense of honor. He would have died before he would have committed an action contrary to the dictates of his honor. So when Walter, who was under considerable obligations to the Colonel for the exercise of his political influence, commenced to persuade him to do that which honor and gratitude suggested he ought not to do, it nettled his feelings, and he replied, in rather rough and profane language:

"D—n it, Walter, do not talk to me thus, and attempt to persuade me to a thing I will not do. Had it not been for that man, my sister's body would have floated down the Mississippi River."

"You would better say, had that man not been aboard, your sister never would have been in any danger. He is undoubtedly a spy of the most diabolical cast."

"I care not what the h—ll he is, sir. This much I do know; the boat was sunk, and I was powerless to save Emily, and Winston rescued her from the waters; and, more than that, would not receive the large reward I promised. And now you would have me turn against her benefactor, and assist to take away his life. Should I do it, I hope h—ll might open and swallow me up alive," he said, giving the table a tremendous rap with his fist. "I tell you now, you need not put my name as a witness to your charges. If you are determined this man's life shall be taken, his blood shall not be on my hands."

"I am willing," replied Hallam, "to shoulder the whole responsibility in this matter; for I feel that I am discharging a sacred duty to my country. Your name, however, shall not appear in the charges, if you do not wish it. The evidence I have already obtained will be, I think, sufficient. It will doubtless hang him, and that is all I want to make sure of."

"I fear, Captain Hallam, you are laboring more for the gratification of your revengeful feelings than for any particular good you expect to accrue to your beloved country," said the Colonel, in a tone of irony. "I never knew you before to undertake any thing with such decidedly religious zeal. You may not be to blame, however, for it must be rather disagreeable and unpleasant to have an enemy in the world whom you may meet at any time and in any crowd. It becomes doubly so when that enemy is so unceremonious and uncivil as to lay one flat on his back, and deliver a lecture which one would not desire all the world to hear."

Walter reddened at this cutting speech; but he did not wish to lose the Colonel's influence. He, therefore, replied in language which he probably would have scorned to use had their relations been different. But Walter remembered this cut for many months afterward.

"I think, sir, as you were an eye-witness of the scene to which you allude, you might do me justice. I was laboring under several disadvantages. My strength was almost exhausted by the unusual exercise of swimming the Mississippi River on a cool, dark night. I was, therefore, in no condition for the vulgar practice of pugilism. I do not believe in such a barbarous custom. Powder and lead are the materials which gentlemen prefer."

"Yes; but," said the Colonel, "I thought you said that you did not consider him a gentleman."

"That is true, sir—I did say it; nor do I consider him one now. I am sure he has never done any thing since our first difficulty to give me a higher opinion of the exalted virtues you seem to discover in him. But, then, there are some insults which level all distinctions of caste temporarily, and which a man can not overlook without lowering himself in the world's estimation. I am, therefore, forced by the code of honor to waive considerations of this character; and I should be willing to meet him as an equal and a gentleman, until he should be punished for his impudence."

"Or until you should be chastised for your temerity," remarked the Colonel, who generally said pretty much what he pleased to Walter; "but I suppose you will not allow him that privilege now, will you?"

"Of course not; I could not do it if I so desired. He is now in the hands of the military authorities, and when they are through with him, he will be in no condition to accept a challenge. If he should happen, possibly, to disprove the charges against him, which I know he can not do, then it will be time enough to settle our personal difficulties."

"But, according to your own showing, he has no chance for his life, and can never meet you in personal combat."

"I can not help that, sir. He has laid himself liable to the law, and he must abide the consequences."

At this point the conversation was interrupted by the entrance of a waiter, who announced that he had a note for Captain Hallam. Walter received it and perused its contents. It was a solicitation from Emily that he would meet her in the parlor. He lost no time in complying with this, to him, strange and novel request. After informing the Colonel where he was going, he hastened into the parlor, where he found Emily.

"You may think this rather a strange proceeding on my part, Walter, after what I said to you yesterday," said Emily, as Hallam entered the parlor and seated himself.

"I confess my surprise, after listening to the beautiful and graceful epithets you applied to me, and the lady-like curses you imprecated on my head. I shall, however, leave it to you to explain this sudden change in your feelings."

"I desire to make an apology for my rudeness. Will you forgive me for my conduct yesterday?"

"I will, upon one condition; which is, that I am not again to be blessed with a repetition of yesterday's scene."

"I think I had some little cause to be angry, when you were attempting to tease me for half an hour together, and to frighten me by hints in regard to something I could not understand. You have certainly found out, by this time, that I am not destitute of temper. Indeed, I have more probably than a woman ought to have, and sometimes it is impossible for me to control it."

"I should like to know what fortunate event has wrought this wonderful revolution in your feelings. You disowned me yesterday—pronounced a withering curse upon me, and spurned me from your presence. And now, to-day, you are all smiles. Is there any particular favor you desire to ask? or is this unexpected turn really the result of true repentance?"

"I have no favor whatever to ask," she replied. "Will you not allow me the privilege of offering an apology for a rudeness committed in the heat of passion? And when I make such a statement, is it not sufficient, and ought you not to accept it, without requiring me to give a minute history of the process by which it was brought about? You might do me the justice to suppose that my case is not out of the line of the experience of ordinary mortals."

"The truth is, Emily, I never know how to take you; you turn from white to black, and from black to white, so often. I never know when to expect sunshine or tempest. You rail at me sometimes when I do not expect it; and then you apologize when I have fortified myself to receive your eloquent maledictions with proper dignity."

"Is that the case on the present occasion?"

"I can not say that it is, or it is not. I knew that you had no right to drag or decoy me in your presence for the purpose of re-cursing me. I could not think you would dare to do this—especially after I had tacitly agreed to your desired disruption of our friendship, and your annulment of ties which no human power can destroy. I came, I may say, prepared for any thing that might 'turn up.'"

Emily, who was not particularly anxious to dwell longer on this topic, now changed the theme of conversation, with the usual tact of woman. Her manner considerably puzzled Walter. He could see plainly that her words were uttered with constraint, and in a manner contradictory to her actions. He could not divine her motives. He thought, and rightly, too, that this unexpected turn in affairs was not the result of any desire on her part to renew their former doubtful friendship. He therefore awaited the *denouement* with patience, feeling certain that Emily had some other object in view than a mere apology for her rudeness on the day before. Emily proposed a game of chess, and Hallam readily assented. While they were engaged in this interesting and absorbing amusement, ten o'clock came, and then eleven. Still they played on, and at last the hour of one arrived. Emily's object was now accomplished—at least, partially—that is, as far as the detention of Hallam contributed to its achievement. Announcing that she was tired of the game, and being desirous, woman-like, to know if she had been successful in her *ruse*, she began to question Walter.

"I am afraid I have caused you to neglect your business this morning, have I not?"

"Not that I am aware of," replied Walter, with a look of inquiry, caused by the tone and manner of Emily's question.

"Are you sure you have neglected nothing?"

"I am certain of it."

"Think again. I am afraid I have detained you too long."

"Not the first thing. But, see here, I would like to know what you mean by such pointed interrogations? I confess, your manner all the morning has been puzzling to me. Your words and actions are somehow incompatible. In fact, this whole proceeding appears rather extraordinary. You ask if I have neglected any of my affairs, just like your life or your salvation is dependent upon my negligence."

"The reason I ask is, because the idea has just struck me that there was something which required your attention this morning."

"What is that, pray?"

"Have you not forgotten to prefer charges against your prisoner?" she asked, with a curious blush.

"And suppose I have; what of that?"

"Is it not too late now?"

Walter made no reply for the space of a minute. He now saw clearly why Emily had been so anxious to keep him interested at the hotel. She had apologized merely that she might detain him, and cause him to forget the trial.

"You have played your part finely, my dear cousin," replied Walter, with a laugh, in which slight mockery could be discovered. "You would make a most excellent *diplomat*. I think I see now why you have been so exceedingly kind and entertaining all the morning. Since I reflect, there is a paragraph in the regulations, which says, that if charges are not preferred against a prisoner within twenty-four hours after his confinement, he shall be set at liberty. Our friend Winston was put in prison yesterday, about ten or eleven o'clock. It is now," continued Walter, looking at his watch with provoking deliberation, "it is now after one. So by this time he may be six or eight miles from the city."

Emily was completely surprised and nonplused by Walter's coolness.

"There is one thing, I fear," continued Hallam, slowly, "you have overlooked; which is, that the clause in question is applicable to Federal prisoners only. Of course, a spy would not be released if charges were not preferred in twenty-four hours."

Emily's face brightened, as she thought that Walter was relying solely on the fact he had just stated for the safety of his prisoner.

"But it is not known," said she, in answer to Walter, "that he is a spy, as you assert."

"How do you know it is not?"

"I had it from authority competent to act in the case."

"So, that is where you went last night, is it? You think you have outgeneraled me, do you? Why, even if he were at liberty, he could again soon be apprehended. He can not have gone far. Are you sure he is free?"

"You had better go and see."

"No, I am perfectly satisfied he is safe. I shall not trouble myself at all about it. I know the authorities are not such fools as to turn that man loose, with the plain proofs of his guilt."

"The Provost Marshal informed me that he would be released at eleven o'clock if the charges are not brought forward."

"He did, eh? Well, I will warrant that if you will go to a certain room in the Irving Block, there you will find Mr.

Winston. Do you think I would allow myself to be outwitted by a mere school-girl, who has relied for the success of her plans upon a most trivial technicality? The Provost can have no possible excuse for his action, should he do as you desire."

"Nevertheless, he may have done it."

"I am sorry, since we are now good friends, that your hopes are doomed to disappointment. When I tell you the whole truth, I can hardly expect to retain your favor. I do not generally transact my business by halves. So, if you are trusting for the salvation of your very particular friend to my remissness of duty, you are relying upon a broken reed. Your ingenious *ruse* has completely failed; for I made out the charges this morning, and they are now in the hands of the proper authorities. Our friend is, therefore, doubtless in the Irving Block. I am looking now every minute for a summons to attend the trial."

Poor Emily had had all her trouble for nothing; for it was as Walter had said, and the disappointment sank deep in her heart. Hallam would undoubtedly have beheld yesterday's scene re-enacted, had not Emily felt herself under some obligation to restrain her feelings.

"I am very sorry," continued Hallam, "that you have put yourself to so much trouble and inconvenience. But, my dear cousin, you did not expect to outwit me by such child's play, did you? The next time you undertake to play against me, you must study better the premises upon which you act. But never mind; if you have failed this time, you may be more successful the next. Every dog has his day, you know. However, I will say no more about it, as we are good friends."

"We *never* can be friends," replied Emily, in a choking voice.

"Come, now, cousin, you will undo all your pretty apology. You forget that you sent for me. You have no right, then, to *curse* me again. Even if you did, this is no place for the display of such a lady-like accomplishment. I did not seek to make up our little quarrel. It was all your work. I would suggest the propriety of not widening too much the breach between us, as it might possibly be necessary on some future occasion to solicit my good will, when any of your friends are in danger. You are not a very shrewd *diplomat*. You ought to have kept me in ignorance of the fact that you were foiled in your schemes. I am sure, if you had said nothing, I never would have suspected the sincerity of your apology. But women can not keep secrets. It is a wonder that you had not told me two hours earlier than you did. You wanted to enjoy your triumph too soon; and you expected to see me overwhelmed with surprise and rage. But your weapons have recoiled upon your own head. There is another thing yet; do you know I can have you *arrested*, were I so disposed, for your disloyalty? It is a good thing for you that the prisoner did not escape. For if he had, and you had rejoiced over it, I do not know what I might have been tempted to do."

Emily did not venture to reply to these last remarks of Hallam. Rising, with a full heart, she left the parlor without uttering a word. She retired, crest-fallen, to her room, in a state of feeling that may be easily imagined. Walter sat for a few moments reflecting; but he was soon notified to appear before the court-martial sitting on Winston's case.

The result of this trial may be summed up in a few words. Two witnesses appeared against the prisoner—Hallam and Williams. The former testified that he had once captured the prisoner, who belonged to the rebel army, and that since he had seen him twice within the Federal lines, acting in all respects as a Union soldier. Williams made a full confession in regard to the destruction of the gun-boat, relating the conversation which took place between himself and the prisoner on the night of the catastrophe. As Winston, of course, could make no defense, and all the evidence being against him, he was, in a very brief space of time, convicted and condemned to be executed as a spy. Courts-martial are much less merciful than civil tribunals; they care nothing for the soul of a victim. Our reader will not be surprised, therefore, to learn that Winston was informed, before he returned to prison, that the hour for his execution would be on the next day at eleven o'clock. This is the way the Yankees did business while the war was in progress.

Our hero was reconducted to the prison, and, as he saw no prospect of escape, began making immediate preparations for his approaching death. There were few ties to bind the spy to this earth. Beyond the natural desire to live, implanted in every human heart, there were few inducements to make the prolongation of life desirable. His life never had been happy. Disappointments had embittered his existence since the days of childhood. All of his relatives had gone down to the republic of dust and ashes, and he was destined soon to follow. He cared not. He had nothing to live for except to serve his country. He felt that if it should be the will of the Almighty that his days should be few, he would bow with submission. He did not consider the loss of his life as any very great sacrifice upon the altar of southern independence. Could he have that night raised the vail of futurity, and have foreseen beyond the possibility of a doubt that the freedom of the Confederacy would be established, he would have welcomed death with all his grim horrors; for he thought that when peace should finally come, bringing joy to millions of suffering hearts, amid all this rejoicing he would be in the crowd, but not of the crowd. It might be for the best, then, that he should die now, and leave a world in which he had never found any thing but mental suffering. His whole life had been but a series of melancholy events. He had never known a mother's love nor a father's care; no brother nor sister had ever with him roamed the hills; an orphan he had lived, unpitied on the earth. Once a gleam of sunshine played over his darkened pathway, but it was only for a moment. Those few brief moments constituted the only bright spot of his whole career; they were the only green oases in the past. He could, indeed, exclaim, in the language of Moore:

> "'T was ever thus: from childhood's hour
> I've seen my fondest hopes decay;
> I never loved a tree or flower,
> But 't was first to fade away."

Why then should he care for death? It was about ten o'clock that night, and Winston heard his prison door open. The Provost Marshal stood before him.

"I am sorry, Mr. Winston," said the officer, after the customary salutation, "to see one to whom I owe so much in this situation."

"Do not commence to pity me in that manner, Captain," said Winston, interrupting him. "I do not see what you expect to gain by mentioning what you owe, unless you choose thus to discharge your debt by continually reminding me of it, and expressing your sense of the obligation. To one in my condition, thanks are needless and useless. I told you last night I had no favor to ask, neither have I any now; so, if you please, do not revert to this subject again."

"Are you a Mason, Mr. Winston?"

"I am," was the response. And in a few seconds the two men knew that they both belonged to the great fraternity which has diffused untold blessings even in the remotest corners of the earth.

"I can now no longer hesitate, my brother. My obligations are double. I therefore offer you your liberty."

"Our order, Captain, does not require us to make such sacrifices of principle."

"I have been hesitating some time whether to do violence to my allegiance or my conscience. After carefully weighing both sides of the question, I have come to the deliberate conclusion that the law of nature and the requirements of gratitude are higher than the demands of loyalty. Since, in addition to this, I find you to be a brother of the mystic tie, my resolution is confirmed. You must allow me to think, though, I am extending that charity to a distressed brother which our sacred institution enjoins. I can then give you your freedom the more cheerfully."

"Think as you please, Captain; I shall certainly accept your kind offer. I see in it too plainly the hand of Providence, not to avail myself of the means of escape. But still I will reject the offer if your own life is jeopardized by your kindness; that would be too great a stretch of charity."

"Give yourself no uneasiness on my account. But we must talk no longer. Here is a key which unlocks your door, and here is a Federal uniform. You know how to use both. About midnight you can make your escape. When you come out, leave the key in the door. I hope you may be successful; but before we part, let me remind you of one thing: if you are again apprehended within the Federal lines, I will not be able to favor you to such an extent. Farewell."

Winston warmly thanked the officer, who immediately left the prison. The spy was soon in darkness, and kept still until the appointed hour arrived. When the hour of twelve approached, he cautiously arose and opened the door. Taking up a musket which had been pointed out by the Provost, he easily made his way out as one of the guard. Once out, he did not consume much time in widening the distance between himself and Memphis. At daylight the next morning he was in no danger of pursuit, but was still rapidly making his way in the direction of the Confederate lines.

Early the following morning it was known throughout the city that the spy was gone. It was reported that some secessionist had furnished him with a key to his prison door. All search proved in vain. Emily was greatly rejoiced, and Hallam smothered his rage as well as he could. That same day Colonel Burrell, Emily, and Walter took the boat for Washington City; and here for the present leaving them, we will follow the footsteps of the spy.

CHAPTER XVIII.

"Murder most foul, as in the best it is;
But this most foul, strange, and unnatural."

A SHORT time after the events narrated in the preceding chapter, Henry Winston might have been seen in a building rather dangerous for a spy, in the city of ——. He was busily engaged writing among the adjutants and clerks of one whom we will distinguish, for obvious reasons, by the name of General Robespierre. How he came to be in such a strange and unusual position is not known; but one thing is certain—Henry Winston, a rebel of the deepest dye, was a clerk for the most cruel, despotic, vindictive officer that could be found in the Yankee army. The people of —— will long remember with feelings of horror the numberless indignities, insults, and abuses heaped, with inhuman malice and with hellish delight, upon all who were in the most distant manner connected with the cause of the Confederates. Female honor and delicacy and childish helplessness were no more regarded than if modern civilization had been utterly ignored, and its place usurped by the barbarism of the darkest ages. Abu-Bekr and Atilla were saints compared with General Robespierre—the personification of all the low, abject, grovelling passions of human nature. An assumed zeal in the cause of his country was a mere pretext for the gratification of a malignant disposition, which loved misery for the pleasure it afforded his own vile, unnatural heart. With truth did Madame Roland, standing upon a scaffold erected during the stormy days of the French revolution, exclaim: "O, liberty! how many crimes are committed in thy name!" Many a sufferer in the city of —— might have uttered the same exclamation during the still darker days of the American revolution of 1861. The French revolution produced Maximilian Robespierre, whose name has been handed down as synonymous with tyrant. But some excuse can be found for his atrocity in the fact that he, depraved as he was, was urged on by a mob of enthusiastic fanatics, who clamored for innocent blood. But what apology can be made for the American Robespierre, who had all the infernal passions of his French namesake without the one thousandth part of his intellect?

Reader, this is no caricature; it is a very brief sketch of the true character of a living fiend in human shape. There is but one man in the United States who will answer to this description, and the true name of that one no person can be at a loss to imagine. So we will proceed.

One day, when this vile monster had gone out, and Winston happened to be left alone in his private office, a most ungovernable curiosity seized him to examine Robespierre's desk. The day before the spy had seen him busily engaged writing an epistle, which he accidentally discovered was addressed to President Lincoln. Winston felt what in "the piping times of peace" would have been deemed a most impertinent and unjustifiable curiosity to see this document, over which he had seen Robespierre studying and poring for several hours. So to the desk he went, and, searching eagerly among the papers of the inhuman wretch, found the much wished-for composition. Without further ceremony he sat down at the desk and read the letter to the end. An observer could have known that the document was an extraordinary one, by watching the spy's countenance, which turned red and pale as the various and conflicting emotions of anger, fear, indignation, and sympathy worked on his palpitating heart. And well might he tremble when the safety of his country was imperiled. For cold-blooded atrocity and inhuman villainy, a more diabolical composition could not have emanated from the brain of a fiend. The proposition it contained was like the forbidden tale of Hamlet's ghost,

>   ———————"Whose lightest word
> Would harrow up thy soul; freeze thy young blood;
> Make thy two eyes, like stars, start from their spheres;
> Thy knotted and combined locks to part,
> And each particular hair to stand on end
> Like quills upon the fretful porcupine."

History will never show a darker page than that upon which this famous letter is recorded, which, had it not been for the spy, would have been hidden among other unknown crimes clandestinely committed by the agents of the United States Government. We feel bound to give it to the reader entire, as it was read by Henry Winston.

As we have already stated, it was addressed to President Lincoln, and then proceeded as follows:

Your excellency's favor reached me a day or two since. I perused it with an unusual degree of interest, as it was partly devoted to the discussion of a subject upon which I have reflected anxiously for some time past. My mind is now, however, made up, and I do not hesitate to say that your proposition in regard to the treatment of the rebels is, I think, entirely too lenient and merciful. I have endeavored to study the character of this southern people, and if my opinions, based upon personal observation, are correct, they are a stubborn, proud, high-minded, obstinate race. The educated slaveholder is characterized by a contemptible *hauteur*, which would cause him to spurn any offers of peace except upon the basis of a separate nationality. This class, I find, controls public sentiment in the South. Therefore, by treating these people with kindness, leniency, and respect, and by offering a general amnesty for past offenses, upon the condition of a return into the Union, you would not only compromise the dignity of your high position, but would create in their minds an idea of our inability to achieve our object; and thus you prolong the struggle to an indefinite extent.

The wall of this people's pride can never be broken down by

kind treatment. They hate the Union; they despise the time-honored flag under whose protecting folds they have lived and prospered for the last eighty years. I am hated; you are hated; in short, the whole northern race is hated, with all appertaining to it, and is cursed and execrated with a malignity and bitterness truly astonishing. This feeling of malice extends to the women and children, and, in numerous instances, to the silly negro, whose freedom is at the bottom of the contest. Consequently I have had to rule here with a rod of iron. By way of parenthesis, I hope your excellency will consider it as a proof of my zeal in the cause of liberty and truth, that I am known throughout the South by the rather unenviable name of "Robespierre, the ——!" Sometimes I think the whole vile race, negroes and all, will have to be exterminated utterly before the Union can be restored.

The negro is a strange animal. It is impossible to make him appreciate the advantages of liberty, or even understand them. The boon of freedom, for which a white man would shed his blood and give up his life, has no charms whatever for the negro. Born and bred a slave, his mind early receives an idea of inferiority, and of incapacity to pursue any of the common avocations of life upon his own individual responsibility. He moves only as he is moved upon. Those who have fled to us for protection, and have joined our standard, have done so, I am persuaded, under mistaken notions and ideas. They look upon the North as a kind of El Dorado—a land flowing with wine, milk, and honey, and think that when they once get to a free state there is no further necessity of labor.

As to the abstract idea of freedom and independence, to which a white man will cling even unto death, and which would cause his form to dilate with pride, though he should beg his bread, and hide his nakedness with rags, they have no correct, no definite idea. It is impossible to force into the negro's dull mind the nobleness and sublimity of such a principle. He would sell his birthright for a mess of pottage without reflection, and barter his freedom for a dram without sorrow. I confess my mind has undergone a change in regard to the blacks. I have been grievously disappointed in my expectations. I calculated that wherever our victorious banner should appear, the negroes would rise up, murder their masters, flock by thousands to our standard, and thus crush the rebellion at once. But they have not done so. On the contrary, they have clung to their bondage with an affectionate tenacity, which has had a tendency to degrade the negro in my estimation.

I doubt not the whole race would be in a much better condition if allowed to remain where they are in a state of slavery. This language may sound quite strange coming from such an abolitionist. But the truth is, I am no longer an abolitionist from principle, but from hatred. God knows I hate the slaveholding aristocracy of the South. I hate these lordly millionaires, whose gold is stained with negro blood; and I will never be satisfied till they are all put down, and this tremendous power, so inconsistent with the spirit of our free institutions, is forever destroyed.

But this is not the question with which we have to deal at present. The rebellion must be crushed; and, in order to accomplish this desirable result, slavery must be abolished to cripple the South in her resources. As the institution now exists, it is a source of wealth to the insurgents, and a powerful element in protracting the war. I would be in favor of exciting the negroes to servile insurrection, but I do not believe it can be done. I have tried, in fact, but failed most signally. And now, since this has failed, I have another project in view, which I doubt not will meet with your excellency's approbation, when you have duly reflected upon it.

I will preface the proposition I have to make by saying that the South has now few men of pre-eminent mental ability—that is, men who have the capacity to guide and control a great movement like this present rebellion, inaugurated by Jeff Davis and Yancey. If the leaders of the rebellion were out of the way, I believe the great mass of the people could be induced to renew their allegiance, under such regulations as we might see proper to prescribe. *I propose to put them out of the way.* Your excellency must not be surprised at the novelty of such a proposition, nor especially at the means to be used to insure the complete success of the plan. I shall shed no blood, nor use magic either, in the accomplishment of the project. To be brief, my scheme is to carry them off *by the peaceful process of poison.*

With your permission, I shall employ intelligent agents, who shall work themselves into positions in which they can have free access to these men, or at least to their culinary departments. By the use of such men, I do not doubt that in a short space of time your excellency will have the pleasure of knowing that all men in the South who would be dangerous have somehow very mysteriously disappeared from the stage of the rebellion.

There are two men of whom we must be rid at all hazards. One is the chief leader in this movement, who has always been a turbulent and troublesome spirit in the political affairs of our nation. Jeff Davis is about the only man in the South who has the impudence and audacity, the stern nerve and energy, to shape and control the elements of the rebellion, and carry it on until he shall be put down by the strong hand of power. Stephens would be much more easily managed than Davis, and I would be pleased to see him President of the so-called Confederacy. He is disposed to be conservative, and seems not to have lost all his attachment to the old Union; or at least he appears to comprehend the folly of offering resistance to the tide of loyal strength now rolling from the North with crushing power. But Davis possesses a firmness and a courage which no disaster can shake or stagger. He is a man of iron will. No military reverses can damp the ardor of his patriotism, or rather his mischievous but lofty ambition, or frighten him from the position to which he stands with the sullen stubbornness of an immovable rock. The Rubicon is passed, the die is cast, and he will now be "emperor of Rome," or go down to a gory grave covered with an eternity of fame. With him there is no retreat. The bridges are all pulled down behind him. He will establish the independence of his idolized Confederacy, or failing in that, when his last soldier has expired, with the stoicism of a Cato, will stab himself to the heart before your face, with a smile of derision and contempt on his countenance. If he is allowed to remain President, millions of treasure must be expended, and oceans of blood must be spilled, in order to put down a movement which might easily be crushed if he were only *hors du combat.*

The other man to whom I refer is R. E. Lee, who now ranks

as the greatest military chieftain of the age. Of Johnston I have no fears whatever. At present he possesses the unbounded confidence of the whole southern people. There appears to be only one man in the southern states who has measured the shallowness of Johnston's military genius, and that is Davis himself. It is a matter of astonishment to me how a whole people, including their intelligent men, too, could be so woefully mistaken in the capacity of this man. His reputation is based upon no solid foundation. It may be blasted by a breath of wind. The private feud existing between Johnston and Davis, by giving ground for the cry of persecution, has made a mark and a name for the former which he never could have carved out himself. I would much rather Johnston were in command of the rebel armies. With Stephens as President, crying out and begging for peace, and Johnston as commander-in-chief, giving up stronghold after stronghold, the rebels would soon lay down their arms in disgust. But Davis and Lee are dangerous men—capable of directing a grand revolution. In them there are no signs of vacillation or wavering. They have one object in view, and will sacrifice the whole South rather than fail in its accomplishment. I have said this much in regard to the characters of these two men, in order to show the necessity of adopting my plan. I shall use no further argument in justification of the severity of the proposed scheme, but will submit it without comment to your excellency's careful consideration.

In conclusion, I have only to say that if you approve the project, and I should be so fortunate as to succeed in its accomplishment, I shall expect a reward commensurate with the important service thereby rendered to my country.

Your obedient servant,

B. F. ROBESPIERRE.

When Winston had finished the perusal of this slanderous and villainous, but remarkable, document, he returned it to its proper place, and then hastened to his own desk, where he wrote rapidly for ten or fifteen minutes; after which he folded his letter and directed it to General Johnston. He then put the letter in his pocket, intending to forward it through a source not necessary now to mention.

During all this time, while the spy was thus engaged, he was closely and eagerly watched by an eye he did not suspect. And right here a short digression becomes necessary.

John Bowman, to whom we have alluded above, was one of those strange, incomprehensible characters, sometimes to be met with, who seem to have very little common, practical sense, and yet are endowed with a cunning, snake-like sagacity almost supernatural. These fools in external appearance are sometimes surprisingly accurate judges of human nature, and can fathom the thoughts and intentions of the mind, with a degree of shrewdness utterly incompatible with their supposed mental capacity.

Such was Bowman. A little, diminutive creature in stature —a model Zaccheus in size, he nevertheless combined the noiseless motions of the cat with the cunning of the fox. At all hours of the day and night this mischievous dwarf would be stealing through the streets of ——, or through the building occupied by General Robespierre, prying with his small, snaky, restless eyes into every nook and corner, in order to discover something amiss, which would cause the infliction of punishment upon some unfortunate wretch. Bowman was a cross-breed, which means that General Robespierre was a *miscegenator*, and in early life had been smitten very deeply with the sable charms of a stout negro wench. To this happy connection—a connection carrying out fully the idea of Yankee miscegenation—John Bowman was indebted for his existence. John, at an early day, exhibited strong symptoms of his father's disposition. There was the same cruelty, the same love of misery, and the same indifference to suffering. The striking resemblance, in point of disposition, between the son and his illustrious progenitor, created in Robespierre a kind of beastly attachment to the boy. Consequently he had always manifested a peculiar interest in the welfare of this fine specimen of mulatto miscegenation, and trained him up to suit his own purposes. The time had now come when the cunning fiend could be useful, and he was honored with the position of Robespierre's secret detective—an office he filled with great credit to himself, and with singular diligence and fidelity to his father. To this fact a large number of the citizens of —— can testify. Many a gentleman was surprised, on being summoned before Robespierre, to have repeated to him *verbatim et literatim*, a rebellious expression, which he thought had been uttered to his best friend. Many a dignified lady was made to feel the force of Robespierre's wrath and abuse for some thoughtless remark, dropped, as she thought, in the privacy of her own house. Little expressions and hints, in the slightest degree in sympathy with the rebellion, let fall by some unsuspecting individual in an unguarded moment, were faithfully and accurately reported by this eavesdropping imp. He seemed to be *hic et ubique*, at the same time. But yet he moved so secretly and silently, that it was a considerable length of time before the unfortunate sufferers of —— discovered how or whence Robespierre obtained his information. Such was the distinguished man, or rather boy, employed by General Robespierre.

From some unknown cause, Bowman had suspected the loyalty of our hero from the very day he had entered Robespierre's service. It is certain that Winston had not said nor done any thing to arouse suspicion, though he discovered that he was closely watched. Bowman, however, detected nothing amiss until the day that Winston found the letter, which we have already given. When General Robespierre left Winston alone in his office, the little wretch heard the latter carefully lock the door, and turn the key in such a manner as to preclude the possibility of being watched through the key-hole. Bowman's instinct taught him that something unusual was about to take place. So stealing noiselessly up-stairs, immediately over Robespierre's office, he placed himself in a position in which he could observe all the spy's movements. If our hero had thrown his eyes up to the ceiling overhead, he would have seen that in one corner a small portion of the plastering was knocked off. Bowman had done this, and had taken up a piece of plank from the floor, in order to peep through the apertures between the lathing. He could thus, without any difficulty, observe all that was going on in the room below. While Winston was deeply occupied with Robespierre's letter, a pair of twinkling eyes was fastened upon him, with a degree of most intense interest. When the spy had finished his letter, and placed it carefully in his pocket, he resumed his usual business. Bowman moved not, but kept his position, crouched up with the patience of a cat watching for its prey, until toward nightfall.

That night when Winston retired to his room, he locked his door with more than his usual caution. He felt a vague, indefinable presentiment that he was in the presence of danger. Before lying down he searched his apartment, looking under the bed, up the chimney, and into every place in which it would be possible to conceal a human being, whatever might be his size. Having taken all these precautions, he removed the missive he had written from his pocket, and put it under his pillow. Notwithstanding all this, the eye of Bowman was upon him.

About midnight, when Bowman knew from the spy's heavy breathing that he was in a deep and profound sleep, his stealthy form might have been seen creeping through the window of our hero's room. It would have been well for Winston had he examined his window as closely as he had his door. If he had done so, he could have seen that one pane of glass was held to the sash only by three or four tacks, which could be easily removed with the fingers. The spy had, however, prudently fastened down the window. Nevertheless, a few moments after twelve o'clock, Bowman had stolen silently into the spy's apartment. A shadow or a spirit could not have moved with less noise than he did. Stealing up to the bedside, his tapering fingers glided under the pillow, and soon drew forth the letter from its hiding-place. Having now accomplished his object, he vanished from the room with the swiftness and noiseless motions of a dim, silent sprite. Hastening to his own chamber, he quickly struck a light, and his eyes fairly danced with joy as he read the palpable evidence of Winston's guilt. But no time was to be lost; for Winston might soon miss his letter, and might make his escape before he could be arrested. So, in a short time, he was closeted with General Robespierre, who allowed John free access at all hours.

"I suppose, John," said General Robespierre, rubbing his eyes, "something of unusual importance has occurred."

"I do n't generally wake up your honor at midnight for nothing," replied the son, however manifesting no disposition to make known the object of his visit. A silence of several moments ensued.

"Well, John, I am waiting patiently to hear your communication."

"Before I tell any thing, I want to ask your honor a few questions."

"Very well, John—proceed," said Robespierre, eyeing the boy with some surprise.

This was an unusual course for John to pursue.

"Have n't I always served you faithfully?"

"Yes," was the laconic reply.

"Have I ever claimed any thing for my services except my regular wages?"

"Ah, yes; I understand it now. You want money," pulling out his purse and laying a five-dollar gold piece on the table. "I thought, John, you were well supplied. I have always treated you liberally."

22

"You have never heard me grumble at my lot. Your honor has occasionally tossed me a five or a ten, and I have been satisfied; but now I must have something more than tens and fives."

"Well, what amount do you want?"

"Two thousand dollars," said Bowman, slowly.

"Two thousand dollars!" exclaimed the General, starting from his seat. "H—ll and blazes! John Bowman, what do you mean?"

"Bowman would n't be my name if I had my rights."

"The devil it would n't!" said Robespierre, in astonishment. "Who told you this?"

"It do n't matter who told me—I found it out. But you need n't swear at me so; you never did it before, and I think I have done enough to deserve better treatment."

"Well, well, John," said the General, softening somewhat; "I did not mean any harm. But what do you want with so much money?"

"There's no reason why I should keep it a secret, if you want to hear it. You recollect I once had a mother, and you know where she is as well as I do. I never know'd until a short time ago who really was my true *father*. My mother, as you ought to know, is now in New York, and she is in want. I see your honor understands it all; so it won't be needful to bring up old stories. I do n't like to tell it any better than you like to hear it. If you will give me two thousand dollars, and let me take it to my mother, who you left entirely when you was made a general, I will put her in a way to make a decent living; then come back and say no more about it. I think you owe my mother this much for deserting her as you did."

"I never was married to your mother."

"No, I know you was not, and that's what disgraces me. I do n't see why you should leave her now, when you profess to be fighting for the blacks, and to make them equal to the whites. You ought to marry her, and carry out your doctrine, even if she is not as white as your honor is. She did not leave you to freeze in the streets when you used to git dead drunk and tumble into the gutters."

This was rather an unpleasant subject to the worthy father, and he was willing to dismiss it as soon as possible. He did not wish to hear any more of his own history.

"Well, never mind, John; it is a large amount, but I will give you the money upon one condition; and that is, you are not to repeat this story hereafter in order to extort money from me."

"I do n't think I shall call upon your honor again; but the news I have may be worth more than I ask."

"Now we understand each other," said Robespierre, "let us have it."

"You know this man Thompson, who has been with us only a short time?"

"Yes," replied the General, with eagerness.

"I have been watching him since he came here. To-day he searched your desk, and to-night I took this from under his pillow." And he handed the letter to Robespierre.

The brutish monster fairly clutched at it, and fired up with wrath and ire as he read the lines revealing, in a few words, his nefarious plot. He required no further evidence, though no name was subscribed, nor any thing else except a private mark, which might furnish any indication as to the authorship. Bowman's simple word was ample testimony with Robespierre.

"John," said the General, when he had finished the letter, "wake up Sergeant Bowles, and tell him to report at my office immediately, with twelve men."

Bowman disappeared in a trice, and executed the order with such alacrity and speed that in less than twenty minutes the sergeant, with his men, stood in Robespierre's office.

"Sergeant," ordered General Robespierre, "follow Bowman here, and arrest the man whom he will point out, and bring him to me. Be careful that he does not escape."

The sergeant bowed to the officer, and then, following the wiry dwarf, hastened to the spy's room, where he was sleeping, all unconscious of the approaching peril. The sergeant stationed two men at the window, and rapped at the door.

Winston sprang up in an instant. "Hold on," said he, in a low voice, as the rap was repeated. On opening the door, he was thunderstruck to find several bayonets pointing to his breast.

"That is the man," said John Bowman, who was carrying a light.

"I am ordered to arrest you," said Sergeant Bowles, "and take you to General Robespierre's office immediately."

"This is rather a strange proceeding; but nevertheless I will be ready in a moment to appear before the General." And the spy proceeded to don his clothing. While moving about his bed, he took occasion to feel under his pillow for his letter.

"You need n't look for that, Mr. Thompson; it's gone, sure," cried Bowman, in a fit of laughter.

Winston now comprehended the magnitude of his danger; but it was too late to attempt an escape. Putting on the best face he possibly could, he was soon led into the presence of General Robespierre. As soon as the spy entered, Robespierre fastened his eyes, glowing like those of an enraged tiger, upon him, and surveyed his form from head to foot. Winston stood before him calm and collected.

"Sergeant Bowles," at length said the brute, in a stern but suppressed voice, "take this d——d traitorous spy beyond the outer pickets before daybreak, and never let him see the sun rise. Hang him half a mile from the road, and leave his infernal body to rot in the air."

"General Robespierre," said Winston, in a calm voice, "I should like to know the meaning of this unexpected and severe order. I think, sir, I am entitled to a fair trial, at least."

"Meaning? Damnable hypocrite, what does this mean?" shaking the letter in the spy's face. "Do n't feign ignorance, Thompson; you are a black-hearted rebel, doubly guilty, and, by the eternal God, you shall die. Not another word, sir. Take him away, sergeant; and if he escapes, I shall hold you responsible. Go with them, Bowman." And the enraged officer retired to his bed.

Winston was put under strong guard, and closely watched until a short time before daylight. There was no possible chance to escape, nor did he make any attempt to extricate himself from his perilous situation; but submitted, with the best grace he could, to what seemed the decrees of inexorable fate. When the first streaks of the approaching day began to illuminate the eastern horizon, the party charged with Winston's execution were one or two miles from the city. The prisoner was tightly bound, and placed in a wagon guarded by six men. Behind this there followed seven or eight horsemen, among whom was John Bowman. The party moved rapidly until the outer pickets were passed, when they came to a halt. The spy was now taken from the wagon, his feet untied, and then he was made to walk half a mile from the main road, as Robespierre had directed. At length, stopping under a large oak, with a projecting limb fifteen or twenty feet from the ground, Sergeant Bowles prepared to execute the cruel mandate of his master.

"This is ugly work, boys," said the sergeant. "Be quick, and let's get through with it. You heard the General's order," he continued, turning to the spy. "You must die before sunrise. But we will give you time to say your prayers, if you want to."

Winston moved three or four steps, knelt for several minutes, and then, to the astonishment of the blood-thirsty Yankees, uttered a strange, wild shriek, that caused the whole party to start like they had been shot. They glanced at each other in amazement.

"What in the h—ll do you mean by that?" asked the sergeant.

"It is the custom of my church," replied the spy.

"He thinks he's come to a camp-meeting," said another.

"He's one o' the Methodists. I guess he's only happy."

Winston remained on his knees for twenty minutes. By this time the patience of the Yankees was exhausted.

"Why, you must be a h—ll of a sinner," cried Bowles. "You might have got pardon for two lifetimes of sin in all this time, if you had been in earnest. Come on; we can't wait any longer; it is nearly sunrise."

Another shriek, louder than the first, split the air like a clap of thunder, and seemed to jar the very earth on which the startled Yankees stood.

"See here, boys," cried Bowles, "that scream means something besides religion. I'll be d—d if he ain't hollering for somebody. Come on, let's hang him at once. He's after no good. Get up, sir, we won't wait another minit."

"Let me finish my prayers first," said the spy.

"No, sir; you have had time enough to say a dozen prayers. If you aint done, I can't help it. I must obey orders. So come on, or I will use force."

"Will you be so cruel as not to let a dying man say his prayers? What difference can a few moments make to you?"

"Well, go on, then," interrupted Bowles; "but be in a hurry; I can't wait much longer."

Winston still remained on his knees in the attitude of earnest prayer. The Yankees now began to murmur at this delay, and at length their stock of patience was completely exhausted. Their grumblings were suddenly stopped by another shriek.

"By G—d, I will stop that," cried Bowles. "Come on, men; there's treachery in them screams. Hang him up at once."

The rope was adjusted about the spy's neck, and the bandage was placed over his eyes.

"Now, boys," commanded Bowles, "throw it over the limb, and grab the other end, and then pull him up."

Poor Winston felt the cord tighten around his neck as he was drawn us, and he silently commended his soul to God.

"Fasten the rope to that sapling, boys, and leave—quick."

Scarcely had the sergeant uttered this exclamation, when bang! bang! bang! rang out, sharp and clear, from twenty Maynard rifles. The spy felt himself fall heavily to the earth on his back, and heard a confused, dull murmur of groans, shrieks, and yells. It was several minutes before he recovered. The first object which met his eyes when he returned to consciousness was the writhing form of John Bowman dangling from the limb from which he himself had been suspended. Springing to his feet at length, he saw a dozen bodies dressed in blue stretched upon the earth. Every one had passed into "that bourne from whence no traveler returns." Standing around were twenty-five or thirty rough-looking men, who gazed upon the scene with perfect *nonchalance*. At last, one who seemed to be the leader exclaimed:

"There is no time to be lost. To horse, men, to horse!" Having given this command, he turned to Winston. "You have been mighty lucky, friend, mighty lucky."

"Yes, but what made you so slow?" asked Winston. "I thought you never would come."

"We were in that thicket all the time. But we could not fire into the squad until they had drawn you out of the crowd. You might a-thought of this, and saved them terrible screeches which we all understood. I know'd you would n't die before we could git you down."

"Where is Taylor?" asked Winston.

"He's with the horses; but mount that animal," pointing to one of the Yankee's horses, "and we 'll talk more about it when we git out of danger; the pickets aint fur off."

In a moment the whole party dashed away from the spot upon which this gory tragedy had been enacted, and, turning into a dense thicket, in one hour more were beyond the reach of immediate danger. Here we will leave Winston, relating to his deliverers the circumstances which had nearly cost him his life, and enter into more minute details as to the means which led to his rescue. We promise to be brief.

The reader will recollect that when Sergeant Bowles rapped at the spy's door, a short time after midnight, it was opened without hesitation. Had he have known who his visitors were, and what their object was, probably admission into his chamber would not have been so easily effected. He expected to meet at one o'clock that morning an accomplice by the name of Taylor, whose business it was to go in and out of the Federal lines, in order to bear whatever messages might be necessary. Taylor had called upon Winston two hours after the latter had written his letter to General Johnston, but Robespierre was then in the office, and he had no opportunity to put the document in Taylor's hands. So, whispering in his comrade's ear "one o'clock to-night," Taylor retired until the appointed hour should arrive. About the time Winston was arrested, his accomplice was lurking near the office. He was in a position in which he could observe the whole proceeding; and when he saw Winston taken into Robespierre's office, he walked close under the window, and by listening attentively could hear all that was said. While the spy was being removed to prison, Taylor followed at a short distance until he was in a safe place, then whistled a well-known signal, which was understood by the spy, but was unnoticed by any of the guard. As soon as the sound had issued from Taylor's lips, he darted down a narrow alley, and traveled out of the city with a celerity which soon brought him to the headquarters of a band of guerrillas. Here, in a few words, he related the object of his early visit, and the result is known to the reader.

CHAPTER XIX.

"I would outstare the sternest eyes that look,
Outbrave the heart most daring on the earth,
Pluck the young sucking cub from the she bear,
Yea, mock the lion when he roars for prey,
To win thee, lady."

READER, the scene now changes. Let your imagination leave the —— city, and wander to the Federal capital, which, notwithstanding the gigantic war that was scattering its untold horrors throughout the civilized world, was a scene of gayety and festivity. It is night. The bright moon, from a soft, smiling sky, pours down a flood of silvery light upon the streets of modern Sodom and Gomorrah. It is the brilliant eye of Deity peering down upon the gaudy habitations of a sinful race. O, upon how many crimes, upon how many dark deeds of blood, does that same serene eye gaze from the gates of heaven! It beholds the night-walking ruffian, lurking amid the thickets that shade the highway, in order to plunge his glittering knife into the heart of some unwary traveler. It beholds that human form, mutilated and mangled, dragged by rude hands to the brink of some gentle river, and buried beneath the smooth moonlit surface of the placid stream. It looks with pitying kindness upon the wretched miser who, consecrating his soul to the god of Mammon, steals to his coffers, hidden in the "first temples" of deity, and feasts his failing sight upon ill-gotten treasure, extracted from the warm tears of widows and orphans. It peeps through the windows of the presidential mansion, upon the proud tyrant rejoicing, like Belshazzar of old, in the greatness of his power and the grandeur of his fame, but is yet blind to the handwriting upon the wall, traced in letters of blood—MENE, MENE, TEKEL, UPHARSIN. Go on, vile man, unmolested in the ways of sin and iniquity, but when death shall bear thee beyond the murky waves of that river which no mortal crosses but once, and shall confine thee within the narrow limits of the tomb till the great day of wrath, that same holy light, now smiling down upon thy deeds of forbidden wickedness, changed to crimson gore, will frown the mighty vengeance of an offended God upon thy guilty soul! In a little while thou shalt cross the river of death, and answer to God for the suffering scattered by thy sinful hand over the bloody surface of a ruined continent!

In front of a large, handsome building, a number of splendid carriages was drawn up. Reader, enter that magnificent dwelling. Do you discover any indications of the terrible scourge of war, which has changed the "sunny South" from a Shinar's fertile plain into the sad and mournful wastes of a Golgothic land? Would you suspect, from the gay scene before you, that a struggle of most stupendous magnitude was carrying grief and sorrow to millions of suffering hearts? You see smiling faces, bright eyes, lovely forms arrayed in the costliest apparel the world can furnish. You hear lively chat, and the clear, ringing laugh, as it issues from the rosy lips of some happy maid. Indeed, in the midst of life, we are in death.

But, passing by the thoughtless, giddy throng, observe that officer who bears upon his shoulders the insignia of a Federal colonel. His form is well-proportioned, and his noble countenance, at present of a somewhat melancholy cast, is sufficiently handsome to cause the hearts of Eve's fairest daughters to flutter with joy and delight. But the officer seems lost in profound abstraction, and pays little attention to any person of either sex in the brilliantly lighted parlor. Occasionally he casts his eyes in the direction of the door, moves uneasily.

then turns his face to the company with ill-concealed vexation and disappointment. Presently a dress rustles in the door, and again the officer turns his head. A dark-haired, dark-eyed, pale-faced maid, of some twenty-two summers, stands in the entrance. She looked more like a spiritual than a human being. Though this was evidently the person expected by the officer, he yet seemed surprised; his heart beat with uncontrollable emotion, and he blushed to his temples. His secret is revealed. The pale lady moves gracefully through the assembly, and seats herself, with perfect unconcern, on a sofa in a far corner of the room. It was palpable to the most inattentive observer that she was "in the crowd, but not of the crowd." It was Emily Burrell. Poor girl! she had lost all taste and relish for such pleasures and scenes; but, at the solicitation of her brother, had agreed to attend this one party. Under the weight of her crushed affection, she was slowly but surely sinking to a premature grave. The bloodless cheek, the sunken eye, the vacant look, the sluggish step, the listless attitude, were all indications of a bruised and broken spirit. Had it not been for the bright, dark eye, she might have been mistaken for a fine piece of marble, chiseled and fashioned into a human form by the hand of man. Yet she was beautiful, angelically beautiful; it was almost the beauty of a spirit— the beauty of an etherealizing form. Colonel Burrell had done all that affection for his suffering sister could suggest to alleviate her distress; but it was all unavailing. She seemed to occupy an intermediate position between the living and the dead, like an unculled flower that stands between two seasons, and perfumes the last summer breeze with its sweet fragrance, then scatters its fading leaves upon the first rude blast of the wintry winds.

As soon as our officer could change his locality with decency and propriety, without betraying the secret of his heart too plainly to be unnoticed, he moved to Emily's side. Numerous eyes were at first fixed upon the strange-looking pair, but the officer managed to retain his self-possession, and conversed with so much intelligence and feeling, that Emily could not but listen with an unusual degree of interest. In the course of the evening, Emily, who had declined all solicitations to dance, was induced to promenade with the Colonel. They walked in the long gallery, illuminated only by the rays of the moon, and talked of the beauties of nature—a subject upon which the officer expatiated with so much pathos and feeling and sympathy that Emily actually forgot her sufferings. At length the topic was changed.

"Do you know, Miss Burrell," said the Colonel, in a slightly tremulous voice, "that this night has been one of the happiest of my life?"

"No, sir, I did not; but I am glad somebody can be happy?"

"But more than that," continued the officer, not replying to the last remark, "do you know it depends upon you to make it the most happy or most miserable of my whole life?"

There was no reply.

"I see you are not good at taking hints, Miss Burrell. I was in hopes that I had met my spirit's mate, and that I could be easily understood, without even the customary agency of language."

"I shall not pretend ignorance, Colonel Ellsworth, of the subject to which I think you allude. If I have not misinterpreted your words, we may as well change the subject."

"Say not so," he exclaimed, with great earnestness; "say not so. Do not thus blight the tender flower which I have cherished in my heart until it has become the sole study of my existence. But let me talk to you of that holy emotion which has now taken possession of my whole being."

"It will all be in vain, Colonel. The subject is an unpleasant one to me; but if you insist upon making it the theme of our conversation, I tell you in advance, and I give you fair warning, that your words will fall upon a heart of ice."

"You slander yourself," exclaimed the officer. "Your very manner contradicts the unjust statement you have made, and you do not understand the nobility of your own nature, if that is your opinion. No being of your personal appearance can own a heart of ice."

"You see that beautiful moon, Colonel Ellsworth?" she said, pointing upward. "The language of love can no more reach my nature than it can change the cheerful countenance of that glowing orb of light—I am *love-proof!*"

"I can not believe it. *Mon Dieu!* one of your appearance, one with your sparkling eyes, destitute of all that ennobles the nature of woman! I will not slander you by believing it. Do not, then, doom me to a lifetime of misery."

"Well, you can believe it or not. Even were it otherwise, and I should be disposed to reciprocate the feeling you profess, there would be an eternal barrier between us."

"What, in the name of heaven, can that be?" cried the officer, starting in surprise at the energy with which the words were uttered.

"Since you ask it, Colonel—since you want a reason, I trust I can presume upon your honor not to divulge a secret which might endanger my safety in Washington?"

"I would lay down my life before I would betray your confidence."

"Then I could never give my hand to one who helps to sustain this wicked war, or who affiliates with those now devastating the South, and turning her broad fields into a wilderness."

"Why not?"

"That is a strange question. You know what Halleck says?

'They love their land because it is *their own*,
And scorn to give aught other reason why.'

But I am not so ill-natured as that; I will give you a reason why. Because, then, I am a native of Kentucky; because I love the South; I love her social and political institutions; I love her sunny plains, her magnificent rivers, her hills and her vales, her fountains, her streams, and her floods. I was born in the South; educated in the South; my feelings, sympathies, associations, affections, are all in the South. She nurtured my childhood, witnessed the sports and triumphs of my girlhood, and when I die the only thing I shall crave is a quiet resting-place in her bosom — yes, in her bosom, now torn, bleeding, and bruised by the most cruel, savage, and unjust war ever forced upon an oppressed and down-trodden people. I have witnessed her heroic struggle for independence; I have seen her noble sacrifices—the dearest and most trying that liberty ever calls upon her devotees to make; I have pitied and grieved over her unparalleled sufferings; and I have wept when her once happy people have been reduced to ruin, poverty, and beggary. Cast your eyes, Colonel Ellsworth, cast your eyes over the southern states, and what do you see? Happy homes burned and razed to the ground. And where are the owners? They have fled from the fell destroyer, and have sought, as refugees, an asylum in other states, or hidden in the wilderness like hunted beasts of prey. You see our women and children driven to the woods, our domestic animals butchered, our farms made an inhospitable waste, and even our wearing apparel wantonly torn to fragments. Our churches, dedicated to the living God, have been desecrated; our cemeteries, adorned and beautified by the labors of mourning friends, despoiled, and the bones of the sleeping dead disturbed by a worse than vandal foe, in the search for hidden treasure. In the days of yore, Colonel Ellsworth," continued the girl, moved to tears by her own eloquence, "when a Roman citizen had been guilty of any misdemeanor, and wished protection against his enemies, he fled into the temple of the sea god, and not even the unbelieving heathen dared to pollute the sanctity of that holy spot. But, in the South, where is the sacred sanctuary to which our defenseless women and children can flee from the insults of the barbarous foe? Not even the church—the *sanctum sanctorum* of modern religion—the church in which we are required to lay aside human passion and human pride—escapes the argus eye of northern avarice. Not even the Masonic temple—that time-honored institution, which has withstood the shock of more than a thousand years, which has come down to us from the days of Solomon over the forgotten ruins of kingdoms and empires, and which is now venerated and reverenced for its antiquity and its sacred traditions among all nations, both civilized and barbarous—not even the arcana of that wonderful temple of mystery, whose only object is to unite the bonds of brotherly love between men of different tribes, races, and religions, and to pour the balm of consolation into the bleeding bosom of distressed man, and which professes no connection with the political schemes and rebellions of this earth—not even that meets with the respect a Goth or a Vandal would pay. But its doors have been forced open; its jewels, visible emblems to inculcate lessons of virtue, morality, and religion, have been snatched from the sacred adytum, and sent back to the North as trophies wrenched from offending rebels. Not even the graveyard—that silent, peaceful home of departed friends—is free from the intrusions of UNION soldiers. But the very tombstones, bearing the last tribute of respect and affection that mortality can pay, have been torn down, and used as tables in the Federal camps. Sir!" she exclaimed, wild with the intensity of her own deep feeling, "men who could do this would attempt to rob a saint in the presence of the Great Redeemer, or pilfer gold from the throne of the invisible God! Men who could do this"——.

"In the name of heaven, Miss Burrell, pause—pause!" cried Colonel Ellsworth, somewhat alarmed, as he saw the fragile form quivering, the dark eye flashing in the moonlight, and the lip trembling with deeply aroused feeling.

It was a picture of personified patriotism, indignant at the heathenish outrages and wrongs inflicted upon a proud race—a picture upon which Colonel Ellsworth gazed with a strange mingling of fear, sympathy, and admiration. Emily, recalled to herself, continued more calmly:

"You doubtless think I am an enthusiast or a fanatic, Colonel. Well, I shall not deny it. Upon this subject I am immovably fixed. If I marry, a rebel shall be my husband; his people shall be my people, and his God my God; and when the South goes down beneath a sea of blood, if that is to be her dreadful fate, I would not survive the wreck, and reside in the North, a living monument of disgrace to the dead heroes, the noble martyrs of liberty, whose moldering bones repose in the soil of my own native land. But when all have gone; when her last son has fallen upon the battle-field; when her last daughter has famished in the wild woods; and her last babe has breathed out its young life at its dead mother's breast; O God! let me too follow their shades beyond the reach of northern oppression! Let me die—let me rest in the bosom of Kentucky's dark and bloody ground, where sleep my own dear father and mother!"

Nature gave way to this sudden transition of feeling, and as the heroine ceased from talking by reason of exhaustion, a flood of tears gushed down the pale cheek. Will Colonel Ellsworth be called weak if his eye moistened? Reader, at that moment he would have exchanged places with the humblest soldier in the Confederate army could he have clasped that weeping girl to his breast, and have wiped her tears away. But it was absolutely necessary that he should say something in his own defense, or he might lose the eloquent rebel girl forever. After a brief, thoughtful silence, he slowly replied:

"I appreciate your feelings, Miss Burrell, and your extreme sensibility. But you must not allow the ardor of your nature to force you into an excess of patriotism, and of hatred against those who deem it a sacred duty to sustain the Union. War, I know, is a terrible scourge, and no one deprecates its horrors more than I do; and while I admit that the state of things so graphically and eloquently described by you exists to some extent, yet pardon me when I say the picture drawn by your brilliant imagination appears to be rather highly embellished. Death and suffering are the natural, legitimate, and inevitable consequences of war; and a war without distress would be an anomaly in the history of man. But you take altogether a one-sided view of this question. You throw the whole blame upon those who would restore the Union to its former integrity and its pristine glory. Now, while I am not disposed to exonerate my party from just censure, I nevertheless believe the South is as much responsible for the inauguration of this war as the North. I blame both parties. I believe this awful calamity could have been averted. You will find that one is to blame as much as the other. Now I ask you who fired the first gun—who first insulted that flag which you see streaming from the heights of the capitol in proud defiance? Under that same flag you were born, Miss Burrell. It waved over and protected your infancy. You were taught in your childhood to love and revere it as the emblem of the proudest nationality this world ever saw. Your heart once beat with joy when you beheld that glorious streamer unfold its "stars and stripes" over a free, contented, and happy people. After the lapse of nearly a century, when that flag was recognized and respected throughout the wide world, up springs a man in the South, goaded on by the demon of unholy ambition, who tears it into fragments, and tramples its shreds under his unhallowed feet. Who that has a single spark of patriotism glowing in his heart would not rush to that sacred emblem representing the honor, dignity, and power of his insulted country? The Union, Miss Burrell, was a splendid inheritance, bequeathed to us by our forefathers, purchased with their blood, nurtured and fostered by their protecting care for many long and trying years, until it came down to us the wonder and admiration of man, and the favored institution of God. Washington with his dying breath admonished us to beware of dismembering this great country, this magnificent bequeathment. We have been told, time and again, by Clay, Webster, and other great statesmen, that the dissolution of this Union could never be accomplished without bloodshed. With all this warning, then, I ask you again, who is responsible for the suffering and distress occasioned by the war? Not I, and others like me, who wished only to see our nation go forward in its career of unexampled prosperity; not Mr. Lincoln, who only desired to fill the position to which the voice of the nation had called him, and to hand down intact to his successor the Union in its entirety, with all its blessings and privileges; but it is Jeff Davis, who, not satisfied with his high, dignified place in the United States Senate, must persuade the southern states to secede, form a confederacy, and place him at its head. Like Cæsar, he would rather rule in an insignificant village than be a private citizen of Rome. Suppose we had recognized the right of secession, and the different states should begin to set up for themselves. In a few years this vast country would be severed into numberless little republics; not republics either, but petty kingdoms, quarreling among themselves, and filling a continent with confusion and trouble. In course of time foreign despots would interfere, and the horrors which you depict as now existing in the South would sink into insignificance compared with the evils inflicted by an invading army of French, English, Spanish, and other ambitious nations of Europe. Rather than risk the probability of such a state of things, the South would better submit to the punishment due to her act of disobedience, and like a chastised child return to the embraces of a kind father. But, Miss Burrell," continued the officer, abruptly breaking off, "I have no desire to discuss this unpleasant subject further. I would much rather talk of yourself and the deep affection I feel for you."

"I am not worth talking about, Colonel Ellsworth; and as for your love, bestow it upon some of those gay dancers, who will feel proud of the preference, and whose tender hearts will swell with affection at the approach of the gallant Colonel Ellsworth."

"Do not talk thus lightly, Miss Burrell, and in such a tone of mockery and sarcasm. I am not, I trust, one of those thoughtless beings who bow with reverence at the shrine of Plutus, and who worship and adore the pomp and parade of fashion. But I am one—and I say it not boastingly—who can appreciate those solid and more noble qualities of mind and heart which constitute the basis of all true happiness. I am not one who can be dazzled and attracted by the thin, gauzy surface of beauty; but I am one who can penetrate the shallowness of outside display, and who can esteem the excellences of a true heart. It is not my intention to flatter, Miss Burrell, but you are the only one I have yet met with who possesses in an eminent degree those qualities which I respect and admire. I love the open candor of your nature; your sensibility of soul; your enthusiasm of mind; your indifference to the frivolities and trumperies of life; and, above all, the deep and profound sympathy and ardor of your heart. In a word, I find in you all the indications of a true woman. Can you blame me, then, if I should feel the laudable desire to make such a heart my own? Can you reproach me, having this opinion of your character, for the excusable wish to make you the idolized *wife* of my heart?"

"I would, indeed, be an exception to my sex, Colonel Ellsworth, did I not feel flattered at your undeserved encomium. I thank you for the unmerited compliment bestowed upon virtues which exist, I fear, only in your imagination; but I must say you have one praiseworthy quality in a high degree, and that is perseverance. You must possess a most wonderful amount of that virtue, or you must consider me a very fickle-minded creature, to be changed in a moment after I made the positive and emphatic declaration that I could not return the feeling which you at least profess. If you gave me credit for so much honesty of heart, you should have been satisfied with my answer. But I repeat, Colonel, if there were no other obstacles in the way, I could never be induced to connect my destiny in any manner with one who hates the unfortunate country that gave me birth, and who seeks to rivet upon her bleeding limbs the galling chains of bondage and subjugation. No; let me live in my own native South, and if she can not be free, O, ask me not to forsake my suffering sisters in the hour of anguish, and desert the noble sons of Kentucky, who have immortalized, in story and in song, the 'dark and bloody ground.' While our valiant soldiers are struggling with almost superhuman courage against the terrible odds hurled upon them, and our delicate women, with more than the firmness of Spartan matrons, are sending their adored sons to the gory field, God forbid that I should turn from them in this the day of trial, and mock their libations of tears and blood by my act of apostasy. I could not be so deaf to the voice that cries from the ground for vengeance.

> 'I tell thee that the voice of patriot blood,
> Thus pour'd for faith and freedom, hath a tone
> Which, from the night of ages, from the gulf
> Of death, shall burst and make its high appeal
> Sound unto earth and heaven!'

Methinks I hear that voice to-night; and I can not close my ears against its loud appeal. Rather than be a faithless Helen, and flee my country with a perjured Paris, I would willingly become the Iphigenia of the South, whose death should appease the wrath of the angry sister of Apollo, if it could seal the independence of our oppressed republic. In the language of a true patriot, 'Sink or swim, live or die, survive or perish,' I go with the South. If she triumph, I shall glory in her success; but if she fall, may the Holy One never let me live to see her proud-spirited people become 'hewers of wood and drawers of water'—forced to perform vile drudgeries imposed by Egyptian task-masters."

"I am extremely sorry, Miss Burrell," replied the officer, in whose ears the soft, silvery tones of the rebel girl's trembling voice were still ringing like the mournful vibrations of a funeral bell—"I am extremely sorry that you are laboring under such a strange and, to me, unaccountable delusion. I do not hate the South, as you say; God knows I pity her great sufferings; and I would lay down my poor life, if for nothing else but your sake, to cement the sacred ties that once bound our separated people together. I was a member, Miss Burrell, of the last congress that ever sat in the old Union, and I raised my feeble voice, I spoke with all the power of my whole mind, to ward off this separation which has brought upon both sections calamities and horrors that no description can justly portray. I endeavored in vain to pour oil upon the troubled waters, and to calm the stubborn passions under the influence of which both parties were rushing on headlong to destruction. I failed; and when the first tocsin of war sounded the alarm, I drew forth my sword from its scabbard with a sorrowful heart. Not because I hated the South; not because I wished to spill the blood of her deluded children in wanton cruelty; but because I wished to chastise her with the kindness of a physician who cuts out the foul flesh from the wound that the patient may live. When, therefore, you accuse the whole North of manifesting such an unjustifiable malignity toward their brethren of the South, you do me great injustice to include my name in the category."

"You are found in very bad company, to say the least of it. But, however, it is not my intention, Colonel, to include any but the guilty; and if you disclaim all feelings of bitterness toward my down-trodden countrymen, I could not be so ungenerous and unjust as to force you into a position which you do not occupy."

"I am glad to hear you say so; and now, having done this much, why can you not go a step further, and include my humble self in the number of your friends and well-wishers?"

"Why, I trust you are not an *enemy*, save in a national point of view."

"Miss Burrell," said the Colonel, thoughtfully, "excuse my impudence, but allow me to ask a question upon which I feel a considerable degree of curiosity. I think I have a right to know. *Have you ever loved?*"

"Colonel Ellsworth," said the girl, with moistening eyes, as the thought of Henry Winston flashed over her, and caused her pale face to redden like a delicate rose blushing by moonlight, "*I have loved*, and," said she, with artless candor, "behold the result in these pale cheeks, these sunken eyes, and this wasting form. Let this confession, wrung from a bleeding heart, convince you that *I can never love again*."

"And what kind of a person had the happiness to win your affection?" asked the officer, without noticing her emotion. "What was his form?"

"Rather tall, and straight as an arrow."

"What kind of features?"

"Deep azure eyes; a bold, broad forehead; a small Grecian nose; a firm, well-set mouth; and a face withal you could not pass without stopping to take the second look."

"A rather remarkable personage; but," said the Colonel, fixing his eyes upon her face, "where to-night is your *beau-ideal?*"

"O, Colonel Ellsworth, question me not on this subject. It makes my wound bleed afresh."

Colonel Ellsworth formed the conclusion that her lover was dead; or, if not, he had nothing to fear from that quarter.

"Pardon me, Miss Burrell, if my curiosity has forced me beyond the limits of true politeness. Yours, I see, is a sad history, and I assure you I deeply sympathize in the evident suffering of a heart disappointed in the beginning of life. But if you go on thus, unhappy young lady, to repine over past grief and sorrow, you will tread upon thorns even to the brink of the tomb."

"I need not be told of that, Colonel Ellsworth. My happiness is all gone. My pathway is strewn with withered flowers; and I look upon death only to release me from the weight of troubles I can not endure."

"My dear Miss Burrell," exclaimed the officer, with great earnestness, "let me win you back to life and happiness. Throw not thus away the noble gifts of mind with which God in his wisdom has endowed you. Waste not the bloom of your womanhood and the affections of your tender heart in useless repinings and regrets over past disappointments. Come back to this beautiful earth which can be made a paradise. The bright world is before you with all its charms. They are placed here for the pleasure of man, and the Almighty never intended that his creatures should pass through life in sorrow, totally indifferent to the bright, gay flowers blooming in beauty around. It is sinful to shut our eyes in stoical indifference to the brilliant scenes the world presents, when God made them to please the eye and gratify the taste. No one has the right to withdraw himself from society, and waste the powers of an extraordinary mind in unavailing sorrow, when his influence and his talent might contribute so much to the improvement of man and the advancement of God's glory. Be mine, then; seal my happiness this night. I will lay my fortune, my all, at your feet!"

"Colonel Ellsworth," cried Emily, interrupting, "cease this talk. You know not to whom you are speaking; besides, your words are thrown away. Let us leave this place."

"Before we part, Miss Burrell, promise me that I may call upon you two weeks from to-night."

"Why, certainly, Colonel Ellsworth, if it will afford you any pleasure. I am not in the habit of receiving company, but I will violate my rule once in your favor. It is, though, upon the express condition that you are not to mention this unpleasant subject again."

The officer sighed. Emily was escorted to the room she had left, and Colonel Ellsworth bade her good night; then, seizing his hat, he left the apartment and rushed into the street. He had met with an enigma he could not understand; but yet he madly worshiped the strange enthusiastic girl, who appeared to him like the visitation of some heathen goddess described by the pen of Virgil or Homer. That night he dreamed of the battles in which he had figured, and he saw a pale, beautiful creature in the thickest of the fight, entreating him not to spill the blood of her oppressed countrymen. The intense vividness of the dream caused him to awake. Before he slept again, he made a vow, which is recorded in heaven. The sequel will show he was true to his word and paid his vow.

CHAPTER XX.

"Let me tell you, Cassius, you yourself
Are much condemned to have an itching palm;
To sell and mart your offices for gold
To undeservers."

WE will now return to the spy. Having narrowly escaped an ignominious death, as described in a previous chapter, he reported, as soon as practicable, at the head-quarters of General Johnston, in obedience to orders received from that officer. His services were now needed in a higher but more dangerous field of labor. During the time Winston had been acting in the capacity of a spy, he had rendered important service to the Confederacy. The information which he very frequently gave prevented many military disasters, and contributed greatly to the achievement of victories. Yet the names of our distinguished chieftains will be engraved in brass and chiseled in marble, while that of the humble spy will not find a lodgment even in some obscure corner of history. The southern people know not what a debt of gratitude they owe to this class of men, who have risked so much without the prospect of reward, and without the chance of preferment and promotion within the reach of every private soldier. If justice were done these self-sacrificing men, it would be found that they are as indispensable to successful military operations as the commanders of armies.

We have not time or space now to enter into particularities and to specialize all the secret services rendered by Henry Winston. Suffice it to say that he had done much for the cause of independence; and that while he was little known to the great mass of the soldiers, yet among the general officers he was recognized as a man of most remarkable and extraordinary ability. In fact, in the year 1863, he was the most reliable spy within the limits of the Confederate States. But, as we have said, his talents were now to be exercised in a position in which he could do an incalculable amount of good. Soon after reporting to General Johnston, he was ordered by that distinguished officer to proceed without delay to Richmond, and receive instructions from President Davis. In compliance with this order, a few months before the spring and summer campaigns of the year 1864, Winston was alone one night with the President of the Confederate States. Our limits will not allow a narration of all that passed. The President, we will say, was well pleased with the spy who had so frequently imperiled his life for the good of the Confederacy, and he listened with much attention to Winston's opinion of the future programme of the Federal Government. Mr. Davis was also thinking of something else which showed his sound judgment of men. But we will not anticipate.

"The country, Mr. Winston," remarked President Davis, "is under lasting obligation for the invaluable services you have already performed. There is, however, much to do yet. You have acquitted yourself so creditably and honorably that I must request you to undertake a mission of vital importance to our cause."

The spy signified his willingness to perform any duty for which the President might think him qualified.

"Your views," continued Mr. Davis, "coincide exactly with mine in regard to the next campaign. But I would still prefer to have something more substantial than mere opinions upon which to base military operations. The enemy's whole programme can, I think, be ascertained by a person of shrewdness and intelligence. The knowledge of Lincoln's intentions at this time would prove of incalculable advantage.

I would like much to know whether the enemy places a sufficient estimate upon Richmond to justify the concentration of his whole force against this one point."

"I think your excellency would hazard little in relying upon the information I have already obtained; but still, to make assurance doubly sure, I am perfectly willing to undertake to procure their whole programme, as far as it is developed."

"And to do this, Mr. Winston, it will be necessary for you to invade Washington City. You must, then, by some means ingratiate yourself into favor with some of the high officials, and you may learn from them all that will be necessary. Dr. Vernon, whose address I will give you, can aid you materially. He is a Confederate in the disguise of a Yankee surgeon."

"What man," asked the spy, "would you suggest as the most suitable to become the 'cat's-paw?'"

"I should not like to advise you upon that subject, for my advice might place you in a very embarrassing situation. The best plan will be to leave you free to act in accordance with the dictates of your own judgment. You will have to be governed by circumstances altogether; and the man whom I would probably suggest might be very difficult of access."

"It may not be amiss, then, to tell your excellency that I have been thinking of a character, and I would like to have your opinion of my selection. It is Lincoln himself."

"I fear that will be a troublesome undertaking; but Lincoln is a plain, blunt man, and can be managed more easily than Seward. If you can only obtain some position which would allow you to approach him freely, he would be a very proper personage for your purposes."

"If my usual good fortune attends me," said the spy, "I shall be able, in less than two months, to furnish you all the information you may require."

"You have been remarkably successful heretofore, Mr.

Winston, and have aided our generals to a great extent in thwarting the schemes of the enemy. Besides, I am under personal obligations to you, as I learn from General Johnston, for having probably saved my life. The wicked plot of Robespierre's, which you discovered, would no doubt have been carried out, and our country would have sustained an irreparable loss in General Lee, Hill, and others. We are contending with an inhuman foe, Mr. Winston. I am surprised that some of our people are talking of reconstruction; as for myself, having once cut loose from the despicable race of hypocrites and Pharisees, I would as soon trust myself in a den of thieves as to form a union with them again. I can not see how any man can be in favor of such a movement. After three years of privations and hardships, it would now be an eternal disgrace to our people to lay down their arms and quietly submit to the humiliating terms imposed by a proud, boastful despot. Our people are too easily discouraged and disheartened by disasters. Independence is within their reach, if they will only stand firm till Lincoln and his followers shall see the folly of a further prosecution of the war, and shall desist from this unholy purpose of subjugation. I foresee, from the alternations of success which have characterized the contest, that the next year will be marked by great reverses. Our citizens will then be dejected, and the demoralization will spread to the army. There will be general discontent and disaffection, and a disposition to abandon the principles of freedom which we pledged our fortunes and our sacred honors to maintain. At this juncture the danger will be that the enemy may take advantage of our momentary despondency, and propose some disgraceful terms of compromise which our despairing people may be disposed to accept. And if they should," continued the President with considerable vehemence of manner, "they will live to regret their folly; but it will be when they are bound hand and foot, and a Nero rejoices over their political and social degradation. I say *they*, Mr. Winston, because I do not include myself in the number of those who will manifest a disposition to reconstruct. My course is marked out clearly and distinctly; and, so help me heaven, this hand shall be severed from my body before it shall subscribe to any treaty or instrument, acknowledging the downfall of this Confederacy, and entailing misery, ruin, and infamy on its deluded citizens." And the President paused and looked thoughtful and serious.

"If," said the spy, "my study of Yankee character has not been in vain, Lincoln will never propose any terms the southern people would be willing to accept. I venture to predict that his first and last proposition will be unconditional submission."

"I hope you may be right, Mr. Winston," replied the President, looking thoughtfully into his face—"I hope you may be right; and I myself am inclined to the same opinion. I would even make some proposition to the Federal Government, in the certainty of its being rejected, merely to convince our people of the absurdity of the idea of a restoration of the Union, but for the moral effect such a step would have upon our enemies, Europe, and our own people. But this reminds me that I have omitted to communicate to you something in regard to this subject which may be of great use in Washington. I need not say to a man of your sound practical sense and intelligence that this is one of the political secrets with which only a few must be intrusted."

The President drew nearer to where the spy sat, but spoke in such a low tone of voice that his words could not be distinguished by any outside listener. After talking thus for some few moments, they were disturbed by a rap at the door. However, Mr. Davis had now communicated all he thought necessary, and the spy took his departure.

We can not follow Henry Winston through all the various

little incidents which transpired between the two capitals—
Richmond and Washington. He met with many exciting adventures, which would be highly interesting to the reader, but
would swell this volume beyond its intended limits. In seven
days after his interview with President Davis, the spy was in
Washington City. And now commenced a series of the most
remarkable occurrences ever contained in the unwritten annals
of espionage. The next day after his arrival Winston visited
Mr. Chase, and showed to that worthy testimonials as to character and qualifications in which not a single flaw could be
detected. They were signed by well-known citizens of New
York. The intention of the spy was to procure a situation
with some of the cabinet officers until he could work himself
into the good graces of Mr. Lincoln. Chase, in answer to
the spy's petition, replied that he had no place at present, but
if Mr. Smith (the assumed named of Winston) would call
when a vacancy should occur, he would be happy that Mr.
Smith should fill it. The spy next called upon the Postmaster-general, who was very much pleased with our hero's
personal appearance; but who still pleaded Mr. Chase's excuse, and made the same promise.

"I would advise you, though," said the Postmaster, as he
was about leaving, "to see Mr. Seward."

The spy thought he would not follow the officer's advice
until he should consult with Dr. Vernon, the surgeon to
whom he had been referred by President Davis. That gentleman, who was in the employ of both governments, but who
was faithful only to the Confederacy, was soon found. After
satisfying himself that the spy was no impostor or detective,
and after listening to his account of his ill success with Mr.
Chase and the Postmaster-general, the Doctor remarked:

"It was well you came to me as soon as you did, for with
your *modus operandi* you never would have found a place.
You are too honest, Mr. Smith (as I must call you), you are

too honest to succeed with Yankees. Tell a Yankee that 'honesty is the best policy,' and he will set you down for a fool. Positions are obtained here with money. Gold will buy any thing from a Yankee."

"I know that, Doctor; but I felt doubtful about trying its effects upon many high in office, like Chase and others."

"Pooh! Chase and others are no better than the common herd. They will jump at five cents with as much avidity as any rear-rank private in their army would. Why, for gold the best of them can be induced to sell the fee-simple to their souls. Now, when you present your testimonials to Seward, put among them, as if by accident, a pair of golden eagles, and I will insure you will get a situation. It will take twenty dollars to bribe Seward. If that, however, does not buy him, double it, and he will give you a position."

After some further conversation with Dr. Vernon, the spy proceeded to the office of Secretary Seward. Before presenting his testimonials, he took the precaution to deposit in one corner of the papers a couple of shining pieces of yellow metal. Mr. Seward received the documents, and his face brightened when he discovered they were not destitute of weight. Winston watched as closely as prudence and propriety would allow, but the officer was so dexterous and sly that the spy saw not by what a skillful maneuver the gold was taken out, but he heard the two pieces as they fell with a slight musical jingle to the bottom of Secretary Seward's pocket. No juggler could have performed the trick with more dexterity.

"So you want a place, Mr. Smith? You come well recommended as an intelligent, honest young man;" and at the word honest the Secretary slyly thrust his hand into his pocket and felt the weight of the two eagles, in order to discover if the honest young man had not imposed spurious coin upon him. He, however, seemed satisfied with this manipulation test of the docimastic art, and then continued: "'Honesty is the best policy,' Mr. Smith; and I am glad to find that you *are* honest;" by which declaration he referred more to the genuineness of Winston's two golden eagles than to any other evidence of the spy's integrity.

"I have many applications of this sort, Mr. Smith; but, nevertheless, I will take pleasure in assisting you. I have no vacant position at present, but the President, I learned to-day. is in need of a secretary. If you want the place, I will speak to Mr. Lincoln, and I doubt not you will get it."

The spy expressed himself satisfied, and under obligations, and then promised to call next morning, according to Seward's request. Having now, as he believed, succeeded in obtaining the situation he so much desired, with less difficulty than he expected, his next care was to find a boarding-house convenient to his place of business. This was soon done; and the remainder of the day was spent in examining the fortifications around the city. That night the spy again visited Dr. Vernon, in order to perfect the arrangements of secret communication between them, after which their acquaintance was to cease, in appearance at least. The next day Winston was installed into office as a secretary of the President of the United States. All this happened about three weeks before the occurrence of the event recorded in the preceding chapter. After a residence of that length of time in the Federal capital, the spy had not learned that Emily Burrell was a temporary inhabitant of the same city. During the night of the party, which she attended, Winston was sitting in his room, gazing out thoughtfully upon the moonlit city. He was, however, not thinking of the brilliant scene before him. His mind had wandered far back into the days of childhood, and was tracing out, one by one, the incidents of his eventful and checkered life. The year 1860 was reached. He saw Emily Burrell, and poured out the affections of his whole nature upon the beautiful girl. At the very moment she was, with sadness, giving a brief description of his personality to Colonel Ellsworth, Winston heaved a deep sigh, and then banished the painful subject from his mind. Had he known her locality and her unchanged feelings toward himself, this history would probably have terminated in a different manner. But he knew it not, and he was hastened on by an invisible power to the events of his remarkable life.

The spy had now been three weeks a secretary of Mr. Lincoln. Although he had studied the character of the President closely, and had endeavored to draw him out upon the war, yet Abraham had thus far eluded all of his cunningly laid snares; and, save an expression of opinion in general terms, such as he could hear upon the streets every day, Winston had gathered few items that would suit his purposes. But all men have their faults; and one of Lincoln's weak points was at last discovered. The President loved a good *dram*, though he was not a habitual drunkard. Our hero procured a bottle of the very best wine the city of Washington could furnish, and just before the entrance of Mr. Lincoln into the office drew forth the cork, that the fragrant fumes might have the "desired effect." Mr. Lincoln stopped in at his usual hour. It happened that nobody was in the room but himself and Winston. Presently the chief executive laid aside his pen. He could stand it no longer.

"Smith," said he, rubbing his great fists, "what is that which smells so sweetly? It reminds me of the fabled nectar of the ancient gods of Greece."

"Well may your excellency call it nectar," quickly remarked the spy, handing the bottle. "It is wine of a most rare and excellent quality.

'One sip of this
Will bathe the drooping spirits in delight,
Beyond the bliss of dreams. Be wise, and taste.'"

"You are a sly dog, Smith," punching him good-humoredly in the side, "to tempt me thus with Milton. I fear you are a wicked boy; but here's to your health." And raising the glass with his huge hand, he quaffed down the sparkling beverage. His excellency then resumed his pen, and commenced again to write; but the merry god Bacchus was playing havoc with his mental machinery.

"Smith," said the President, throwing down his pen in a very energetic manner, "hand us some more of that heavenly juice. I can quote poetry, too, Smith, as well as you. Here goes:

> 'Wine—bring wine!
> Let the crystal beaker flame and shine,
> Brimming o'er with the draught divine;
> Not from the Rhine—
> Not from the fields of Burgundian vine—
> Bring on the bright Olympian wine!'

Smith—I am glad your name is Smith. I like a name which can be easily remembered. I abominate long, uncommon names. I was some time ago introduced to an English lord by the name of Hartington, and I told his lordship that I could recollect his name only by its similarity to Partington, which seemed to plague the peer considerably." The President turned off the third glass, and gulped it down with a noise somewhat similar to that made by water running from a tank into a steam-engine. "Smith, it was lucky you came to me to find a place. Not many young men have the same access to the President of the United States that you have."

"I feel very highly flattered by your excellency's ready acceptance of my humble services, and I am honored, I fear, beyond my deserts, to be upon such intimate terms with the most erudite, most distinguished, and greatest statesman of the age."

"You are a young man of parts, Smith—excellent parts; and I saw at a glance that your discernment and judgment were good, and I employed you because I love to give an honest, sober, steady young man a start in life. I have had a 'hard row to weed,' Smith, in my young days—split rails, you know—worked on a flat-boat. I'm proud of it, Smith, because it shows conclusively that if I surmounted all these difficulties, and made my way up to the very highest political position in this glorious land, there is something more than common ability about me.

> 'Honor and shame from no condition rise;
> Act well your part, there all the honor lies.'

Never be ashamed, Smith, of honest labor. Some of the very greatest men of the world were necessitated to labor in their boyhood days—such as Ben Franklin, Dan Webster, Henry Clay, and in latter times, Abe Lincoln"—poking Smith in the side—"and Andy Johnson. Genius, Smith—genius is a great thing. You can't keep it down in this God-favored country. Hem it in, surround it with difficulties, yet it will rise by its own innate energy and power, and make itself known and felt. Smith, old boy, go ahead—press right on, you will make a man yet; and if you should ever get into a strait, call on 'Honest Old Abe.'" Smith received another punch in the side.

"Though I confess to some ambition," replied Winston, "yet I can never aspire to the dignified position to which your excellency's genius and talent unaided have raised you. Even if I should, I could never hope to gain as much glory and world-wide fame as you have reaped from this bloody war."

"Ah, Smith, this is indeed a bloody war—it's a big war—a much bigger one than I ever expected to see. I wish it was ended. I have tried hard to bring it to a peaceable and honorable close. I would have no objection to some other man's trying his hand at a job of pacification. But I do n't think I can offer any terms now. It would result in no good. The insurgent leader would listen to no conditions save a severance of the Union, and that we can not stand. My proclamation of last January stands open yet, and all the rebels who are in a condition to make a choice can avail themselves of its merciful provisions. I fear it will be necessary, in the course of time, to withdraw even that favorable proposition, and adopt a system of severity toward the insurgents which makes my heart bleed to think about it. But we must succeed in restoring the Union, even if the whole South has to be exterminated. We have lost too much now, and our debt is too large to acknowledge the independence of my old friend Jeff's little Confederacy. The South must pay the expense of this piece of luxury. I shall fight it out, and if go down I must, I will go with flying colors."

"I trust your excellency is sanguine of ultimate success?" said Winston.

"Well, I say so in all my messages and public documents; but it reminds me, or rather my experience reminds me, of a man whom I once knew out in Illinois." Here he related a long anecdote, which we have not time to record. "Well, now, Smith," continued the President, after a hearty laugh at the end of his story, "that's my case exactly. I'm sometimes up and sometimes down. I have moments of despondency, and I sometimes feel like letting the rebels go with their bantling of a government. But there's too much at stake to back down now. If, in the beginning of the war, or rather before it commenced, I had had any idea the insurgents would have made such a stubborn resistance, I believe I should have concluded that 'discretion is the better part of valor,' and have submitted to a dissolution of the Union. But, Lord! I can't do that now; my name would be handed down to eternal infamy. No, Smith, I *must* whip; I *will* whip them; and, mark it, Smith, I shall whip them!" and Smith received a most tremendous poke in his ribs.

"I suppose your excellency's plans are all well laid, and will no doubt succeed admirably."

"I rather think the 'secesh,' as our boys call them, will be taken by surprise next spring. They are expecting that I will sacrifice every thing for Richmond. I did want Richmond once, but there were too many 'sour grapes' growing in its vicinity, and I don't care so much about it now;" and he broke out into a horse-laugh. "But I will get Richmond yet; not by a direct attack, though; that is, I will not stake all upon the rebel capital. I shall first demolish the insurgent army in Georgia, cut off all communication from my friend Jeff's home, and Richmond will then die a natural death."

Mr. Lincoln was thus rattling away, giving all the details of the next campaign, when Secretary Seward stepped in. That wily old politician looked in astonishment at this unusual and undignified spectacle. At last he could endure no longer to hear the President's maudlin expose of state secrets.

"I hope, Mr. Lincoln," said the Secretary, in a tone indicating surprise and mortification, "that you have not forgotten who and what you are. If you have, I beg you not to attempt, in your merry moods, the discussion of questions of state policy, and especially the divulging of state secrets, which are in the keeping of the proper officers."

"Smith!" cried Mr. Lincoln, "tell me the name of the President of these United States!"

"The Hon. Abraham Lincoln, of course."

"Very well. Mr. Seward, Smith says *I* am President. If so, I ought to have sense enough to steer the old ship of state. *Ergo*, keep your advice to yourself. You remind me of the fable of the frog and the ox. The frog commenced swelling and puffing out in the vain attempt to attain to the size of the ox; the consequence was, he split wide open. Now, Bill Seward, for the application. I was elected, sir, to the important position of President of these United States, by the people of these United States, sir, and it is not presuming too much to say that they must have supposed the man of their choice to be endowed with sufficient capacity to transact the affairs of this great government. And I have yet to be made aware of the fact that they have appointed an adviser for my special benefit. People who try to swell up till they are as large as some others, may happen to meet with the fate of the unfortunate frog."

"I am not so certain," said Seward very coolly, "that the people of these United States did not commit a most flagrant blunder, and, instead of an enlightened, dignified statesman, stuck up into the chair of the chief magistracy a circus jester or a baboon."

"You remind me very much of a man out in Illinois," said Mr. Lincoln, seeming not to notice the last remark of Seward; and he related another long anecdote. "Now then," he continued, "for the application. William H. Seward should have been President of these United States, and not Abraham Lincoln. But come, Seward; come, old fellow, there's no use of hard words and ugly names," said the President suddenly changing his manner. "There ought to be no private quarrels among government officials while this great national difficulty is going on. Let us all put our shoulders to the wheel, and every man repair to his post. I am President of the United States; the free people, the sovereign people, saw proper to put me in that position. They must, of course, have thought that I was best qualified for that place. To you they have assigned a duty somewhat more humble than mine, but nevertheless a duty you ought to perform with fidelity. As for myself, I think I can paddle my own canoe without unasked assistance."

"And as for myself," said the Secretary, "you can have the pleasure of paddling your own canoe. I notify you that to-morrow I shall tender my resignation. You can now select my successor." The mortified official withdrew in supreme contempt and disgust.

"That's a sly old fox, Smith—a smooth, oily-tongued politician; but nevertheless a man of considerable talent, and one whose services could not be dispensed with at this time."

"What will your excellency do, then, when he offers his resignation?"

"Ha, ha, ha! I say, offer his resignation! He has no more idea of that than of flying to Richmond. He frequently threatens me in this way. He reminds me of one of Æsop's fables—that one about old Mercury, when he assumed a human form and visited the habitations of mortals to find out in what estimation he was held among men. That's just Seward's way of testing his popularity and importance. Some time I shall treat him just like the shop-keeper treated Mercury. Resign indeed! Why he'd resign half his soul first. Billy Seward is too fond of office for that. He is an old office-seeker, Smith. It has been the grand business of his life. He has studied the art day and night, and understands it to perfection; but still he is a man of powerful mind, and was once looked upon as the great leader, the exponent of the Republican party. It was thought at one time that he would be Mr. Buchanan's successor, but when the day arrived for the selection to be made it was discovered that honest old Abe Lincoln was best qualified;" and he nudged Smith again in the side. "Smith, I will tell you the fact, the people like *self-made* men the best—and why? Because they are generally *honest* men—men of nerve and energy of character. I tell you it takes a man of unusual and extraordinary intellectual capacity to walk right up, over the heads of ten thousand and one aspirants, into the upper story. There is always room in the upper story, as Mr. Webster says. Get into the upper story, Smith, get into the upper story, and you will always have plenty of room."

"No doubt your excellency has plenty of room in the upper story; for the present age is furnishing few men of distinction."

"That's so, Smith. The present age is rather scarce of great men. There are some, however, who deserve an honorable place in history. Even the rebels can point to a few who are worthy of the fame they have acquired. There is that old hoary-headed sinner, Bob Lee, for instance. He is the very life and soul of the rebellion. I would willingly give one hundred thousand men if he were on our side, or to get him on neutral ground. He has already been the death of twice that number. I look upon him as a much greater man than Jeff Davis; that is, he is a greater general than Jeff could be. Jeff, however, is not a man to be 'grinned at,' as somebody says. He has the stubbornness of a mule and the sullenness of an opossum. He would not make half as good a *diplomat*, though, as that crafty little dwarf of a Stephens. Jeff wants to get up a great character for honesty. To do this he has made exposures of the military conditions of affairs in the South, which I never would have made had I been in his place. He is too weak for that bold game. He ought to use more strategy. I guess I could beat Jeff at a game of chess, Smith. I am rather inclined to the opinion that I would be a great strategist, and sometimes I have half a notion to take the field. Grant is a poor strategist. He loses too many men, and accomplishes nothing by it. I believe I could crush the rebellion sooner by taking immediate command of the army."

"Doubtless your excellency would be a very distinguished chieftain. Your plans, as far as I have learned them, for the next campaign are indicative of an amazing knowledge of military science. I doubt not the rest are equally as good."

"I did not communicate the whole of my plans, Smith; and probably, as Seward said, it would be best not to do it."

"Your excellency is as good a judge of what is right and proper as Secretary Seward."

"That's so; but old Bill knew that something had loosened both ends of my tongue, and he did not want me to divulge too much."

"I think it was a most excellent hit," said the spy, who was now fearful that Mr. Lincoln would follow Seward's advice, "when you told him that he had not been appointed your special adviser. It nettled him considerably. If your excellency saw proper to talk with a friend about military matters, it seems to me he was rather presumptuous in meddling; and, if you should choose *now* to reveal the remainder of your deep-laid plans to one who is deeply interested in your excellency's success, I do not think it would be his business to dictate what you should say."

"That's so; but you must not speak disrespectfully of a government official, especially one high in office like Secretary Seward. However, you seem so deeply interested in my plans that I will disclose them to you at some future time, to show you how I can solve the problem of the rebellion."

"I assure you that no one could take greater interest in your excellency's solution of the knotty difficulty than I would. I should like so much to hear it while your excellency seems to be at leisure. If it is postponed, you may not have an hour or so to talk with me, and I should lose the benefit of your instruction."

"Not now, Smith, not now; I am not in a condition to do the problem justice. But I will tell you, I will beat Mr. Jeff at the game of war. He can never force Abraham Lincoln, the President of these United States, to recognize the independence of the so-called Confederate States. No, sir; not so long as I can find a soldier who has patriotism enough to fight. It is a sort of a Kilkenny cat fight; but, as General Grant says, our cat has the longest tail, and consequently we will worry out the insurgents in the course of time. They are becoming very tired of it now. Next year, I think, they will accept peace upon any terms. The only condition upon which I will ever agree to the reconstruction of the Union, is the abolition of slavery, and a voluntary return to the good old Union under such regulations as I shall prescribe. The majority of the rebels—that is, the 'small fry'—shall be pardoned at once, and the executive authority will be used with clemency and liberality toward the balance. But, then, somebody must suffer for this rebellion; somebody must pay the penalty of high treason; but it will be only those who got up the rebellion and have sustained it—who have kept the ball in motion since its commencement. After that the rebels must pay the whole of the war debt, and furnish homes to my destitute soldiers, who have covered themselves with glory and honor in this mighty struggle. Then the era of peace and prosperity will begin; our whole nation will be free, blacks and all; and in a hundred years no traces of this horrible contest can be found, except the blessed results which must grow out of it; and the name of Abraham Lincoln, as Billy Seward says, will be handed down to posterity, along with that of Wilberforce and others, as a benefactor of the human race. But I have been talking to you too long, Smith. I must go and chat Mrs. Lincoln awhile." And, without more ado, his excellency went staggering out of the room.

The spy, who saw that he could gain nothing further from the drunken official, made no attempt to detain him; but let him go, with the intention of *pumping* him at some future time, when his plans would be more fully matured. Our hero had gained much valuable information from the President, and had placed himself in a position to glean still more; and he resolved to wait with patience until Mr. Lincoln should be seized with another communicative humor. An unfortunate accident prevented the arrival of that time.

CHAPTER XXI.

"Thou art come to answer
A stony adversary, an inhuman wretch,
Incapable of pity, void and empty,
From every dram of mercy."

VERY unluckily for the success of Winston's plans General Robespierre arrived in Washington City two days after Mr. Lincoln's little "spree." It was now necessary for the spy to absent himself from all places in which he would be likely to meet with his former employer. This was done under pretense of sickness. The spy had, before this, taken precautions to be seen as little as possible in public; for he had seen Walter Hallam once or twice, though at a distance. But, nevertheless, he had been watched, as will be seen in the course of this chapter.

The very next day after Robespierre's arrival, he, Mr. Lincoln, and Secretary Seward were seated in secret conclave. The reader must have, incidentally to our story, the consultation of this interesting trio, or at least a portion of it.

"I suppose," said Robespierre, addressing himself to the President, "you received a communication from me a short time since in regard to a very particular subject—a darling scheme of mine?"

"I did; but I did not choose to give an answer upon my own responsibility without the advice of some of the cabinet officers. I have been so pressed for time by other weightier matters that I have not had an opportunity to reflect upon your proposition. I am doubtful of its success, though. I, however, showed your letter to Secretary Seward, and he may be prepared to express an opinion."

"The enterprise," said the crafty Secretary, with a shrug of the shoulders, "will be attended with considerable difficulty, and whether it should be successful or not, if the plot should ever be discovered, the Government of the United States would be eternally disgraced in the eyes of all nations. The truth is, we have already violated over half the recognized laws and usages of civilized warfare. If we had been at war with any other people but the southern rebels, our total disregard of international law, and our wholesale trespass upon the common rights of belligerents, would have aroused the wrath and indignation of combined Europe against us. From the fact, though, that the South holds on to the accursed institution of slavery, she is hated by nearly all enlightened nations; and, in consequence, our violations of the established usages of war have been connived at. But there must be a limit to our transgressions. The world will not always look on in silence. It has already extended to us unexpected charity. If we now stoop to such an act of national degradation as you desire, the cry of persecution and foul play may be raised against us, and the tide of sympathy may be turned in favor of our enemies. It will be rather a dangerous experiment, and I think we had better let it alone."

"My opinion, General Robespierre, is that Secretary Seward is right, and I agree with him."

"Gentlemen," was the reply of General Robespierre, "I admit that the opinion expressed by Secretary Seward, and concurred in by your excellency, is a strong argument against the scheme. The plot has its objections as well as its advantages. But the strongest argument in its favor is that the rebellion must be put down. If it can not be done in one way, it must be done in another. If we do not succeed, we are politically and socially damned. We will sink below a fifth-rate in the scale of nations, and will become a prey to the ambition of every petty kingdom of Europe. If we fail, our prosperity and our glory will be overwhelmed by a mountain of debt."

"That's so!" cried Lincoln, interrupting; "that's so. It is much easier, I find, to pay a large debt than a larger one, and if we fail our debt will certainly swell into the comparative degree of large." And with that his excellency laughed immoderately at this self-evident proposition, which no political economist ever advanced before. Secretary Seward could not repress a smile of contempt at the President's silly witticism.

"Yes," replied Robespierre, humoring Mr. Lincoln by joining in the laugh; "the debt will not stop at the comparative degree. It will scarcely be contained in a double superlative. You will also find, when it comes to be paid, it will be put in the *objective* case, too."

"It reminds me very much," said Lincoln, "of a case which once came before our court out in Illinois. A neighbor called in my office one day, who owed a *large* debt, with the prospect of its growing *larger;*" and his excellency related a long silly anecdote, which is not worth recording. Robespierre appeared to listen with due respect and attention, but Seward, who had heard Mr. Lincoln's jokes and jests thrice and four times repeated, kept his seat in indifference and *nonchalance*.

"I think," said Robespierre, resuming the original topic, after Mr. Lincoln had finished his story, "that if we could get rid of Jeff Davis, and some others whom I could name, we would easily crush the rebellion in a short space of time. But as long as Davis is President of the so-called Confederacy, we never can succeed. It will be necessary to resort to extreme measures."

"I am fearful," replied President Lincoln, "that I will have to adopt a different line of policy—a new and severe mode of treatment; and I can not but feel doubtful of the effect such a course will have. If Davis and others, as you say, General

Robespierre, were out of the way, I should be much more sanguine of success. I admit the cat ought to be belled; but who is to do it?"

"I thought you understood that very clearly. I proposed that I myself would 'bell the cat,' and I suggested the means by which I would accomplish my object."

"It seems to me, General Robespierre," said the Secretary, who had been silent all the time, "that you are pursuing rather a strange course. If you can put these men *hors du combat* as easily as you appear to think, why do you not carry out your darling scheme without the knowledge, much less the consent, of the government? I do not see that the sanction of the chief executive would be of the least assistance to you in the execution of your project."

"Nor I either," said Mr. Lincoln. "You remind me, General Robespierre, of the fox that got his tail cut off. If you get into a difficulty and lose your tail, you want others to be in a condition to lose their tails also."

"No, sir; not that. But if I undertake this dirty job, *money* will be necessary. I do not care any thing about the official sanction of the government. I only want to be furnished with money sufficient to accomplish the work."

"Or, in other words," replied Mr. Seward, with a significant smile, "you want to be well paid for your trouble."

"Of course I do. There are many risks to run."

"I should think so. There might be some little danger of having the poisoned chalice commended to your own lips. It will certainly be a two-handed game; and, if we commence it, the insurgents can practice it on a more extensive scale than we can. I confess I do not like the policy from several other considerations beside that of being continually in danger *myself*. I see from rebel papers that your plot has already been discovered, and you have already lost more of your own men than you have destroyed for the enemy. It is stated that you employed a man who could, without any difficulty, have administered to you a *dose of medicine* that might have done you more harm than good."

"It is true I did; but I shall be more on my guard in the future. I employed the fellow because he was a man of very prepossessing appearance, was well recommended by Fernando Wood and others of New York, and exactly suited me. I am certain that no one would have taken him, with those remarkable blue eyes, honest, open countenance, and smooth tongue, to have been a villain and a spy."

Mr. Lincoln started from his seat, and Seward cast upon him an inquisitive look, which seemed to say, "Have you not been in danger?"

"It may be," said the President, talking partly to himself and partly replying to the look of the Secretary; "it may be. He is recommended by the very same men General Robespierre mentioned, and suits the description. It must be the same."

As Winston's ill-luck would have it, at this very moment a man stepped hastily into the room, after rapping on the door, and handed a note to Mr. Lincoln. It read as follows:

His Excellency, President Lincoln:

I have just learned that you have a man in your employ by the name of Smith. I have seen the man, and I know him. His name is not Smith. Your excellency will doubtless be surprised to learn that this man is one of the most celebrated spies in the South. I have indubitable proofs of his rascality. I appeared against him once as a witness. He was condemned and sentenced to be hanged by a court-martial in Memphis, Tenn. I would see you personally in regard to this matter, but for reasons which I will explain as soon as the fellow is arrested. You would do well to have him arrested immediately. Lose not a single moment, or he may escape. If I do not substantiate the statement I have made, I will pay the forfeit.

Your obedient servant,

WALTER HALLAM, *Capt. & C.*

"My God!" cried Mr. Lincoln, as he thought of the peril he might have been in; "General Robespierre, I doubt not this is the very man you employed!" and he handed the note to Robespierre.

"I would advise you," said Robespierre, returning the document to Mr. Lincoln, who gave it to Seward, "not to lose any time. Have him arrested, and if he is the same man I will know him."

"I would suggest," said Mr. Seward, his lip curling with contempt, "that as Mr. Smith is now in possession of valuable state secrets, communicated by your excellency, his immediate arrest is of vital importance to the government."

Mr. Lincoln reddened in the face; then rose without speaking and sallied from the office. After the lapse of a short time his excellency returned.

"You have," said the Secretary, inquiringly, "given orders to have the fellow arrested?"

"I have ordered him to be brought before us, to see if he can be identified by General Robespierre."

"I fear your excellency did not act with your usual prudence in talking so freely to a comparative stranger."

"You remind me very much," replied the President, "of the boy who was learning to swim, and was in danger of drowning. A traveler passed by, and began to reproach the youth for his folly in getting himself into such a predicament. 'Get me out first,' said the boy, 'and then chide me.' So wait, Mr. Seward, until I get out of this difficulty, and then talk to me about imprudence, and so on."

"This circumstance," said the Secretary, "I hope, will convince you, General Robespierre, of the impracticability of your scheme. But if you are determined to attempt it, I do not wish to be a party to such a doubtful enterprise, in which, it seems to me, there would be as many chances against us as for us."

"Secretary Seward is right, General Robespierre. As for myself, I do not care about taking physic from the hands of rebels."

"Very well, then," replied the General, "if this great *desideratum* is to be outweighed by personal fears, I am sure I have not so much at stake, in case we are defeated, as you two have. I have been under the impression that either of you would be willing to risk his life in order to re-establish the Union. I regret to say I am mistaken; I thought very differently of you both."

"We might," replied Seward to this insinuation, with provoking coolness, "be more willing to engage in the project, if we expected to accumulate the snug little sum of ——, I say not how many thousand dollars."

"That's so, Seward. There is another consideration beside this. We would doubtless be in the condition of Æsop's geese and cranes. General Robespierre being *light*, might easily *fly* away, and leave us to hold the bag."

"As far as that is concerned," said Robespierre, now showing somewhat the ire of his disposition, "I have gone as far into danger as either one of you, and have stayed as long, too. No *living* man has ever called my bravery in question."

There is no telling what might have been the result of this strange quarrel in high life, had it not been interrupted. Secretary Seward was on the point of replying, when the guard, dispatched by order of Mr. Lincoln, appeared with Henry Winston. Their entrance at once put an end to the wrangle of the three officials. The spy stood before them with an air of innocence that puzzled the trio of officers.

"So ho!" exclaimed General Robespierre, "my friend Mr. Thompson, now metamorphosed into Smith, we have met again, under very interesting circumstances. When we last parted, I had no idea of seeing you again so soon; but I feel very happy in forming the acquaintance of Mr. Smith. This, sir," continued the General, turning to Mr. Lincoln, "is the same man. I would know him in any crowd."

"You seem to have been in the employ of General Robespierre?" said Mr. Lincoln to the spy.

"I was, sir."

"And what have you to say against his accusation?"

"I have heard no accusation, sir."

"He accuses you of murder."

"Then I have to say that General Robespierre had the brutality to have me arrested at midnight, sentenced me to be hanged before sunrise, without giving me an opportunity to speak a single word in my own defense."

"Is this true, General Robespierre?" asked Mr. Lincoln.

"Certainly it is. The proof was too plain to admit the shadow of a doubt as to his guilt. His letter to the rebel General Johnston, was ample testimony to justify my course."

"There was no proof that I ever wrote such a letter; and should I have done so, it ought not to be taken as evidence of disloyalty that I should have the humanity to notify even an enemy that the lawful and recognized implements of war would be ignored, and *poison* used in their stead. The common instincts of nature would have prompted me to such a course."

"You acknowledge your guilt, then?" inquired Robespierre.

"I did not acknowledge any such thing; but if this is what I have been arrested for"—turning to Mr. Lincoln—"I only ask a fair trial. I can establish my loyalty as clearly as General Robespierre can. After that I have a few charges to prefer against him, of which your excellency is ignorant. I will prove to your satisfaction that he is the most unmitigated swindler in the United States, and that his wicked plot to poison the rebel officers was only a scheme to raise money for his own use."

"Well, that beats all h—ll!" cried Robespierre, boiling with rage. "Why, d—n your infernal lying heart"——

"Hold, General Robespierre—hold!" cried Mr. Lincoln, interrupting. "Smith shall have a fair trial, and if he can prove his innocence, let him do it. But there is another witness yet, Smith, whom you will see presently."

Scarcely were the words uttered before Walter Hallam entered the office. He respectfully saluted the officers, and then awaited their commands in silence. Winston saw his chances of escape growing slim when his eyes fell upon this last personage, but he betrayed not his emotion by any outward indication of fear, but looked upon the new feature of the case with as much external calmness as any body in the room. After a brief silence, Mr. Lincoln spoke:

"Captain Hallam, do you know Mr. Smith," pointing to the spy, "or Mr. Thompson, or whoever he may be?"

"I do not know Mr. Smith or Thompson, but I have the honor to be acquainted with Mr. Henry Winston. I knew him before the war, and have met the gentleman several times since. I believe he was known in the United States navy by the name of Jones, and under that appellation sunk the celebrated gun-boat M——."

"Mr. Thompson," remarked General Robespierre, who had now cooled down, "can doubtless establish his loyalty. The beginning of his record is very bright and interesting indeed."

"He was," continued Hallam, "a soldier in the rebel army at the battle of Corinth, and was captured at that place by our forces. I next saw him on the 4th of July, dressed in the Federal uniform, and acting in all respects as a Union soldier A few weeks after that I saw him on the banks of the Mississippi, immediately after the gun-boat exploit. To-day I accidentally caught a glimpse of him, inquired his business here, and when I discovered he was in your employ, I thought it my duty to inform your excellency what a distinguished rebel you were entertaining."

"I also," added Robespierre, "lay to his account the murder of John Bowman and twelve other soldiers."

"These are very grave charges, Smith," said Mr. Lincoln; "very grave charges. If you are guilty, which I can not doubt at present, the penalty of your crime is death, and a very ignominious death, too—a dog's death."

"I trust," replied Winston, whose only object now was to gain time, in order to effect his escape, "I trust your excellency will give me an opportunity to refute the charges. It is a very easy matter in these troublous times to swear away the life of a personal enemy. The assertions of these two men are unsustained by any evidence; and I can prove very clearly that some of the crimes imputed to me are infamous slanders. The remainder can all be satisfactorily explained."

"If I were your excellency," said Robespierre, "I would not allow the impudent whelp five minutes to plead his case. I should have him hung as soon as the righteous deed could be performed."

"I would simply say to your excellency," remarked Hallam, "that Mr. Winston is a very slippery character. As I have already informed you, he was not long since convicted and sentenced, but made his escape. A spy, like he evidently is, deserves no time in which to prepare a defense. He will, in all likelihood, escape again."

"You did not talk thus boldly, Mr. Hallam"—and the deep-blue eye shot forth one of those peculiar glances, the meaning of which Walter well understood—"when I met you upon an equal footing. Should we so meet again, you will not dare to manifest so much impudence."

"Very well, sir," replied Hallam, "*when* we so meet, which is not likely to be in this life."

"Smith," said Mr. Lincoln, "I intend that you shall have a

fair trial—you shall have justice. Not even the rebels shall find ground of complaint. I believe, to be plain with you, you ought to be executed forthwith. I am perfectly satisfied of your guilt; but still we will go through the form of a trial for the sake of decency."

"If your excellency is to be one of the jurors, I fear a trial will do me very little good, when you condemn me before you hear my defense."

"You shall have a fair trial, Smith. If you can establish your innocence, I shall be glad of it. But from the testimony now before me, it will be an utter impossibility. Here are already two good witnesses against you—men of undoubted veracity. I can not see how you are to rebut their testimony. But, nevertheless, you shall have justice, if you want it."

"Gentlemen," said Seward, "who had been silent all this while, either because the golden eagles had made a soft place in his heart, or because he did not wish any thing to be said about the transaction, "the man is a *prisoner*, and it has always been considered very unkind, if no worse can be said of it, to trample upon and abuse a fallen enemy. The Constitution of the United States guarantees to every citizen the right of trial. Mr. Smith is a citizen, and is therefore entitled to all the privileges of a citizen. No man ought to judge, or make up his mind, before he hears both sides of the case. The evidence thus far is very strong against Smith, I will admit; but he says, if I understood him correctly, that he can prove his innocence and loyalty. Let him have the opportunity to do so, and if he fail, then let him suffer the penalty. Common justice demands this mode of procedure. I would suggest to your excellency that we are not the proper tribunal to try the case, and that, therefore, the prisoner be kept in custody until his trial can take place."

"Secretary Seward is right," said Mr. Lincoln. "Every citizen of the United States is entitled to a hearing, and he shall have it as long as I have the honor to preside over this justice-loving nation. I am a great lover of justice, as well as honesty, and you shall have it, Smith—you shall have it, even if it costs you your life; for, if you can not disprove the charges, you shall surely die. Mark that."

Then, turning to the guard, he ordered that the prisoner should be kept in close and strict confinement until the day of his trial should arrive.

"I shall follow you to your grave this time," said Hallam, in a low voice, as the prisoner was led away.

Winston was not long kept in suspense as to the result of his trial. As we have already remarked, the Yankees had a way of committing political murder rapidly in the dark days of 1861. In three days after his confinement a court-martial, by request, sat upon the case. Colonel Ellsworth was president of the court. This officer had been wounded in some of the numerous battles around Richmond to such a degree of severity as to disqualify him temporarily for active field service, and consequently had received from Mr. Lincoln the appointment to the office which he now filled. The spy's case was one which did not admit of much discussion. The evidence was all on one side. General Robespierre and Walter Hallam appeared as witnesses against the prisoner, and swore to all the facts within their knowledge, with which the reader is acquainted. It was in vain Winston pleaded that he had no opportunity to procure testimony.

"Where are your witnesses?" asked one of the court.

"Some are in Memphis and some are in New York. If I only had the opportunity, I could prove my loyalty."

"No doubt of that," remarked Robespierre. "He has sufficiently proved his loyalty, but to the so-called Confederacy. Any man who would risk himself in the place he has, his loyalty, I suppose, will not be questioned by any body."

"I should like to know," said the prisoner, "if General

Robespierre is prosecuting attorney or the judge for the court. If he is not, I shall call upon the court for protection. He is well aware that I can not now defend myself. If I could, I should chastise the base-born churl as he deserves. Under ordinary circumstances, I could not forget my own self-respect so far as even to bestow a thought upon a man like him, who has disgraced the insignia he wears, and who has brought a lasting reproach upon the cause he pretends to sustain with so much zeal."

"Order, sir!" exclaimed the presiding officer, sternly, interrupting him. "Such language will do you no good before this court. It will only make against you."

"I already know what your decision will be," answered the spy. "The court is a mere sham; I was condemned before I was arrested, upon the testimony of these two men, who both richly deserve the fate you will doom me to suffer. I saw from the outset the intention was merely to go through the form of a trial. I have been kept closely confined for three days, and not allowed to consult with any one who could be of the least assistance to me. Your minds were made up before I appeared before this mock tribunal. It is useless for me to attempt a defense before such a court as this. I shall therefore make none; so do your worst. You can but condemn me to death, and I am satisfied you will do that. You will be guilty of *legal* murder. But I tell you now the day will come when some of you"—and his eye rested on Hallam—"will repent this proceeding. That day *will* come. 'The race is not always to the swift, nor the battle to the strong.'"

"Does the prisoner," asked another member, "expect to frighten the court by the use of such enigmatical language? This body is one which can not be made to swerve from the path of duty by distant hints and threats of doubtful import. If this is all you have to say, your words are thrown away."

"My words," replied the spy, "would be thrown away, no matter what I might have to say. Nothing that I could now say would change your minds; and I scorn to bandy words with a court so trammeled and foresworn as this. I have no further defense to make."

The testimony being all now given in, the spy was remanded to prison, and more closely guarded. The court soon determined upon the case. The verdict was "*guilty*," and the prisoner was condemned to be hanged as a spy. The proceedings and sentence in the case were approved by Mr. Lincoln, and the following Friday named by him as the day when the execution would take place. Poor Winston was at once cast into a loathsome cell, set apart for convicted criminals, where he was to remain until he should die—a martyr to the cause of independence.

CHAPTER XXII.

"The love that is kept in the beauty of trust
Can not pass like the foam from the seas,
Or a mark that the finger hath traced in the dust,
When 't is swept by the breath of the breeze."

THE evening following the day of the spy's trial, Colonel Ellsworth called upon Emily Burrell, in accordance with the proposition he had made, and to which Emily agreed. She was in her room, and promptly responded to the Colonel's card.

"I am happy to find you looking so much better than you did at the party," said the Colonel, after the customary salutation, and some uninteresting conversation in regard to city matters. "I hope your health is improving."

"I fear not," replied Emily.

"I am sorry, Miss Burrell, that you look upon yours as such a hopeless case. I fear your malady grows worse by your unwise determination to exclude yourself from society, and your resolution to cherish your feelings of melancholy. The mind exercises a vast influence over the powers of the body; in fact, the recovery from the ills that 'flesh is heir to' very frequently depends upon our resolution not to yield to the griping hand of disease. It is known that when a patient once makes up his mind to die, and resolves that he will not live, there is no power in the healing art to save him. I have no doubt we often sow the seeds of disease and death in the constitution by continually reflecting upon and grieving over the disappointments inseparable from human life. It is the part of philosophy and wisdom to forget ills to which no remedy can be applied."

"It is very easy to talk, Colonel Ellsworth, and to preach up philosophy and fine theories, when one is in perfect health, and has never felt the throes of mental pain. If all the various and diverse theories in the world which have been advanced could only be put in practice, this earth would indeed be a paradise. I am very fond of the 'art sublime,' Colonel, and, if not disagreeable, I will reply to you in poetic language:

> 'It may be that I shall forget my grief;
>   It may be time has good in store for me;
>   It may be that my heart will find relief
>   From sources now unknown. Futurity
> May bear within its folds some hidden spring,
>   From which will issue blessed streams; and yet,
> Whate'er of joy the coming year may bring,
>   The past—the past—*I never can forget.*'"

"I do not often quote poetry, Miss Burrell, but I will condemn you by the art of which you are so fond:

> 'It is not well to brood
> Thus darkly o'er the cares that swell
> Life's current to a flood.
> As brooks, and torrents, rivers, all
> Increase the gulf in which they fall,
> Such thoughts, by gathering up the rills
> Of lesser griefs, spread real ills,
> And with their gloomy shades conceal
> The landmarks Hope would else reveal.'"

"Have you," asked the Colonel, after a short silence, "have you bestowed a thought on the subject upon which we conversed at the party?"

"Your question is a very indefinite one," Emily replied. "If I recollect aright, we talked upon several different subjects."

"I mean that which lies nearest my heart—my own deep and lasting love for you."

"Colonel Ellsworth," she replied, while a shade of vexation flitted across her brow, "I requested you never to mention this to me again. I thought I was sufficiently explicit upon this point, and I told you distinctly that I could never be interested in such a topic. You will forfeit my respect and esteem if you continue thus to annoy me with such vain and useless importunities."

"You are cruel, Miss Burrell, cruel. I have endured an age of torture since I last saw you. The fervor with which I worship you is more than the human heart can bear, if it is to continue long. I have felt so sensibly the utter impossibility of living without you, that I have removed all the obstacles I could, which you mentioned as objections to my suit. I will abandon all—country, friends, parents—all, to secure your love. If my position in the Federal army is an objection, I will resign it. If the North suit you not, we will leave it; we will go to the South. I will change my principles; and, if you insist on it, I will even recant so far as to take up arms against the land of my nativity. O," added the officer, with much feeling, "reject not the terrible sacrifice with scorn and contempt. At least be merciful."

Emily was sensibly affected by the Colonel's earnestness and his evident suffering. She could now feel the full force of that beautiful line of Virgil, uttered by Dido, when shipwrecked. Æneas sought shelter in the Tyrian land—'*Non ignara mali miseris succurrese disco.*' She therefore replied, in a softened, melancholy tone of voice:

"I am not one, Colonel Ellsworth, to treat with levity the offering of a bruised and bleeding heart. I appreciate very highly the compliment implied in the great sacrifice you would make. But were you to make such a sacrifice of principle and honor, even I would lose my respect for your manhood, and could not but regard you as destitute of moral sentiment. Every man's honor should be sacred, and he should die rather than be false to himself, his country, and his God. Beside, Colonel, I fear the sacrifice would not be made from true principle, or a conviction of error. Desertion of one's native country is bad enough, but when done through mercenary motives, or to gain some selfish end, it becomes disgraceful and dishonorable. You would not be respected in the South, for southerners are like Philip, and while they 'love the treason, they hate the traitor.' Your whole life afterward would be wretched and miserable. Were I to pursue the course suggested by you, and comply with your wishes, you would, in a very short time, be left alone; and you would regret, through your remaining days, that you sacrificed your principles, abandoned your country, for a pale, sickly girl, whose wretched existence could not be prolonged to compensate your loss of honor. Where, then, could you find any to pity you? You would be a traitor in the North and a deserter in the South. No, no, Colonel, I could never permit you to bring eternal disgrace upon yourself, and blight all your blooming hopes for a withered flower. Leave me alone in my wretchedness and solitude. Life possesses not a single charm for me. I am not worthy of the great sacrifice you propose to make. You have talents; you have ambition; and you can make a name for yourself which may win the affection of the proudest lady in the land. Go, then, seek out some one who can stimulate you in the path of honor and fame; who can add to your glory and your luster by her charms and her beauty; and who will and who can rejoice in the proud laurels blooming on your brow."

"Talk not in this style to me, Miss Burrell. Your words enter my heart like sharp-pointed daggers.

> 'What is honor? a silly, vain opinion,
> That hangs but on the rabble's idle breath:
> For them we court it, yet by them 'tis scorn'd.'

I value happiness more than honor. What to me is the vain, silly praise of the world, when my heart is barren and desolate? I care not for the vain applause of a thoughtless multitude, whose admiration is often bestowed without reflection, and whose censure is given without justice. You mistake my character if you suppose me to be one of those who delight in the jars and discords of political life, or who seek after the fleeting bubbles of the *beau-monde*. I want a heart to love and adore. I want a companion, a congenial spirit, whose emotions respond to those of my own soul and heart. I want a *guardian angel*, to purify the depravities of human nature; to restrain the evil propensities of my disposition; to elevate my thoughts above the hollow schemes and pursuits of this sinful globe, and thus foretaste the joys of eternity. To possess such a heart, I would defy the scorn and hate of twenty generations of men, and smile at the condemnation of a world. I would not so much as bestow a thought upon the united frowns and reproaches of North and South. To own a heart like yours, for the space of a month even, I would renounce all claims upon human society. Life, Miss Burrell, is but a span—a very brief span; and it matters not to me in what clime I may dwell, or among what races of men my lot may be cast, if only the intense longings of this heart can be quelled, and that aching void which demands the communication of soul with soul can be filled. What, though, as you will have it, you should be taken from me? Will our connection cease here? I trust I have a higher, holier, nobler aim in view. Think you not I could watch over you with love and tenderness in your sleep? Our connection as human beings might, as you anticipate, cease, but that of the immortal soul, never. If the result should be as you predict, I would daily visit the spot whereon you should repose, and look far beyond the skies, by the aid of religious faith, to the realms of eternal light, and hold communication with the soul of one who had been an angel on earth. I would thus pass on through the brief period allotted to human life, indifferent to the taunts of men till we would be reunited in that bright world in which sorrow and grief can never enter. The prospect is, therefore, not so gloomy as you picture it, but is much more inviting than the other you have pointed out. Do not, then, send me away a disappointed wretch, to mourn through my whole life, and to regret that I ever lived."

"If you should mourn thus, Colonel Ellsworth, you will be rather inconsistent, and will fail to practice the precepts you preach to others. I shall remind you of your poetic quotation, and tell you to apply it to your own case. I shall advise you," she continued, with a mournful smile, "to call to your aid some of that consoling philosophy that you recommended to me."

"Do not attempt thus to turn my love into ridicule, and treat my protestations of fidelity with contempt," said Colonel Ellsworth.

"'Say that you love me not, but say not so
In bitterness: the common executioner,
Whose heart the accustomed sight of death makes hard,
Falls not the ax upon the humbled neck
But first begs pardon.'

I can endure any thing better than the contempt and mockery of her whose life I would lay down my own to save."

"You misunderstand me, Colonel Ellsworth, if you suppose it my intention to make light of your emotions. I have suffered too much myself to give pain to others, and especially to those who may be passing through the ordeal of fire which has prostrated my hopes and blighted my affections. But it is useless to dwell upon this unpleasant topic. I tell you I can never love again, and you certainly would not desire me to perjure myself before the altar. You ought not to wish to link your destiny with one who could never fill the position of 'guardian angel' you have described."

"The idea of loving but once is rather romantic and fanciful, and I would willingly risk that."

"Then, Colonel, practice your doctrine. If it be but a romantic idea, go find some one else, who can listen with eagerness to your burning words, and respond to your feelings. You can love again; as for me, *I shall never love but once;* and to convince you, look at this." She drew forth a small miniature, and handed it to the officer. He looked upon it earnestly, with an expression of wonder, and then suddenly started, in seeming surprise. He was on the point of speaking, but Emily continued her remarks, and he remained silent: "I told you at the party, in answer to your inquiry, that I had loved, and I described my *beau-ideal* at your request. That miniature is an exact representation of the features of him to whom I gave my heart years ago. You asked me where he was? I know not; but I love none the less. He may live for aught I know; but if he be dead, then are my affections buried in his grave. And now, Colonel, after this brief but to me sad history, ask me no more to change my purpose, but leave me wedded to my sorrow."

"This picture," remarked the officer thoughtfully, "bears a striking resemblance to the features of a prisoner who was tried to-day by a court-martial. When I first saw him, I thought of the description you gave at the party. This, however, can not be the person in whom you are interested, for he is a celebrated spy, and was convicted, and is to be hanged next Friday."

Emily slightly started.

"I never saw a bolder looking man in my life, and one of such prepossessing appearance. He defied the court to the last, and, I understand, heard his sentence with the stoicism of a heathen philosopher. I feel extremely sorry for the young man, who must yield up his life in the prime of manhood, and die a dishonorable death. But he was guilty of the charges preferred, and attempted no defense. It was useless, because the testimony was furnished by two very creditable witnesses—General Robespierre and Captain Hallam. But I fear you are *ill*, Miss Burrell," said the officer, breaking off in surprise, as he noticed the deathly pallor of Emily's countenance. She was looking at the Colonel with a fixed, agonizing look of inquiry, which was painful to behold. It was in vain she essayed to speak. Her words died on her tongue. "You *are* ill, Miss Burrell," exclaimed the officer, in painful embarrassment; "let me ring for assistance."

"No, no," she cried, partially shaking off the death-like stupor; "it will leave me in a moment. Continue your story; tell me the name of this unfortunate southron," she added, with as much indifference as she could assume.

"He seems to have been known by several names," said the Colonel, after a brief pause, in which he appeared to be troubled with an embarrassing thought. "He has passed himself off as Smith, Thompson, Jones, and probably Brown. But his true name, as Captain Hallam testified, is Henry Winston."

Emily did not faint, or go into hysterics, as some would have expected. But her bloodless face turned a shade paler, and her limbs slightly quivered with an imperceptible shudder. She felt for an instant a sense of blindness; her head became dizzy; a sickening sensation crept over her; and she sat as fixed and immovable as a statue of brass. Colonel Ellsworth gazed at her with an expression of profound sympathy.

"Miss Burrell, you are ill."

"I do feel unwell," replied Emily, in a feeble, choking voice. "If you will excuse me I will retire."

With a painful effort she slowly rose from her seat, bade the officer good evening, and sought the solitude of her own chamber. After her departure, Colonel Ellsworth sat a few moments in deep abstraction; then, suddenly rising, he muttered to himself, "I thought so. I thought so;" hastily walked out into the streets, and wended his way homeward. "I will," thought the officer, as he was moving along the street; "I will lay down this life before I betray her. She can not, though, be an accomplice. Her ignorance of his whereabouts and her palpable suffering preclude the idea. It is her lover; it *must* be. O heaven!" he cried, in agony, "I would exchange places with him this night." He was not the only miserable being in Washington that night.

Poor Emily, as soon as she left her visitor, went reeling into her room. "God of truth!" she cried, "desert me not in this hour of trial!" She sank down into a chair by an open window. A gentle breeze came stealing into the chamber, and played with the raven locks of the drooping head. The noiseless moonbeams danced, in the sheen of heavenly splendor, around the bowed form; but the stricken child of sorrow looked as one dead to the beauties of nature and art. The broad blue sky stretched out its wide canopy, glittering with myriads of twinkling stars that peeped forth from their cerulean height in unearthly brightness, but the grief-worn spirit felt not the cheering influence of the magnificent scene. The sweet, soft tones of a musical band, not far distant, came trembling upon a sighing zephyr, but the ear heard it not. But, one by one, these beauties of the night began to fade away. The city was buried in profound silence, and its inhabitants had yielded to the healthful sway of Morpheus. The moon rolled on, up to its zenith; then went, marching in solemn grandeur, its downward track behind the western hills. The stars disappeared, one after another, as if wearied by their long nightly vigil. But the bowed form in the open window moved not.

> "At last the golden oriental gate
> Of greatest heaven 'gan to open fair;
> And Phœbus, fresh as bridegroom to his mate,
> Came dancing forth, shaking his dewy hair,
> And hurl'd his glist'ning beams through gloomy air."

Morning dawned. "Night's swift dragons cut the clouds full fast, and ghosts went trooping home, here and there, to church-yards." The sun rose above the eastern horizon, and some of his straggling rays stole in at the window and seized the disheveled locks of Emily's head. The city was rife with confusion and the hum of business, but the mourner rose not.

When breakfast was dispatched, and Emily still had not appeared, Colonel Burrell left the table, and knocked at his sister's chamber door; but there was no answer. Opening the door, he entered, and gazed in surprise at the unusual spectacle. Just before day, Emily, completely exhausted, had fallen into an uneasy slumber. She looked the very picture of death, and might have been mistaken for a corpse had not the labored breathing of the sleeper told that she lived. Her lips were slightly apart, and she murmured distinctly, "God, save him!" Colonel Burrell stood looking on, and, listening a few moments, touched her face. Emily started up, and gazed around with a wild stare.

"Emily," said the brother, looking at the smooth, unruffled bed, "what means this? You have sat up the whole night."

"I am so glad you have come, brother. I had such an ugly, frightful dream. But sit down; I want to talk with you. I want your advice; and I want you to do me a favor."

"Not until you have eaten something; then I will listen to you."

The Colonel rang for a servant, and ordered Emily's breakfast to be brought up to her room. She rose, laved her face, and brushed back her tangled hair; she then sat down, and dispatched a very small portion of the breakfast, which had been brought up, in a few moments. Colonel Burrell looked on in sorrowful silence. She rose, and the waiter was carried away.

"You have eaten scarcely any thing," remarked the Colonel,

as she seated herself by his side; "but never mind; tell me what is the matter. Why did you not sleep last night?"

She fixed her large lustrous eyes upon his face.

"You heard of the trial yesterday, brother?"

"No, I did not. What trial?"

"The trial of Henry Winston."

"Where—in this city?"

"Yes; he has been hunted down, tried, and condemned to die."

"And the favor you have to ask relates to him?"

"It does."

"I feared so. Emily, I wish to God you had never seen this man," said the Colonel, with an angry frown.

"O, brother," she said, while her eyes moistened with tears, "look not thus darkly upon me. I wish it as much as you do. I wish I had never been born. O, my God! I wish I was dead!" And she buried her face in her brother's breast.

This was more than the Colonel could endure. The dark frown quickly passed away, and was succeeded by an expression of tender sympathy. Colonel Burrell was not the first man that had ever felt the power of a tear "in woman's eye, the unanswerable tear," that appeals to the heart more strongly than words—the tear

> "Which melts me to the softness of a woman,
> And shakes my best resolves."

"Emily, my poor little sister, I did not mean to be angry with you. I only made the wish because I thought it would have been best for you. This man has been the bane of your life, and you have sacrificed your happiness for an eccentric lover. On his account you have rejected the most brilliant match in the city. Colonel Ellsworth is a man of acknowledged worth, of superior education, and of boundless wealth, and loves you to madness. Why, then, have you cast such a man aside for a rebel spy who is awaiting sentence of death?"

"Because," she replied, rising up, "I do not love him."

"But you might learn to love him. I wish you would give up this silly notion of your girlhood, and act like a grown woman. Colonel Ellsworth is all that you could desire, and will make you a good husband. There is not another lady in Washington City who would refuse such an offer."

"Why should I marry, brother, if I do not wish to?"

"Because it will be best for you. I can not always be with you; and I want you to have a protector."

"I feel that I will not be with you long, brother James. I shall not trouble you a great while longer."

"I did not mean that," quickly interrupted the Colonel— "I did not mean that. All the trouble you are to me is a pleasure. But the day may come when we will have to separate; then I want you to be in somebody's hands in whom you can with safety confide. As a matter of course, you can now never *see* this man Winston, much less marry him."

"But, brother, *you* can see him, and I may see him."

Colonel Burrell looked earnestly into her face, as if he did not understand her words.

"What mean you by that, Emily?"

"I mean that I want you to visit the man whom you call a rebel spy this very day. If he still loves me, I shall prove true even unto death. If not, then I will marry whom you will."

"I anticipated this," said Colonel Burrell; "but let me ask if you have considered the impropriety of such a thing?"

"I see no impropriety in your visiting a prisoner."

"No, not if the affair should end with that; but then you propose that you will visit him afterward."

"I did not say so. I want you to find out the relation which subsisted between him and Carrie Hallam. After that, I will tell you what I shall do."

"And what is that, pray?"

"I scarcely know myself; but I want to know this for my own satisfaction. I can not die content without it. An effort ought to be made to save him, if possible. You can find out whether there is any chance to procure his pardon."

"Do not begin to talk that way," said the Colonel, shaking his head. "You will get us both into a difficulty."

"Brother, we, or at least I do, owe Mr. Winston a debt of gratitude. The time has now come when I can be something more than grateful. I do not wish this opportunity to pass away without an effort on my part to liquidate the obligation."

"I am willing to pay the amount I promised, and consider the debt discharged. I do not consider myself, nor you either, under any obligations to be forever attempting to get the fellow out of his scrapes. I will pay him, and be even."

"Gold to one in his situation can be of but little use now. He needs something more substantial than that."

"What, in the name of God, do you expect me to do? It is not to be supposed that I can release the man. Even if I could, I do not know that I would be doing right to do so. He is evidently a dangerous character to our cause. What would be thought of me in Washington City and elsewhere were I to ask the pardon of one who has made himself a notorious spy? My loyalty to the government would be at once suspected; because I have no reason whatever upon which to base a petition for his release. It might become an ugly piece of business, and a more serious affair than you imagine. I will not undertake it."

"You can at least find out for what he has been condemned. I shall not ask you to do any thing inconsistent with your position. As far as I am concerned, individually, I care not for the opinion of Washington City, even of all Yankeedom. Could I do any thing for the Confederate States by assisting even the humblest soldier in the southern army, I would do it.

if the act should forever degrade me in the estimation of the whole Yankee nation. God knows I *hate* them all—the vile, thieving set that is now plundering the state in which we were born. O God, forgive me! but if I had the power I would set fire to the North, even if the bones of every man, woman, and child should add fuel to the flames. Methinks I could laugh at their wild shrieks, as they would come howling and screaming through the fire. I could be like old Nero, who fiddled over the ruins of burning Rome."

"My God! Emily, you are mad—you are deranged!" cried Colonel Burrell, looking at her in terror and alarm.

"No more mad than you are, brother. I tell you," she continued, calmly, "if I had the power, I would blow up the whole North, and scatter its disgraced soil throughout the universe. I would, if I could, Samson-like, tear down its foundations, if I should be buried beneath its ruins."

"This is sheer nonsense, sister. You do not know what you are talking about."

"Let us change the subject, then, brother. Will you grant my request? I have sacrificed something for you, James. I never did want to leave the South, but I came here merely because you desired it. I think, therefore, you might do me this little favor. You will not have to repeat. The poor prisoner will soon be *murdered*. They will put him to death, and I will soon follow him down to the tomb."

She burst into another flood of tears, which overthrew the Colonel's resolution. Woman triumphed, and Colonel Burrell had to yield.

"Hush, sister, hush. I will do almost any thing if you will stop crying. I can not stand your tears. I will go and see Winston; but you must excuse me after that. What must I say to him? What is it you want?"

"May God bless you, brother, for this kindness," she said, wiping away her tears. "I want you to find out why he left

Kentucky so abruptly; whether he ever loved Miss Hallam; and if he is—is true to me. That is all."

Colonel Burrell then left the apartment, went to the proper officer, and procured a pass, then visited the prisoner. Upon his return, several hours afterward, during which time Emily was in a dreadful state of suspense, he related to her substantially what will be found in the next chapter.

CHAPTER XXIII.

"It is a noble constancy you show
To this afflicted house: that not like others,
The friends of season, you do follow fortune,
And in the winter of their fate forsake
The place whose glories warmed them."

WHEN Colonel Burrell, in obedience to the request of his sister, visited the prison, he found Henry Winston in a dark stone cell. It was several seconds before the Colonel's eyes were sufficiently accustomed to the darkness to distinguish objects. As soon, however, as it was practicable to use the organs of sight, he saw in one corner a pile of straw, which served the prisoner as a bed. Near by was a stone pitcher, filled with water, and a tin cup. A rugged stool occupied a conspicuous position near the center of this gloomy abode, set apart exclusively for those who were under sentence of death. These were all the articles of furniture of which those doomed to occupy the cell were deemed worthy. The appearance of the apartment was calculated to remind one of the dismal regions of Pluto. The reader need not be told that this wretched cell had been very frequently applied to the purpose for which it was intended since the commencement of the bloody war of 1861. In fact, hardly would one unfortunate victim to the fury and fanaticism engendered by the hell-born spirit of terror's reign vacate this receptacle of felony, before its creaking door would close in upon another, sentenced to expiate his real or supposed crime upon the gibbet. Sometimes half a dozen would occupy it at once. Many names, traced by hands which were now cold in death, could be plainly seen upon the cold gray walls. A little apart from the long black list the name of Henry S. Winston appeared, in a bold hand, and immediately under it those beautiful lines of Goldsmith:

> "The wretch, condemned with life to part,
>   Still, still on hope relies;
> And every pang that rends the heart
>   Bids expectation rise.
> Hope, like the glimmering taper's light,
>   Adorns and cheers the way;
> And still, as darker grows the night,
>   Emits a brighter ray."

But to what hope the spy had reference, in his present condition, is difficult to imagine, unless it was to that bright beam of comfort which lights up the Christian soul in the "valley and shadow of death."

When Colonel Burrell entered the cell, Winston seemed not to have heard the heavy door that harshly grated on its strong iron hinges, as it opened and shut. He was sitting upon the stool, with his back to the entrance, and held open before him a large, red-bound book, amid the pages of which he appeared to be totally deaf to all external sounds. It might be supposed that a prisoner, condemned to die in the course of a very few days and nights, would certainly devote his last moments to the study of Holy Writ. But such was not the case. The book contained only the lives of celebrated robbers, who had been distinguished for shrewdness in the annals of crime. It is not known whether Winston made special arrangements to procure such a work, or whether it had been accidentally left, or because no other disposition could be made of it by his predecessors, who, too hardened by vice to think of the eternal world, had pleased fancy in their last hours by living in imagination with notorious highwaymen. We know not what consolation could be derived from such a collection of facts, especially by a man of Winston's intellectual capacity, refined sensibility, and religious principles. It may be that he found the book in his bed of straw, opened it, and became deeply interested before he was aware of it. At all events, Colonel Burrell stood still for several moments, and surveyed the apartment and its occupant without speaking. At last, seeing that the spy was unaware of his presence, he advanced and broke the gloomy silence.

"You are so highly entertained with your book, Mr. Winston, that you do not notice the entrance of an old acquaintance."

The spy started in surprise at the voice, which seemed to come from the pages of the book; then rose from his seat, cast a glance at the face of the speaker, and instantly recognized the man whose presence was calculated to revive so many melancholy recollections and sorrowful associations.

"I have good reason to know you," answered the spy, throwing the book aside and extending his hand with a mournful smile; "but, strange to say, I have never yet learned your name."

"Indeed!" said the officer; and then added, after a brief pause: "My name is James Burrell."

"You are, then, related to Miss Emily Burrell, I presume?" said the prisoner, in a tone of anxious inquiry.

"She is my sister."

"Your sister!" exclaimed the prisoner, with an expression of countenance that baffled description. "Great God! how *terribly* I have been deceived!"

The two men looked at each other in mutual embarrassment.

"Excuse my want of politeness," at last said Winston, noticing that the officer used a crutch; and placing near to him the solitary stool. "This is the only convenience with which I have been furnished, in the way of chairs."

The Colonel sat down, and the spy placed himself on his bed, and then continued:

"You need not wonder at my surprise, when I inform you that I had the stupidity to take you for your sister's husband."

"I am aware," replied the officer, "that you have been laboring under some kind of a delusion, and I supposed it was of this character when you left us so suddenly on the banks of the Mississippi."

"No doubt you have thought my conduct very strange in some respects, but I trust this delusion, as you well name it, will be a sufficient explanation; for it has been a delusion fatal to me."

"It is no secret to me, Mr. Winston, that you were once engaged to my sister; and I do not see, under the circumstances, that I should conceal the fact that she has suffered—yea, still suffers—from what she conceived to be a disappointment in the days of her girlhood. I never have believed that you wantonly trifled with her affections; but, nevertheless, Emily was considerably troubled by a letter addressed to you and a miniature found upon your person by Captain Hallam, when you were supposed to be dead."

"I do not recollect," replied the spy, "of having had any letter about me at the time to which you allude. If I had a miniature, it was that of Miss Hallam."

"Just so," replied Colonel Burrell. "There was also a letter, as I said, addressed to you by that young lady, and which seems to have embittered Walter Hallam against you ever since that time. And I must say, that at the time, and under the circumstances, and owing to the strange language of the letter, it placed your character in a very unenviable light."

"Is it possible," asked the spy, "that Miss Hallam's own family never heard of the unfortunate circumstances relating to her, which was published by several newspapers when it occurred?"

"Walter, at least, seems never to have heard it. I am,

however, too fast. He may have heard it, for aught I know to the contrary. I never knew much about my cousin Carrie's history, and should be glad to hear the circumstance to which you allude, especially since it seems to be connected with the affair you are explaining."

"Miss Hallam's history," replied the spy, "is rather a sad one, and sounds more like romance than reality; but, if you wish to hear it, I will relate it in a few words."

The spy, after seating himself more comfortably on the pile of straw, related the story as follows:

"I graduated in the University of Mississippi. When I first entered that institution, I boarded at a private house, with a gentleman who had a son in my class. The gentleman's son and myself roomed together, studied together, and in a short time we were as intimate as David and Jonathan. In fact, we called each other David and Jonathan, as our names happened to be the same. For three years we thus lived, until we were in the senior class; but at the end of the senior scholastic year the unfortunate occurrence transpired that deprived me of that friend forever.

"Not more than a mile from the University was a female college. Miss Hallam, from Kentucky, was a student in that seminary. She was a young lady of great personal beauty, but, begging your pardon, rather destitute of that which would recommend her to a man of solid intellect, such as my friend was. In fact, I never could see the attraction which so completely drew forth the affections of his noble heart. I never met with two characters in my life, more opposite. He was sober, serious, and thoughtful; she was gay, volatile, and seemed to think no more than if she had been a child. He was a hard student, was plain in his dress, and heartily despised the common frivolities of fashion; she, on the contrary, rarely made an effort of mind, or, if she did, it was in regard to her apparel, or some other frippery of fashionable life. I never could account for his fascination, save upon the phrenological principle that we are disposed to choose our opposites. I once presumed so far upon our great friendship and intimacy as to ask him what he discovered so peculiarly attractive in Miss Hallam; but he laughingly replied in three lines of Spencer:

> "'Lover's eyes more sharply-sighted be
> Than other men's; and in dear love's delight
> See more than any other eyes can see.'"

"Miss Hallam was in the habit of visiting my friend David's (as I shall still call him) sister. David at first was rather shy, but his timidity, under the gay attacks of the young lady, gradually wore away, and his feelings soon ripened into a warm friendship; next changed into love; and finally settled down into a passion of romantic madness. The consequence of this unfortunate attachment was an engagement of marriage between the two, to be consummated in a few months after their graduation.

"Time rolled on, and commencement-day arrived. The exercises on this occasion were unusually interesting, and were witnessed by the largest audience that ever gathered in the little village of Oxford. My friend was one of the orators of the day; and he had selected a subject which he handled with masterly skill. It was known that he was a good speaker, and when he arose expectation was on the tip-toe. For twenty minutes he delivered his composition with a power and a pathos that held the vast assembly perfectly spellbound. He surpassed even himself, and it seemed that the goddess of eloquence had seated herself upon his lips, and directed his burning words into the inmost recesses of every heart and soul under the influence of his powerful but musical voice. But all at once he came to a dead halt, in the middle of a beautiful and thrilling peroration. I thought the composition had escaped his memory. His prompter very readily repeated the first two or three words of the next sentence. His gaze was intently fixed upon some one in the back part of the chapel. I involuntarily cast my eyes in the direction in which he was looking, and there beheld Miss Hallam engaged in what appeared to be a very interesting conversation with a student of dissipated habits and notoriously immoral principles. How long she had been thus engaged, or how long my friend had seen her *tete-a-tete*, I know not; but when he took up the words from his prompter, and proceeded with his speech, it was in such a changed voice and awkward manner, the contrast with his previous tone and graceful gesticulation was so great, that the whole house was filled with surprise and disappointment. He proceeded thus, in this strange, unnatural, and uncouth manner, to the end of his oration, and when he took his seat, not a single plaudit was heard. I was glad, for his sake, that the piece was finished. He sat down apparently deeply mortified and disappointed.

"When he first saw Miss Hallam thus interestingly engaged with a young man for whom he had no respect, the thought must have suddenly flashed over his mind that, while every other person in the house was completely absorbed in his speech, she alone was utterly indifferent to his mighty effort. The thought staggered him, and so worked upon his feelings that he entirely lost control of himself, and proceeded with the remainder of his speech like a bird taught to pronounce phrases and sentences, one word of which he does not understand. The young lady appeared not to be aware of the impropriety of her conduct, and her want of respect for her intended husband; for when the exhibition was ended, and the audience was dispersing, I noticed her manifestation of surprise and vexation at my friend, who, under the influence of a fit of jealousy and disappointment, passed out of the chapel without taking the least notice of Miss Hallam. That evening his dejection and melancholy were so great that I ventured to say, 'She is unworthy of you; banish all thought of such a fickle creature from your mind, and give your love to some other who can appreciate your talent and return your affection.'

"He seemed vexed that I should be aware of his mortification, and he replied, with an angry flush of the countenance: 'He who says she loves me not *lies* in his foul throat, and I cast it in his teeth. By Jove! she *does* love me; and there are some people who would do well to attend to their own affairs, and let me manage mine. I have asked nobody's advice, and I think it is the height of impoliteness and impudence to thrust one's opinion even upon a friend, when it is unasked and undesired.' I choked down my feelings of anger aroused by this cutting reply, as I saw plainly my friend was not himself. I did not venture to return an answer, but instantly left him alone, intending to talk with him when his angry mood should wear off.

"That night I attended the ball given in honor of the graduating class. A ball of this kind is given annually, at each commencement, in compliment to those who were about to quit the scenes of the college curriculum, and enter upon the trying realities of life. My friend, with a dark, murky countenance, entered the hall, in which there was assembled a large crowd for the purpose of dancing. Miss Hallam was there also, but my friend did not seem to notice her in the least. She appeared to be evidently piqued at this intentional neglect, and, I supposed, resolved to repay the slight with compound interest. No sooner did St. Clare, the young man in whose company she had been so highly entertained while my friend was speaking, enter the hall, than he made up to where Miss Hallam was sitting, and was received with a smiling face. I observed that she cast a sly glance at David, to discover if he had noticed this turn of events. He was looking at her with an **expression** upon his gloomy face that I never can forget. She was satisfied with having attracted his attention, and entered into a flirtation with St. Clare, that occasioned David perceptible annoyance. I saw that in this lover's quarrel, this contest of mutual jealousy, Miss Hallam would be triumphant. She danced with St. Clare, chatted with him, laughed with him, as if she were perfectly delighted with her companion. David got off into one corner of the hall, and maintained a moody, sullen silence. At last the dancers paused, and Miss Hallam took her seat. David could stand it no longer. I suppose he resolved to make the first advances toward a reconciliation. He walked slowly up to where Miss Hallam was sitting, and politely asked her to dance the next set with him.

"'I am engaged,' she flippantly replied, and turned coldly from him, without another word, and commenced talking to St. Clare.

"David stood like one confounded for a moment. Her coldness and indifference seemed to penetrate his inmost soul. He suddenly turned upon his heel, with a haughty curl of the upper lip, and went from the hall, while the demon of jealousy was poisoning his heart. When Miss Hallam saw that he was gone, her manner instantly changed, and she appeared to repent of the cool manner in which she had treated him. But her face brightened up in the course of half an hour, when David re-entered, and she commenced anew with her volleys of 'small talk.' David remained standing a few moments, with his gaze sternly fixed upon the chatting pair. She talked more loudly and lively than ever, and St. Clare seemed beside himself. At last David marched straight up to where they were sitting, and beckoned St. Clare aside. They at first talked in a low tone, but presently St. Clare was heard to say, 'You are in no condition to listen to reason now. Wait till to-morrow. You are drunk.'

"'Damnable liar!' exclaimed David, in a loud voice, which

at once produced a breathless silence in the hall. 'You have stolen more than gold from me. You have robbed me of my happiness, and, by all the gods! I will be revenged!' and, before St. Clare or any one else was aware of his intentions, David drew a glittering dirk, and plunged it to the hilt in his breast. St. Clare reeled, staggered, and fell into the arms of a bystander.

"'You have killed me! you have killed me!' cried St. Clare.

"Miss Hallam came running up to where poor David was standing, looking at the reeking knife.

"'O, what *have* you done?' shrieked Miss Hallam.

"David turned upon her with a fierce, wild expression of countenance.

"'Perfidious, faithless wretch!' he cried, in a voice of thunder. 'This is all your work. You are a *murderess*. I was only an instrument in your hands. *I* am no murderer. You have done all this. You have murdered St. Clare. Carrie,' he continued, wildly, while the horror-stricken crowd stood still in speechless amazement, 'Carrie, I did love you—yes, I did love you—but now it is all gone. I hate you—I utterly abhor your very name. You have transformed me into a Cain; you have made me an outcast from human society; your damnable folly will bring me to the gallows. But you are the one who ought to swing, for St. Clare's blood is on your head. You are the *murderess*—I repeat it, you are the murderess. When I am hanged, you will have murdered two. You are cut off from heaven, Carrie, and hell is your doom—hell is your doom!'

"With a loud, unearthly laugh, he fell flat upon his back to the floor. Poor Miss Hallam was borne from the room in a fainting condition. The horrible scene seems to have been too much for her delicate constitution; for the letter which you say was found upon my person shows plainly that her mind was wandering. She left Oxford the very next day, and I learned, several weeks afterward, that she pined away, and died of a broken heart, or rather from the shock she received upon the night the tragedy occurred. St. Clare lived only a few hours after the fatal stab. My friend became a perfect maniac, and never uttered half a dozen sentences afterward. His reason was completely prostrated, and he survived the awful deed only three days. Miss Hallam, from her letter, seems never to have heard of his untimely end. Such, sir, is the history of this unfortunate young lady."

"There is one thing about the matter," said Colonel Burrell, when the spy had paused, "which I do not understand. This letter of Miss Hallam's is addressed to you, and you seem to be the person upon whom her affections had once been centered. No other name is mentioned in the letter but yours."

"She had no allusion to me whatever."

"How do you make that appear?"

"The letter was not addressed to me. I have already told you that my friend's name and mine were the same, with a very slight difference. My name is Henry S. and his Henry T. Winston. We were, however, not at all related. Miss Hallam's T's and S's were formed very much alike, if you noticed her letter closely. I had left instructions with the postmaster at Oxford to forward my letters to my place of residence. When, therefore, Miss Hallam's arrived, the postmaster, knowing that my friend had been dead for several weeks, and mistaking the T for an S, forwarded it to me, together with her miniature. I suppose I must have put them both in my pocket. I had forgotten it, and did not know that I had them about me until so informed by you. When her brother called upon me for an explanation, my mind was so much occupied with another matter that it did not once occur to me that he could be unacquainted with this melancholy event of his sister's life, and that I had been taken for the person to whom the letter was addressed. I was so stung with madness and jealousy that I really did not comprehend the import of his words. As for myself," continued the spy, with a perceptible blush, "it may not be improper to say that I have never loved but once in my life. But, of course, under the circumstances, it is useless to say more on that subject."

To this, Colonel Burrell made no direct reply. He expressed his regret to find the prisoner in such an unpleasant position, and manifested a willingness to ameliorate his disagreeable situation as far as he could, consistently with the demands and the requirements of the law; after which he took his leave.

No sooner had the heavy door closed again than the spy seized the red-bound book, and commenced reading eagerly among its soiled and torn pages.

Colonel Burrell immediately went to the office of Colonel Ellsworth, and learned from him all the particulars in regard to the charges preferred against Winston. From Colonel Ellsworth's statement, he saw the folly at once of attempting to procure the prisoner's pardon. He gave up all thought of this, therefore, and immediately went to his sister, who was awaiting his return in painful anxiety. He related faithfully to her what had taken place in the prison; also the substance of the interview with Colonel Ellsworth, omitting, however, the name of that officer, by his own request. The reason is obvious.

Emily listened with the most profound and eager attention to all her brother said.

"You think there is no doubt that he still loves me?" asked Emily, after her brother had ceased speaking.

Colonel Burrell could not tell his sister a falsehood, though he felt tempted to do so.

"I am certain of it," said he; "but there is no use of even thinking of Winston now; he is as good as dead; there is not the shadow of a chance for him."

"I will at least see him *once more*," she said, very calmly.

"You will do no such thing," replied the brother, in a tone of vexation. "I will not permit you to disgrace yourself by such an act of madness."

"Disgrace myself, brother! And where is the disgrace? What care I for the people of Washington, or of the whole North. Their opinion is nothing to me. Provided my conscience tells me I am right, the disgrace attached to the act may be trumpeted all over the Yankee land, for aught I care. I shall prove true to my country to the last."

"People will put a different construction upon the act from that. You will be looked upon as true to the *man*, and not to the *rebel*."

"I do not care how they construe it."

"Sister, for heaven's sake, let me persuade you out of this notion. What do you expect to gain by it? The man can live for only a few days. He is sentenced to die an ignominious death; and, by this visit, you will bring disgrace upon both of us. If you could possibly be benefited by it, I should have no objection; but you can gain nothing whatever. On the contrary, your future prospects will be forever blasted."

"Talk not to me of prospects, brother. I do not expect to survive this southern patriot's death but a short time. I have no desire to live. I never more expect to enjoy happiness on this earth, and only long for the time to come when I can lay down and die. Then what to me are the opinions of men, and the dazzling prospects of ambition? I can not now be influenced in the least by such motives."

"You are determined on this step, then?" asked the Colonel.

"I am," was the firm response.

Colonel Burrell saw that it would be useless to offer further opposition to his sister's wishes and intentions. He, therefore, agreed, with great reluctance however, to accompany her to the prison. Having made all the necessary arrangements, the brother and sister proceeded, without delay, to the dark, cold cell that shut out Emily's lover from the bright, gay world.

CHAPTER XXIV.

> "The ample proposition, that hope makes
> In all designs begun on earth below,
> Fails in the promis'd largeness."

THERE is a touch of romance attached to the idea of a young lady meeting her lover in a prison, especially when she had been separated from him several years, and kept constantly in a state of doubt, suspense, and uncertainty. In Emily Burrell's case it indicated great depth of affection, thus voluntarily to renounce all her brilliant prospects in life, and sacrifice, to some extent, her claims to respectability, at least in Washington City, for a rebel spy, condemned to death. We shall make no apology for her course of action, but will simply ask the reader to extend some little charity and pity to one who could thus give up all for love.

It was with ineffable emotion that Emily stood before the huge iron door that concealed her lover from view. She shuddered as it screaked upon its hinges, and the jailer motioned her to enter. All within was silent and still. The ponderous door had closed behind her. Poor Emily, blinded by the natural darkness of the cell, and by a sense of fear and shame, and by the intensity of her own emotions, arising from the peculiarity of her position, said nothing. She was beginning to think that she had, by mistake, entered an uninhabited cell, when the outlines of the spy's form, at first dim and indistinct, attracted her attention. By degrees he began to assume shape and form, like the gem in the "Arabian Night's Entertainment;" and, in a few seconds, Emily beheld her lover, after a long and bitter separation. He was, however, in the same position in which Colonel Burrell had left him—his back to the door. He was sitting on the solitary stool, bending over the old red-backed book with a concentration of mind rather unnatural to one whose situation was so perilous. His whole mind and soul seemed to be entirely absorbed by the red-covered book, and he knew not that a visitor had entered the cell. Emily could not speak. She stood still, with her feelings in a tumult of confusion and embarrassment. She had been thus standing for two minutes, in an awkward and painful situation, when the spy suddenly threw down the book and commenced to pace the floor. Emily moved, and Winston halted in extreme astonishment at the apparition that met his sight.

"In heaven's name, who are you?" quickly asked the spy, as he looked at the pale, ghost-like form.

"Henry, have you forgotten me?"

"My God, Emily, is it you?"

He clasped the trembling form in his arms. Emily wept upon her lover's breast, with feelings which the reader may imagine, but we can not describe. The holy joy diffused through their hearts, mingled with the sad truth that they must soon part to meet no more, gave to the scene a most melancholy and painful interest. These were the first tears of joy she had shed for many long and weary months. When her feelings had become more calm, and had somewhat subsided, the spy tenderly seated her on the stool.

"It grieves me, my dearest girl," said he, "to meet you again, after such a long period of separation and suffering, in such a place as this, and with a prospect of gloom and darkness before me; for you certainly can not be ignorant of the fact that I am a condemned rebel."

Poor Emily did not know what reply to make.

"But," continued the spy, "I am dishonored by no crime save that of serving my native country. To die for that country, even in the lowest grade of military rank allotted to the humblest of her defenders, is a privilege which takes from death half its bitterness and its horrors. I do not know, though, that I am speaking to one who can enter into my feelings, and who holds to the principles of political faith I have espoused."

"Yes, yes," she said; "I am a rebel, in principle at least, although my brother is an officer in the Federal army. He is, however, not in service, having lost his foot at the capture of Vicksburg, on the 4th of July."

"On the 4th?" asked the spy. "I did not know there was any fighting on that day."

"It was not done in battle. It was caused by a shell, supposed to have been fired by some of the Confederates, when the Yankee army was marching into the city. I never was sorry for it much, because I am glad he has been forced to leave the army."

Winston did not reply to this. He thought it would do no good to inform Emily that he was the Confederate who had made her brother a cripple for life.

"Is it not strange that I was so stupid as to take your own brother for your lover, and then your husband?"

"It is, indeed. I do not know how you could have made such a mistake, unless you wanted some pretext to break off the engagement."

"You do me great injustice by such a supposition," said Winston. "I did not think I could possibly be mistaken, nor do I now know what you meant, when I heard you say to your brother in the bower, '*I do not love Henry Winston.*'"

"Did you hear nothing else?" asked Emily, while a blush mantled her cheek.

"Yes; I heard you tell the person, who has since turned out to be your brother, that you loved him. I could endure no more. Stung with jealousy, and supposing that you had proved false, I fled from the spot, and returned to Mississippi.

But what did you mean by saying so emphatically you did not love me."

"I must first ask you," said Emily, "whether your feelings have changed in regard to me?"

"Not in the least."

"Well, then, I will answer your question. If you had remained longer, where you were, you would have heard me say, 'I do not love Henry Winston—it is more than that—*I adore him.*'"

"Is it possible," said the spy, imprinting a kiss upon the blushing face, "I could have been such a numskull? But I have paid for my folly and rashness a thousand times over. I wrote you a cruel letter, and threatened to forget you, but my efforts to do that met with ill success. Sometimes I have been able, for a short time, to banish your image, under the pressure of military business, but not often. The harder I struggled to forget, the more vividly would your form rise up before my imagination, and would seem to reproach me with my cruelty and faithlessness. Very frequently would the conviction come into my mind that I had acted rashly; that I alone was to blame; and sometimes I did not care whether I lived or died. Had not our bleeding country needed and demanded my services, I would have preferred death to a life of solitary misery."

"I, too, have suffered," replied Emily. "No human being can tell what bitter pangs I have endured, and what griefs have rankled in this aching heart. My case was different from yours. I have had nothing to occupy my mind but my own disappointment. While you could forget your cares and troubles amid the exciting vicissitudes and adventures natural to war, I have brooded in silent selfishness over my own private sufferings. In vain have I visited scenes of gayety; the phantoms of blasted hopes and slighted love have embittered every moment of my wretched existence. There is too much proof of what I say, in this wasted form and these pale cheeks."

"Ours, my too faithful girl," said the spy, tenderly, "has been an unhappy lot; but we ought not to murmur at the decrees of Providence. God, perhaps, for his own wise purposes, intended that we should thus live; and we should console ourselves with the reflection that he has done all for the best. We are not to expect much happiness, my dearest Emily, in this world of privation and trial. We were not placed here to adopt the old epicurean philosophy—'eat, drink, and be merry, for to-morrow we die.' Life is a mere state of probation, granted us to prepare for eternity, and we are happy or miserable, in a worldly sense, as it affects our eternal destinies. God deprives us of happiness if he sees the deprivation will be best for the welfare of the immortal principle. We ought, therefore, to submit with Christian resignation to the wise dispensations of Providence. We can find no true happiness this side the Jordan of death; it may please the great Creator soon to call us both from this state of wretchedness. Our only aim, then, should be to be ready when the summons comes. In all probability, I at least will soon be called to try the fiery ordeal of death. We may soon part; but, my dearest, let us meet beyond the skies," said the spy, in a low, solemn tone, that touched the poor girl to the heart.

"O, Henry," said the wretched girl, with tears in her eyes, "do not talk thus; you will *kill* me. You must not leave me. You must not die. You must escape. You must leave here."

"Emily, my sweet one," said the spy, sorrowfully, "you scarcely know what you are saying. I wish I could live, if only for your sake. If you were gone before, to the eternal world, God knows I would lay down my poor life upon the altar of my country as freely as I now breathe. You are the only tie that binds me to this earth. But we will not long be separated. Life is but a span. I may go on before you down to the darkness of death, but you will follow, in a few years at most; and then we will meet, I trust, to part no more."

"No," replied Emily, "we will not be separated long. If you die, I do not wish to live; I *must not* live; I *will* not live. But Henry," she cried, springing up, "you must *not* die; you must not be murdered. You SHALL NOT die! God will not allow it. I tell you, God, if he is just, can not allow it!"

Henry Winston gazed in surprise at the wretched girl as she uttered this wild, strange language. He greatly feared, from the unearthly brilliancy of her eyes, and their curious expression, that her intellect was staggering. He could not well conceal the deep emotion of his own heart when he looked upon the frail, fragile form, trembling and quivering like the aspen. He, therefore, remained silent for a moment, in speechless agony; then rising from the floor, where he had been kneeling at Emily's side, he made a few strides across the cell. "God of salvation," prayed the spy aloud, "suffer me not to drink this last cup of bitterness." He was interrupted. A soft, thin, emaciated hand was placed tenderly upon his shoulder. Emily gazed with a degree of startling eagerness into his face.

"Henry, you shall not die yet; I feel it. God will not let you die upon the gibbet. If he does, there is no justice in heaven."

"O, wretched, wretched girl!" cried the spy, folding her to his heart.

He could say no more, but pressed the yielding form to his heaving breast, and silently prayed to the great High Power, to shelter, to protect, to guide the soul of his faithful love, who had indeed proved true "even unto death." At last he reseated her upon the stool, knelt by her side, took her trembling hand in his own, and spoke in a soft, humbled tone:

"Emily, listen to me. I am deeply pained at your blasphemy and profanity. Call not in question the justice of God, though heaven and earth should fail, and every human being should perish. It matters not how I may die—whether upon the gibbet, upon the battle-field, or of old age, surrounded by friends—it will be in accordance with His will; and His wise purposes, mysterious though they be, will thus be accomplished. God gave us life, and he will take it from us at the appointed time, however severe and trying the bereavement may be to those who would have us live. We are very frequently necessitated to witness dispensations that conflict with our notions of right and justice. The righteous often go mourning all their days, cramped by adversity and scorned by the world, while the wicked flourish and enjoy all the pleasures of earthly prosperity. The case of Dives and Lazarus is not the only one which could be placed upon record. Again, we are forced to surrender our friends—our fathers, our mothers, our brothers, and our sisters—and then poor, tried human nature is disposed to attribute injustice and cruelty to the great Creator. But all these things, be assured, are right and just, though we may not be able to see it, clogged as we are by the desires and propensities of mortality. Death is the common lot of all. All must sooner or later yield to his merciless shafts. He comes unbidden at all hours, like a thief in the night. We should always be ready to meet the dread, inevitable summons. Now, Emily, we must soon part. In all probability we will never meet again. Let me, then, advise you, let me beseech you, to devote your remaining life to the service of the world's Redeemer. Consecrate your heart to that God by whose mysterious power it now pulsates. The time will come when you will be compensated, even in this life, for all the sacrifices you may make upon the altar of religion. When you come to lie upon the bed of death, and all the glory of this earth shall fade into insignificance; when all mortal means have failed; when all human philosophy is powerless to furnish a single ray of comfort and hope to the troubled spirit, thanks be to the God of Abraham, Isaac, and Jacob, you will be sustained and soothed by the philosophy of religion."

"I acknowledge," said Emily, "that I have been hasty and rash. It was a thoughtless expression which I used, and one which I really did not mean. But I can not bear the idea of your calmly submitting to an ignominious death, when you might possibly avoid it. You have doubtless often met with difficulties as great as this. Have you no hope, then, of escape; or do you intend to yield tamely?"

"I do not wish," said the spy, slowly, "to flatter you, or myself either, with vain illusions. Of course I shall do every thing in my power to save my life; but, as yet, I can not say that I have found any thing tangible upon which to base a reasonable hope. All, you know, may fail. If so, I can but resign myself to my fate, and drink of that bitter cup which soon must come to all."

"Do you not think," asked Emily, "as a *dernier* resort, you could take the oath, and afterward return to the South?"

"No, no, Emily; I could not take the oath. My enemies would not suffer that now, were I disposed to do so. Besides, I would die before I would disgrace myself by such an act of degradation. I am too proud, and I care too little for life, to humble myself to that extent before these savage vandals, who have reduced the South to ruin. They have already robbed me of every thing but my good name and my honor. Let them take my life, but they can never make me ask it at their hands. I have endeavored to discharge my duty. I believe the South is in the right. I have espoused her cause, and have never regretted for a single moment the course I have pursued. Some of our countrymen, I know, are violently opposed to the Confederacy, but as for me, thank God, I have never yet 'sighed for the flesh-pots of Egypt.'"

"I admire your nice sense of honor and your patriotism," replied Emily; "but pride and conscientious scruples, in my opinion, should give way to the preservation of life. As in your calling you could not always have adhered strictly to the truth, I do not see that you should hesitate now to adopt any plan by which you could save yourself."

"It is true, as you say, Emily, I have not always adhered to the truth; but then I have never done violence to my conscience for personal aggrandizement. Very frequently I have been forced to prevaricate. But in war spies are indispensable, and I believe all nations have recognized the system of espionage as right and proper, while at the same time they have attached a heavy penalty to its practice. Belligerents, therefore, say, 'Deceive me if you can, but if I can catch you, the consequence is death.' I have never yet, though, taken the oath, and I never will do it, and thus bow before Yankee oppressors, even to save my own life."

"You can surely have no objection to the process of bribery. That will require no sacrifice of honor and principle."

"I have been thinking of that," said the spy, thoughtfully. "The attempt will, however, be attended with extreme difficulty. I have had no opportunity yet to try any thing. The sentinel at the door is not allowed to hold any conversation with me. Besides all this, in my present condition, I might not be able to raise the necessary funds, for more than one must be bribed into silence."

"That shall be no impediment, Henry. My whole fortune is at your disposal. Take it; use it all, if needed, and consider it one sacrifice for the Confederate cause."

"God bless the true woman!" cried the spy, again folding the blushing girl to his heart. "I never can repay your generosity, my dearest one, unless I should be so fortunate as to escape, and then I hope to make amends for all the suffering which I have caused you. But I do not wish you to embarrass yourself, or jeopardize your own safety, in order to effect my rescue. You have already sacrificed too much in honoring me with this unexpected visit."

"Say not so," said she. "What is friendship or love if it must yield to the first blasts of adversity? But we will talk of all these things after you have escaped. We must now make the necessary arrangements. How do you propose to try the experiment?"

"The only way I see is to bribe the guards. They may be induced to release me at night. If I can once get into the city, I think I can possibly get out and away before it could be discovered The difficulty is, I can have no opportunity to talk with the soldiers on post."

"Then I will manage it all," replied Emily.

"No, no; I can not suffer that," cried the spy. "I will not allow you thus to endanger your own life to save mine. You have already run sufficient risks."

"It must be done, Henry, it must be done. You must escape this very night if possible. Do not attempt to dissuade me from my purpose. Only do your part, and before tomorrow morning you will be free."

"I would rather, my dear Emily, you would not take so much upon yourself."

"Suffer no uneasiness on my account. I believe the affair can be very easily managed. These Yankees will do any thing for a little gold; let me manage it."

"Have your own way, then, and may heaven crown your efforts with success. But if we fail, my dearest one, and it should be our sad destiny to meet no more on earth; if I must die, and leave you, strive to obtain that inheritance which fadeth not away. Live for God, and when we meet in the eternal world, we will still love with an affection higher, holier, and nobler than that which belongs to human nature."

They parted. When Emily had gone, the spy stood in a kind of bewildering stupefaction. It all appeared so like a dream of the night. He could scarcely realize the fact that after a long, painful separation, marked with such a diversity of mournful events, checkered with the scenes of a savage conflict, and variegated with the natural changes inevitable in the progress of time, he had again met Emily Burrell, unchanged in her feelings and affections. Those whose experience justifies the oft-quoted line, "the course of true love never did run smooth," who have felt the pangs of jealousy and disappointment, and who have afterward made up, of the famous *lovers' quarrel*, can, without any difficulty, imagine Henry Winston's emotions, and the wild joy of his heart. But those who have felt the sweets of reconciliation amid blooming bowers, have never tasted of the bitter cup which the spy drained to the dregs in that dark, loathsome cell. It has been the misfortune of few to make the *eclaircissement* of the lovers' quarrel with death staring them in the face. God forbid it should be the lot of many!

The spy, however, was not a man to indulge in unavailing regrets, or to yield submissively to the despondency and despair which would have paralyzed the most of hearts in such a trying hour. Arousing himself from his gloomy and melancholy stupor, he sighed, uttered in a low voice, "It may all fail," and commenced pacing the floor. He then turned to the stool; Emily's handkerchief was lying on it; he observed that it was carefully rolled up, and, upon opening it, what was the spy's surprise to find five thousand dollars in "greenbacks!"

> "O, woman! in our hours of ease,
> Uncertain, coy, and hard to please,
> And variable as the shade
> By the light quivering aspen made:
> When pain and anguish wring the brow,
> A ministering angel thou."

Presently the gloomy door again opened, and a feeling of joy swelled in Winston's heart, as he expected it was Emily about to re-enter; but not so. It was another visitor of a different character, whom the spy nevertheless welcomed with a degree of eagerness and vehemence rather foreign to his disposition. After some few common-place remarks, they entered into a long conversation, in the course of which the old red-backed book was very frequently called into requisition. They spoke almost in whispers, as if they feared the very walls had ears. At the end of two hours, the visitor took his leave, and the spy was again left to the solitude of his narrow cell. He was disturbed no more during the day.

That night, at the usual hour, the spy's supper was brought in. The guard, heretofore, had merely opened the door, and handed in the provisions without the utterance of a word; but this time, contrary to his usual custom, he entered the cell, and remained while the meal was being dispatched. Winston, however, made no remark, but still waited anxiously for the soldier to break the silence. He was not disappointed, for no sooner had he finished his supper than the man spoke.

"It is necessary to move you to new quarters," said the Yankee.

"Why?" asked the spy. "I should think this apartment is sufficiently safe."

"Safe enough," replied the fellow, "for some purposes; but it is thought best to put you in a *safer* place."

Winston saw from the man's emphasis that "safer" was an ambiguous term, but he greatly feared to put upon it the construction he would have desired. He moved to the "new quarters" with mingled feelings of doubt and hope. He thought it best not to ask any questions, which might arouse suspicions as to his intentions. He was very soon placed in another cell, which differed from the one he had previously occupied by having a window, which, however, was secured by stout iron bars. The soldier entered with him. When they were fairly within, Winston cast a searching glance at the fellow, which appeared to be understood; for the soldier pointed to a rope lying in one corner, and then at the window.

"What do you mean?" asked the spy.

"You must be dull if you can't take a hint," was the reply.

"It is fast," said Winston, pointing at the window.

"They work like *draw-bars*."

"What, then, am I to do?"

"If you can't understand it, I sha'n't explain it. I have done my part. I've no time to talk now. I have already tarried too long. I don't think I will bring your breakfast to you." So saying, he left the cell, and closed and locked the door.

Winston laid down on his bed, similar in all respects to the one he had just left, but he did not sleep. He was thinking of Emily Burrell, and the strange events of the last few hours, and wondering if Providence would again favor him in his effort to escape. He lay thus musing until the hour of eleven arrived, and then arose, stood upon a stool, and listened at the window. All seemed to be silent without. He went boldly to work, confident that all the necessary precautions with the guard had been taken. The iron bars easily yielded, and worked as the Yankee had said. In less time than it takes to write it, the way was clear. The cell was three stories from the ground. So taking the rope he fastened it to the lower bar in the window, and then climbed down with little noise to the pavement below. No person was visible, and the spy walked rapidly down —— street. He halted not till he came to a window, in which two lights were burning. The reader need not be told that this was Emily Burrell's room. Winston made the signal agreed upon, and Emily, after removing the candles, raised the window and beheld her lover.

"Thank heaven, Henry. you are here. I have been anxiously looking for you. But the danger is not over yet; you must leave instantly."

"Not till I have thanked you, dearest, for your generosity, and learned where we shall meet again."

"This paper," she said, handing him a letter, "will explain all, and give you all the information you will need as to my whereabouts. Now leave at once."

"Do not be in such haste, my dear Emily. I have plenty of time."

"You do not know all that I do, or you would not loiter here. I have no time to enter into explanations now. You have not a moment to lose. Fly, Henry, fly, or all will be lost."

It would have been well for the spy had he taken Emily's advice sooner; for just as he was on the point of turning slowly and reluctantly away, he found himself suddenly surrounded by half a dozen armed soldiers.

"Yes, Miss Emily," exclaimed a voice, which both the lovers had reason to hate, "all is lost. A beautiful piece of business this is. I declare"——

But Walter Hallam suddenly checked himself, for reasons which will be obvious in the sequel. A thought seemed to strike him just at the beginning of a tirade of abuse, and he walked up close to the window, and whispered in her ear:

"Beware, Emily, beware! No harm shall come to you if you are only discreet."

Poor Emily was so overcome with feelings of fear and mortification that she made no reply. She had again been foiled by the very man whom she could not even think of but with sentiments of utter abhorrence and detestation. She, however, concealed her emotions as well as she could, silently closed the window, and seated herself, because she could not stand, while thoughts of fearful apprehension were playing through her mind. The impossibility of her lover's escape produced pangs that shot through her despairing heart like jagged arrows.

> "No thought within her bosom stirs,
> But wakes some feeling dark and dread;
> God keep thee from a doom like hers,
> Of living when the hopes are dead."

"I presume your *tete-a-tete* was quite interesting, Mr. Winston," said Hallam, in a tone of mock politeness, as soon as Emily had disappeared. "I beg your pardon for interrupting you so unceremoniously. But in these war times, you know, we are frequently disturbed even in our dreams, much less our pleasant waking moments. You have been guilty, Mr. Winston, of great ingratitude, in your attempt to leave your friends without notice or a farewell. Here you have been furnished with comfortable quarters, and nice food, all *gratis*, but still you depart without thanking those who have put themselves to all this trouble for you. However, in the future, your kind friends will not allow you so much latitude. They have too much love for you."

To this unmanly sarcasm Winston did not deign to reply, and they moved back to the prison. He was then confined in the very same cell which he had at first occupied.

"I am happy, Mr. Winston," producing a pair of handcuffs, when they had entered the cell, "I am happy to present you these nice bracelets, which some of your good friends have had the kindness to procure. Here is also a very pretty chain, from the same benevolent source, for your ankles. We do not wish you to take too much exercise; it is not good for your health. You see, we have an affectionate regard for you."

Accordingly the spy was manacled hand and foot, and then left alone to his own gloomy reflections. What they were we leave the reader to imagine.

He remained in this condition until the day of his execution arrived. Emily had done all that affection could suggest to procure her lover's release, but it was all unavailing, and she gave it up in utter dark despair President Davis also made an effort to save the hero, and proposed to Mr. Lincoln to exchange a Federal spy, by the name of David McGibbons. "If Mr. Lincoln would release Winston, he (Davis) would release McGibbons, upon the condition that both should remain in their respective countries during the war." But Mr. Lincoln replied, "that spies could not be treated as prisoners of war, and that he did not feel disposed at this late day to make an innovation upon the established usages of nations. If McGibbons had been found guilty of the charges alleged, it was with Mr. Davis to deal with him as he thought proper," etc. (We may here state, in consequence of Mr. Lincoln's refusal to agree to the humane proposition of President Davis, David McGibbons was executed at Demopolis, Ala., the 11th day of February, 1864. Who, then, is justly chargeable with his death?)

Thus the last chance of the Confederate spy seemed to be gone; and here, omitting minor events, which are of but little interest to the reader, we must leave him until the next day, which was appointed for his execution.

CHAPTER XXV.

> "The last, the fatal hour is come,
> That bears my love from me;
> I hear the dead-note of the drum—
> I mark the gallows-tree."

It is strange with what feelings of melancholy pleasure we witness the last struggles of a fellow-creature in the agonies of expiring nature. We are somehow peculiarly fascinated and irresistibly attracted by the mournful scenes of a death-bed. The ominous silence which reigns throughout the domicil in which the solemn event is transpiring; the strange contrast between this silence within and the jarring bustle and din of the busy world without; the noiseless tread of spectators and friends; the grief and tears of the immediate relatives of the dying man; and, lastly, the victim himself, with his glazing eyes, painful respiration, convulsive shudders, slowly sinking down to the tranquillity of death—all these things possess irresistible charms for the living. When the last gasp is over, and the victim is no longer in a condition to afford pleasure by the drama of dying, we leave the room with a feeling akin to shame—or at least ought to—for our mysterious curiosity, and then hasten to surprise our friends with the sad tidings. Human nature is disposed to deny these assertions, or at least each man will believe them true of every body but himself. Our acts, however, are in direct antagonism to our words. The assertions above made are demonstrated by an indisputable fact we will now mention, which all have probably observed. Let a man be confined to his bed by a spell of sickness—his neighbors all keep aloof, or visit only when it would be a shame not to do so; but let it be announced that the unfortunate man is about to make his exit into the land of dreamless slumber—then all, somehow, feel under sacred obligations, and they endeavor to make amends for dereliction of duty by honoring him with their presence in his last moments. As soon as the exhibition is ended, we are disposed to take our leave at once, with our diabolical curiosity gratified, and let the poor corpse rest in peace. God save you and me, reader, in our last hours of time, from the unholy gaze of

> "The curious, questioning eye,
> That plucks the heart of every mystery."

I would we could die like good old Moses, and be buried in some unknown spot; and thus escape the impertinent, love-to-gaze-upon-death inspection of people who would, if they could, ask us how we felt in the new and unknown clime. Let it be spoken in a whisper, that nobody feels true, genuine sorrow when a man dies, except his close relatives, who are directly interested in his welfare, or rather in their *own* welfare. The world is glad he is gone. It can be written upon every tombstone what somebody put at the head of his deceased wife's grave:

> "My wife is dead, and here she lies—
> Nobody laughs, and nobody cries;
> Of where she's gone, or how she fares,
> Nobody knows, and nobody cares."

These assertions are fully demonstrated and verified, beyond all dispute and controversy, when a fellow-being is to be coolly and deliberately put to death by law, or murdered by the strong hand of civil power. This, in the United States, is a spectacle free for all—a public exhibition, without money and without price—but yet designed to inculcate useful precepts, convey wholesome lessons, and furnish warning to law-breaking sinners. It is, nevertheless, a magnificent show, and a grand entertainment for the public. We venture to assert that the old blood-loving Romans never witnessed a combat between skillful gladiators with greater feelings of eagerness and interest than civilized Americans, including both Yankees and rebels, behold the solemn preparations for a legal execution. The spectacle unaccountably arouses a pleasant, trembling, melancholy excitement. Nearly every body is like the Irish woman in the following anecdote, though destitute of her candor in the confession of her disappointment.

An Irishman, for some offense, was condemned to suffer the extreme penalty of the law. He was to die by hanging. A short time before the execution, his wife visited him in the prison. When about to bid him farewell, she asked, with tears in her eyes:

"May n't me an' the childers come to see you hung tomorrow?"

"No," said the indignant husband; "stay at home."

"That's just like ye," said she; "you never did want me an' the poor little dears to sa iny *plazure*."

An observer who will watch the minutiæ of an execution, will be convinced of the truth of what we have been saying. The day before the occurrence of the tragical scene, two posts, fifteen or twenty feet in altitude, are set upright in the ground. A beam, four or five feet in length, is fastened to the top of each; then a rope is tied middleways of the beam, and the fatal noose is made at its end. Indications of some unusual occurrence are seen early in the morning of the day upon which the execution is to take place. Noisy boys, who have talked and dreamed of the event for days before, and who have flocked from the hills and hollows for miles around, begin to crowd the streets, the prison, and the gibbet. . The parents of the little urchins have had the kindness to promise them this delightful entertainment, for probably a fortnight previous, upon the condition of good behavior in the future.

Wagon-loads of hoosiers and darkies begin to pour in; and by the time the sun is fairly risen, the town is overrun with a motley assembly, gathered together from all quarters, anxious to see a fellow-creature die. With eager looks, they collect around the prisoner's cell, endeavoring to have a peep at the features of the doomed man; and also through fear that he may be lead off to death before they are aware of it. When the prisoner is seated upon his coffin in the wagon, he is honored by a large multitude all the way to the place of execution. Arriving at this dreadful spot, he beholds another numerous audience; some of whom, to have a better view of the beauties of the exhibition, have climbed up the surrounding trees, and perched upon all other elevations in the immediate vicinity of the fascinating center of attraction. The wretch steps upon the platform, takes his position upon the trap-door, the rope is adjusted about his neck, the black cap is pulled over his face, and the executioner steps down to tap the trigger. What a breathless silence now reigns throughout the mighty multitude! But if, at this moment, a courier should hasten up with a reprieve or pardon, the vast crowd would wish the messenger at the bottom of endless perdition for bringing such bad news, and thus checking the interesting performance. (What a "rascal is human nature!") Not until the door falls—the doomed culprit drops and struggles for a quarter of an hour—is the tender-hearted multitude relieved of its blissful excitement. They then disperse, and the urchins hasten home to regale their parents and friends (*i. e.*, all those who were unfortunately prevented from attending the exhibition) with a relation of the scenes of the day, and the sorrowful event which will constitute an epoch in the history of their lives.

All these preliminary remarks find their application in the execution of Henry Winston, which was to take place on that much-slandered day recognized by the superstitious as prejudicial, if not fatal, to success in the inception of undertakings, enterprises, and projects. He was honored with the attendance, customary upon such occasions, of boys, hoosiers, and negroes.

Early in the morning the prisoner was visited by two personages; one a minister of the gospel, and the other Dr. Vernon. These two remained with the spy about two hours, and then retired. Soon after the Provost Marshal entered and informed our hero that the awful hour had arrived. It did not take Winston long to make the necessary preparations for leaving the cell forever.

"It is ordered that you shall wear this *placard*," said the Provost, stepping to the door and bringing a paste-board containing, in large black letters, the words—THE REBEL SPY.

"Why," said the prisoner, "may I ask, is it thought proper to insult a doomed man with such an indignity? Is not the ignominious penalty itself a sufficient degradation?"

"I do not suppose," replied the officer, "it is done particularly as an act of disgrace to you, but more to let the people know for what you have been condemned. I did not, however, inquire of my superior officers the reason for this proceeding. I always obey orders without asking questions. I should think, though, it would make but little difference with you; it will all be over and forgotten in a few hours."

"True, true; it is a matter of little consequence. The Savior is none the less revered because he wore a crown of thorns upon his bleeding head. It matters not with him, then, if the heart be right, whether a man expires upon the couch of Dives or the hard bed of Lazarus. You may disgrace this temple of clay, but, thank God, you can not garb the invisible soul in the habiliments of dishonor." The spy slightly bent his head, and received the placard on his neck.

The procession now commenced. Henry Winston, seated upon his coffin, was attended by several companies of the military—both cavalry and infantry. The vehicle moved circuitously through the city, in order to give all a view of the celebrated rebel spy. One distinguishing and most remarkable feature in this procession was a large collection of LADIES. (Mark it, historians!) By the term "ladies" we do not simply have reference to the vile rabble of females who have lost all self-respect, and are destitute of shame and modesty; nor do we allude to the lower classes of society, born and bred in the backwoods, who have never heard of the letters of Chesterfield; and who, in mind, taste, and manner, differ very little from the "rougher sex." But the truth must be told on the *elite* of Washington City; and the gay belles, who had attended the President's levees; who had conformed strictly to all the artificial rules and requirements of etiquette; who, in a word, had moved all their lives in the "so-called" *upper circles* of society—were now seen mounted upon high-spirited chargers, following an unfortunate rebel to the gallows. Some of these ladies were distinguished authors, whose works have been extensively circulated in the South—*abolition* authors, whose damnable books have extracted princely fortunes from southern wealth, and over whose sickly, morbid sentimentalisms, in regard to the imaginary wrongs of the "poor" negro, southern readers have wept tears of blood. May God forgive you, southern reader, if you be guilty!

We forbear to make any further commentary upon this unusual spectacle; but we must ask the reader to kindly and charitably remember, because these are our "northern sisters," rendered so by *ties of steel* (and therefore much stronger than the bonds of natural affection), that war has both an *im*moralizing and *de*moralizing effect, throughout all the ramifications of human society. But the procession moved on, and many an eye read that day those large black letters—THE REBEL SPY.

Reader, we will, for a moment, leave this motley crowd, and watch the proceedings of a female, in the solitude of her room. Her wild, unnatural appearance would have aroused a sentiment of pity in the breast of a savage. When the procession moved opposite the house at which poor Emily Burrell was staying, she could not withstand the strong temptations of curiosity to look forth from her window. The first object which met her eye was her doomed lover, with the conspicuous placard upon his breast. The sight was too much for her delicate nerves. She staggered, reeled, and fell to the floor, overcome by a sudden rush of feelings of anguish and despair. She could now, indeed, have exclaimed:

"Cursed fate! malicious stars! you now have drained
Yourselves of all your poisonous influence;
Even the last baleful drop is shed upon me!"

Emily lay thus a short time, then suddenly rose and paced the room in indescribable agony and anguish. Then she stopped, gazed vacantly, and again commenced her wild, rapid walk. At last she halted at a small table, and unconsciously opened a Bible. Her eyes fell upon a passage which seemed to arrest her attention, and partially relieve the intolerable commotion of her overcharged heart. She read: "Hear me when I call, O God of my righteousness; thou hast enlarged me when I was in distress; have mercy upon me, and hear my prayer." She came to the fifth verse: "Offer the sacrifices of righteousness, and put your trust in the Lord."

"I will try it. He advised me," she continued, communing with herself, and referring to Henry Winston, "to prove the promises of Holy Writ and the merits of the Christian religion;" and she knelt down by the table, seen only by God, and offered up the earnest prayer of a suffering, breaking heart.

"God of truth and salvation! I call upon thee from the depths of wretchedness. Thou hast promised aid and consolation to the children of men in the hour of distress. That hour has now come to one who feels a sense of her own utter helplessness, and desires the comfort of thy holy truth. All human means have failed. The power, glory, and wealth of the world bring no relief to the aching heart. Comfort me in this trying hour with the outpourings of thy abundant mercy and truth. O God! calm the anguish of this bleeding heart by the power of religion, and I promise that henceforth my whole life, whether it be long or short, shall be devoted to thy service."

The vow was heard, that simple prayer was answered, and He who said "Seek and ye shall find" verified the promise to Emily Burrell. A new light burst upon her soul, and she felt a holy calm diffused through her heart. Emily rose from her kneeling posture. She knew that God had touched her with the finger of his great and holy love.

"Thank God, I can endure it—I can endure it all now! Yes, Henry, I will meet thee in heaven."

The procession had now reached the gibbet. A hollow square, composed of four companies of infantry, was formed around the gallows, to keep out those whose curiosity was stronger than their sense of self-respect. The ladies arranged themselves in military order back of the infantry. In the rear of the ladies the cavalry was drawn up. Behind these was an immense congregation of human beings, of all shapes, colors, sizes, and descriptions. Every civilized race in the world was here represented, thus proving that the love of witnessing death is natural to all "kindreds, tribes, and people."

When every thing was ready, the prisoner ascended the scaffold with a firm, steady step; not a single muscle quivered; no sign whatever indicated that the prisoner felt any unusual emotion. He reminded one of some of the heroes of antiquity—the god-like Achilles, described by the ancient poets. His calm countenance wore its habitual aspect of serenity and self-possession; his tall, manly form stood erect upon the platform; and he looked around upon the vast audience with an expression that caused a hum of admiration to run throughout the motley multitude.

"What a pity! what a pity!" was heard from five hundred mouths.

"The finest-looking gentleman I ever beheld!" cried one young lady, with a sort of semi-sympathizing gaze. "What a pity he should be a rebel!"

"Umph!" exclaimed a fidgety Miss, with more brass than brains and modesty, "I do n't blame that Miss 'What's-her-name' for taking on as they say she did. I could have no objection myself to such a handsome man, if he were only loyal. I declare I do feel right sorry for the poor fellow."

"I do wonder," thought to herself a maid who had culled the flowers of thirty-five summers, "I do wonder what makes men such fools. There are not half enough husbands now for the widows and girls, without shooting and hanging each other in this style. Now, if I had my way, I would pardon the unfortunate man, I do n't care whether he is guilty or not. I don't see any use in murdering a handsome man like he is, when he would make some poor girl a good husband." The old maid sighed, and thought that fifteen years ago she would liked very much to have met just such a man.

Something was now said to the spy by the Provost Marshal, which was not heard outside the hollow square. Winston, however, turned to the audience, and spoke as follows:

"I am asked what I have to say why sentence of death should not be executed upon me according to the decree of the military court. Upon this point I have nothing to say. If the United States authorities deem the crimes imputed to me worthy of death, I must submit without a murmur. I have only to regret that I have not been more successful in serving the cause which honor and a sense of justice to an oppressed people called upon me to espouse. I believe the South is right in this contest; and you may murder me; you may lay to the dust every soldier who fights for the establishment of her independence; you may devastate every foot of her soil, but the victory will be a barren triumph, and the principle of secession will remain as firm and unshaken as ever—guaranteed by your Constitution to every state that entered into the political contract. The self-same moment, then, that you subjugate the South, you sap the very foundations of your own freedom; you subvert the fundamental principles upon which your government is based, and erect upon the ruins of a once proud republic a despotism more galling and oppressive than any tyranny ever exercised over ancient Rome."

"Down with the traitor! down with the rebel!" cried Walter Hallam, joined by numerous rabid radicals.

The spy paused, and manifested no disposition to say more. But suddenly a new exclamation was heard. It seemed to come from a thousand voices at once:

"Go on! go on! go on!"

"Down with the copperheads! down with the copperheads!" now resounded throughout the mighty concourse.

"Free spache, be Jasus! free spache!" thundered an Irishman, from a sapling, in a voice that attracted all eyes to himself for a moment. "Let the ribel talk, if he wants."

The crowd took up the cry, and "free speech!" "free speech!" went the rounds. A scene of general confusion was about to take place, and the consequences might have been serious; but at this moment a government officer, held in great respect in Washington City, quickly mounted the scaffold, where Winston was standing, the most unconcerned of all.

"Citizens and soldiers!" said the officer—immediately a profound silence ensued—"it is not the intention of the government to deprive the prisoner of the right of speech, although he has taken advantage of the privilege granted him to insult you with the utterance of treason. But, however, if he should choose to defend the cause in which he has been engaged, rather than show reason why he should not be executed, let him do so. The cause of the Union is too high and noble to be injured by a rebel under the gallows. Therefore show yourselves worthy of the privileges of freemen by listening without any disturbance to whatever the prisoner may say."

The officer did not really mean what he had said, but he could see that any attempt to silence the prisoner would meet with violent opposition. He waited a moment to see what effect his words would have, and the crowd maintaining silence, he motioned to Winston to proceed with his speech. The hero continued:

"I did not intend to detain you long; but since you desire to hear from me, I will make a few brief remarks. The distinguished officer has just told you that I have the privilege to address you upon whatever subject I may think proper. I do not choose to speak of myself, for the simple reason that, if I die, I die a martyr to the principles which the South is struggling to vindicate. My own character needs no defense. If I should be guilty of any crime, it is only zeal in that very cause which your ancestors died to establish in the first revolution.

"The South did not secede from the old Union until forced by the most stern and absolute necessity. It was with feelings of the deepest sorrow, we saw the confederation handed down by our forefathers, dismembered, and its government set at defiance; for we had no objection to the Constitution, nor to the Union; but we conceived that the government had failed to accomplish the objects for which it was designed. We clung to them, however, as long as we could, consistently with honor and dignity. But when we saw that the powers delegated to the General Government were about to be perverted, we thought, in the language of the Declaration of Independence, 'that whenever any form of government becomes destructive of these ends, IT IS THE RIGHT OF THE PEOPLE TO ALTER OR ABOLISH IT, AND TO INSTITUTE A NEW GOVERNMENT, LAYING ITS FOUNDATIONS ON SUCH PRINCIPLES, AND ORGANIZING ITS POWERS IN SUCH FORM, AS TO THEM SHALL SEEM MOST LIKELY TO EFFECT THEIR SAFETY AND HAPPINESS.' Does not your present form of government derive its existence from the assertion and the successful vindication of this principle? Will you now ignore the declarations of Thomas Jefferson, and the provisions of your Constitution, sanctioned by Washington, and indorsed by all parties for eighty years?"

"Yes! yes!" cried a dozen voices from the crowd.

"Then," continued the spy, in a vehement tone that thrilled like an electric shock, "strike out the last vestige of your freedom; dethrone the goddess of liberty you insult by your pharisaical worship; call your false republic by its true name; and no longer insult the memory of the heroes of '76 by the bare profession of principles which they sealed with their noble blood, but which you virtually discard by your hypocritical pretensions and your political mockeries! Be consistent, and sustain the military despotism which has now usurped all the civil powers of your government, and swept away your last right as freemen."

"That's right; give it to 'em," exclaimed a bystander.

"Why, the right of self-government is as clearly recognized and as explicitly acknowledged in your Constitution as the right of trial by jury. It is the genius of your government; it permeates your whole political system; it lies at the bottom of every political principle; and it constitutes the corner-stone, the very ground-work, of your ancient republic. The right of each state to regulate its own domestic affairs and institutions is clearly set forth in your Constitution in unequivocal language. This none will deny. Why, then, have you made war upon the South? For offering resistance to the encroachments upon her privileges, and the invasion of her sacred rights? We are guilty only of a re-enactment of the scenes of 1776. If high treason can be charged upon the South, it can also be imputed to George Washington; for the very same principles are involved. If you, then, succeed in conquering the southern states, we will be in the same position our forefathers would have occupied had England established her authority over the colonies. In fact, we are more justifiable in this present revolution than the colonists were; because England only claimed the right to tax the colonies; but you go beyond that, and seek to control state affairs, to regulate our internal concerns, to blot out the chief source of our wealth, and thus reduce us to dependence, vassalage, and beggary. You may deny it, but you have repeatedly declared that all the states in the Union must have the same domestic institutions; and you were not satisfied till you elected to the highest offices men whose avowed principles and intentions were to overturn our whole social system. Some of you have gone so far as to attempt to obliterate the distinctions and differences of races which God himself established, and elevate the African tribe to a position of social and political equality, when their true sphere is plainly marked out and limited by their natural characteristics. You may do it; you may temporarily pervert the laws of nature and of nature's God; you may, in fifty years or less, disgrace your illustrious ancestry by a mongrel breed; but you can never induce the proud, chivalrous southron to forget the nobility of his descent by a participation in your unnatural degradation."

"Stop the rebel! stop the traitor!" drowned the spy's voice.

"Go on—go on—go on!" came repeated, so loudly and

vociferously from all parts of the congregation, that it was evident a majority was in favor of "free speech."

"If I am a traitor," resumed the prisoner, as soon as he could be heard, "then have I never understood the nature of our form of government, and the principles that lie as its basis. If I am guilty of treason, it is honest treason, and proceeds from a desire to vindicate the spirit, the genius of true republicanism, rather than to establish a new and separate government. It is a mistaken idea that the South is simply fighting for a confederacy. It is for a principle—a principle, too, which we would much rather have seen engrafted afresh upon the old Constitution, and then have remained in the Union. The South would have been satisfied. If you can construe this into treason, then, in the well-known language of Patrick Henry, 'make the most of it.'

"Now I have told you for what we in the South are fighting. If we fail, you will rue the day that witnesses our downfall. It amounts to something more than a possibility that you may crush this southern movement to perpetuate constitutional liberty. Your resources are abundant; all the necessary munitions and appliances of war are in your hands; you are a powerful nation—powerful in men and money—while the South labors under numerous disadvantages that are plain and patent to the world. If, therefore, you concentrate your full powers and energies; if you persevere to the end, and your whole people are determined to persist until you put us down, it may be done. But when you have accomplished your object, you will have engrafted upon your Constitution a new principle, which can not but prove destructive to republicanism and democracy. You will then present to the world the strange anomaly of a republic held together by military force. Why, what constitutes the first element of a republic? It is the *consent* of the governed. What kind of a republic will it be with one third of it held at the point of the bayonet?

But this will be exactly the sort of government you will have if you conquer the South. It will be nothing but a monarchy or a despotism. Then all you gain, provided the war terminates in your favor, is the annihilation of your privileges as freemen, and the destruction of all your own liberties. The only way, therefore, to preserve your freedom, to check the downward tendency of your tottering republic, and to carry out the democracy of your forefathers, is to recognize the independence of the Confederacy, and thus end a bloody and useless war."

"Hang the traitor! hang the traitor! hang the traitor!" checked the prisoner's further progress. The cry was kept up for several moments, loudly and angrily. The spy stood looking on with a calm, undisturbed countenance, and was watching, nevertheless, with some little feeling of interest, the indications of the storm his words were about to raise. At length there was a dead pause. The multitude was still in breathless expectation.

"*Save the prisoner!*"

It was uttered in a low voice from the outskirts of the congregation, and was barely heard at the gibbet. Then there was ominous silence for nearly a quarter of a minute. The suggestion was taking its effect.

"TO THE RESCUE!" at last exclaimed a tall, dark-looking man, in a short, sharp, quick, decisive, but stentorian tone, that burst upon the startled host like a thunder-clap.

He was a violent copperhead, and was sufficiently acquainted with the passions of the mob to assume the responsibility of leadership. He was not disappointed in his expectations nor mistaken in his calculations; for scarcely had the exciting exclamation issued from his lips when the tumult began.

"To the rescue! to the rescue! to the rescue! to the rescue!"

The mob rapidly collected by the sound of the rallying cry,

The dark-looking man drew forth a pistol, and, waving it over his head, thus became the nucleus around which the elements of the new movement gathered and formed. The ladies, now thoroughly frightened at these unexpected proceedings, attempted to disperse and make their way through the crowd; but the mob was too much excited to respect the privileges of the "fair sex." The horses began to rear and plunge, till many were thrown among the rabble. The loud, piercing screams of the prostrate heroines were heard in various directions. The surrounding trees, whose limbs were bending under loads of human curiosity, were rapidly vacated, as the thought occurred to these lofty spectators that straggling bullets might accidentally find their way to a mark higher than they were intended to reach. All who were not directly engaged in the belligerent proceedings seemed to be actuated by the principle, *sauve qui peut*, and scampered away to a respectable and safer distance. A violent whirlwind was coming on, which would soon be very hard to quell.

At this stage of the proceedings the government officer again mounted the scaffold. He waved his hand to produce silence and secure attention, but his actions were unnoticed, or at least disregarded. The officer then drew forth from a side pocket a paper, and held it up in his hand. It caught the eye of the mob, and silence was presently restored, by the supposition of this document being a pardon. The officer waited until he could be distinctly heard, and then attempted to speak.

"Read the pardon! read the pardon!" thundered the mob.

"Wait a moment," said the officer, unfolding the document, "till I make an explanation. I am sorry, fellow-citizens," he began, "to see this disturbance raised in opposition to law and order. In this free country mob-law is not the proper process by which to correct abuses or redress grievances. As true and loyal citizens of a great, glorious, prosperous country, you should seek to execute the laws of this country, which have been made for your good and your safety, rather than to trammel and retard the progress of justice by unbridling passion and prejudice. Your security in society depends upon a faithful adherence even to the very letter of the law. If the penalties adjudged proper by an impartial court can not be administered, you will soon bring about universal anarchy, and will have no tribunal to which you can appeal."

"Read the pardon! read the pardon! read the pardon!"

"Let me beseech you, fellow-citizens," resumed the officer, "not to resist the law. You will only occasion the useless effusion of blood; because there are more men in favor of law and order than there are opposed to it. You ought by this time to be convinced of the folly of raising the weak arm of rebellion against the Government of the United States. Do you not see that she is raising her millions of men for the purpose of restoring order in the South? How long will it take, then, to quell a mob like this?"

"Read the pardon or get down!" thundered the dark man.

"Fellow-citizens, I do not wish to deceive you. The prisoner has been found guilty of a crime, the penalty of which is death. The paper which I hold in my hand contains the proceedings and findings of the court in the case of Henry S. Winston; the sentence is death, and MUST be executed!"

"G—d d—n the court! Rescue the prisoner!"

Hundreds of pistols were drawn and cocked, and a general rush was made toward the gallows, amid cries, exclamations, oaths, and all the other customary sounds, sights, and characteristics of a wild, frantic mob. The regular soldiers constituting the square immediately around the scaffold "fixed bayonets," and stood ready to receive the charge. But the mob was too powerful; they came like an avalanche; the guard was disarmed in a moment, and the scaffold was surrounded.

"Hurra for the Confederacy! Three cheers for Jeff Davis!" bawled the tall, dark man.

He waved his hat aloft, and a wild shout rent the air in honor of treason under the very nose of ABRAHAM LINCOLN.

"Damnable traitors!" thundered forth Mr. Lincoln (for he it was who had been talking), pointing up the road which led to the city, "damnable traitors! you will soon repent your folly, and pay dearly for your triumph."

It was a whole division of Federal infantry which was stationed in Washington. As soon as Winston had commenced speaking, Mr. Lincoln saw the unmistakable evidences and indications of a lawless spirit, and dispatched a courier with an order to the troops "to turn out." On they came, with glistening arms, at a *"double-quick,"* and halted about one hundred yards from the scene of action. Here they instantly formed into line of battle, and then advanced slowly toward the gallows.

"Now," exclaimed President Lincoln to the mob, whose wild ardor was beginning to abate and evaporate, "I give you five minutes to disperse. If, at the lapse of that time, this spot is not cleared of your presence, I will have every one of you shot!"

He drew out his watch to mark the time. The threat had the desired effect. The mob, now thoroughly cooled, slowly retired, at first one by one, but as the time began to draw to a close they went with a rush, as if afraid to be found leaving last. At the end of three minutes all were gone. The tall, dark man was among the first to leave.

The military again took peaceable possession, and preparations soon recommenced for the execution. The spy was not allowed to finish his speech. A hasty prayer was offered up by a clergyman in attendance, and then the rope was adjusted about his neck. In another moment the fatal trigger was tapped, and the Confederate spy was dangling in the air.

He was allowed to hang twenty minutes, and was then pronounced dead by Dr. Vernon and another surgeon. The body was taken to a grave at some distance from the gallows, and buried with little ceremony, but with extraordinary rapidity. Walter Hallam, true to his promise, saw the last clod thrown on his enemy's grave.

That same evening Emily Burrell, whose feelings we can not attempt to describe, left Washington, in company with her brother, for her home in Kentucky. She could not remain another hour near the fatal spot upon which her last hope had been forever blighted. Her only object now was to return to her native state, and there wait, in peace, with Christian resignation, till the summons of death should come and end her troubles. But with truth it has been said:

"Death comes not to those who mourn."

CHAPTER XXVI.

"Joy never feasts so high
As when the first course is of misery."

SEVERAL weeks had now passed away. Emily Burrell was again amid the scenes of her Kentucky home. Three years before she had been contented and happy; but now her whole manner of life was changed. Formerly she had wandered along the banks of the clear, winding river, and indulged in thoughts that contributed to the cultivation of her intellect. She rarely thought of God, who gave it. Again she stood by the magnificent stream; but she no longer held in her hand the volume upon whose pages she had once concentrated the powers of a solid mind in profound abstraction. She seated herself upon the green moss growing at the foot of a wide-spreading beech, opened her book, and read:

"Since, then, it appears that annihilation forms no part of the plan of the Creator in the material world, is it reasonable to suppose that a system of annihilation is in incessant operation in the world of mind; that God is every day creating thousands of minds, induced with the most capacious powers, and at the same time reducing to eternal destruction thousands of those which he had formerly created? Shall the material universe exist amidst all its variety of changes, and shall that noble creature, *for whose sake the universe was created*, be cut off forever in the infancy of its being, and doomed to eternal forgetfulness? Is it consistent with the common dictates of reason to admit that *matter* shall have a longer duration than *mind*, which gives motion and beauty to every material scene? Shall the noble structure of St. Paul and St. Peter, survive the ravages of time, and display their beautiful proportions to successive generations, while Wren and Angelo, the architects that planned them, are reduced to the condition of the clods of the valley? Shall the 'Novum Organum' of *Bacon*, and the 'Optics' and 'Principia' of *Newton*, descend to future ages, to unfold their sublime conceptions, while the illustrious minds which gave birth to these productions are enveloped in the darkness of eternal night? There appears a palpable absurdity and inconsistency in admitting such conclusions. We might almost as soon believe that the universe would continue in its present harmony and order were its Creator to cease to exist." . . . .

God works wonders and mysteries in his own way. It was necessary that Emily should undergo tribulations; otherwise she might never have read the "philosophy of a future state," and never have bowed to the God that gave her life. Troubles directed her thoughts to the only true source of consolation. She had gone through a fiery sea of trial, but had come out purified, *redeemed*.

Emily finished the chapter from which the foregoing extract has been taken; then, with a silent prayer, rose from her seat and returned to the house. A visitor had come. It was Colonel Ellsworth. Emily welcomed him with a sad, faint smile, that showed plainly the connection of his presence with sorrowful associations. With propriety the truthful language of Shakespeare could be applied:

> "Yet the first bringer of unwelcome news
> Hath but a losing office; and his tongue
> Sounds ever after as a sullen bell,
> Remember'd knelling a departed friend."

They sat in the parlor by a window that opened upon a scene lovely to behold. When they had conversed for an hour or more, Colonel Ellsworth began to explain the object of his visit, which did more credit to his heart than to his sense of propriety.

"I have come far, Miss Emily," he said, after some prefatory and apologetic remarks, "for the pleasure of this interview. It will hardly be necessary to say that I have come upon a mission which you will regard as rather selfish in its nature. I have come to make one more appeal to your heart in favor of myself. In plain language, I have come, after being twice discarded, to ask your *love*."

"And what has induced you, Colonel Ellsworth, to suppose I would change my mind? I thought I was sufficiently explicit upon this subject to prevent a second recurrence to it."

"I will be candid, Miss Emily. I thought, from your peculiar situation, you might be persuaded to alter your determination, and intrust your happiness to another's keeping."

"What is so 'peculiar' in my situation?"

The officer looked troubled and perplexed by the keen, searching gaze fixed upon his face.

"I know," he at length replied, "that you are a lover of candor and plain dealing. I will speak plainly, though I feel a delicacy in saying any thing which may jar upon your feelings. Will you forgive me, then, if I allude to a distressing occurrence, which places you in a different position from that you occupied a few weeks ago? There is no one *now* who has a better right to claim your affection than he who now addresses you."

"This is cruel, Colonel Ellsworth, cruel; it is unkind, ungenerous."

"Do not misunderstand my motives, Miss Emily, nor misconstrue my language. I would not willingly give you pain. I wish you could look into this heart and see what it suffers; for you then would not accuse me of cruelty. I alluded to this painful occurrence only to remind you of the life of solitary misery you must lead if you persist in your determination to shut yourself out from the world. All is for the best, Miss Emily. No one believes stronger in the special providence of God than I do. You have a destiny to fulfill; and this sad event might have been fore-ordained, and doubtless was, to open your eyes to some great truth, which you might otherwise never have discovered."

"I believe you, Colonel Ellsworth, I believe you. It has convinced me of the helplessness of human nature; it has opened my eyes to the fact that we live not for the pleasures of life; it has impressed upon my mind the truth that we are placed here to make preparations for eternity. This is now my only aim and object; and, with God's help, I shall so live in the future as to meet that lover to whom you have referred, and in whose gory grave my affections are buried, in that land where are no sickness and sorrow."

"I am a firm believer in the Christian religion, Miss Emily; not a mere intellectual believer in the general principles of Christianity, but I endeavor to practice the precepts of the Bible, and live up to its commandments. But I can not take the view of its requirements that you do. I am not so much of a Roman Catholic as you seem to be. I do not think God requires his creatures to shut themselves up in total seclusion, in priestly cells, in lonesome convents. The general tenor of Scripture is opposed to such a course. Each mortal has a mission to accomplish; and no one is at liberty, nor has the right, to withhold from society talent that might contribute to its intellectual, moral, and religious advancement. But it is not my profession to deliver lectures. I presume you have as correct ideas in regard to your religious duties as I have. I did not come here for such a purpose; and now, returning to the original subject, I have given up all for you—home, friends, country, reputation, all, to secure your love; I have sacrificed all for you."

"Colonel Ellsworth, what do you mean? Is it possible you have abandoned your political principles?"

"Yes, Miss Emily, yes; I have deserted my cause to espouse that to which you cling. Will you look upon the sacrifice favorably, or will you send me away to bleed and die, unpitied, unwept, in a foreign state?"

"Not unpitied, Colonel Ellsworth, not unpitied. I am deeply moved by your sufferings. But, while at the same time I pity your distress, I can not approve the motive that induced your espousal of southern principles. Excuse me, but it seems to be actuated by a hope of individual gain, rather than an honest, sincere desire to serve a cause in which the heart, soul, and mind are all engaged, or should be."

"You are too hard upon me, Miss Emily. I confess that mine is not first-class patriotism. But what does it matter about motives, provided I am true to the interests of the South. However, I am not quite so selfish as you have said; for my opinions have undergone a change since we talked upon this subject several weeks ago. I have, furthermore, to confess that I never fully examined the grounds upon which the Confederacy set up its claims to a separate independence. I have been taught from my childhood to love the Union, and to look upon any attempt to rend its ties as traitorous. When the war commenced, I could not divest myself of sentiments fostered and cherished in the days of my youth. You are only the instrumentality which led to a careful examination of the principles I have been combating. Recently I have been studying the subject; I find I was wrong, and I am now willing to atone for my error; and, if it become necessary, to even sacrifice my life in defense of southern rights. I am again fit for field duty, and am now on my way to the southern army. I came by to see if I could not induce you to reconcile me to my change of sentiment by the bestowal of at least a small portion of your love, and thus forever preclude the possibility of my regretting the folly of my political repentance."

"You ask an utter impossibility," replied Emily. "I can not change the sympathies and affections of my heart, however much I might be disposed to encourage you. Wherever you may go, you will bear with you my best wishes for your welfare."

"Is this all you can promise? Is there no bright hope to which I can cling in the hours of gloom and despondency? Let me have some hope to buoy me up amid the hardships of camp-life; let me have some reward in prospect to crown my sacrifice when peace returns. Promise me your hand. I will then have something to live for, and I can more cheerfully undergo the privations of a soldier's life. I fear not for the result afterward; I can *make* you love me by my entire devotion to your wishes. I will love you with so much ardor, with so much madness, that you can not find it in your heart not to reciprocate, to some extent, my deep and lasting affection."

Emily maintained a thoughtful silence, and the officer, taking this as a favorable indication, continued:

"Without such a promise, I shall enlist anyhow in the service of the Confederate States, but I will be the most wretched soldier in the army. With such a promise to cheer me on in the path of duty, I could face the scorn and reproaches of a world. Will you, can you, then, still persist in your determination to live and die in solitary grief, when you might secure your own happiness and seal that of another? The chances are that I will fall upon the battle-field; and the probability is you will never be called upon to redeem your promise. Then, while I do live, let me enjoy the enrapturing thought that you will be my bride when peace is restored."

"I am surprised, Colonel Ellsworth, at your undisguised preference for such a sorrowful wretch as I am. What do you want with a creature whose hopes of earthly happiness have all faded away, and whose affections lie entombed in a bloody grave? You know that I once loved, and I have told you that I can never love again. All that you could do would never arouse a single emotion of love in this crushed heart of mine. I respect you—I admire your qualities of mind and heart—but this is all I can do. I freely give you my esteem and my friendship, but I am incapable of any other sentiment. But, nevertheless, I can be as self-denying as you have been; and if it will assist you or encourage you while battling for southern independence, I will make the sacrifice. If, then, at the termination of the war, *I am alive*, and my feelings are unchanged, and you still desire the unworthy boon, I will give you my hand; but mark it, Colonel, *not my heart.*" . . .

The next day after the departure of Colonel Ellsworth Emily was sitting in her bower; her guitar lay near by. After musing a short time, she took the instrument in her hand, and sang, in a mournful voice, that wild composition, "Thekla at her Lover's Grave," which Emily had set to music. When she had finished the song, she was considerably surprised to see Walter Hallam standing in the entrance. She did not speak.

"My cousin does not welcome me as she did four years ago," said Hallam, not moving from his position.

"I am sorry," replied Emily, slowly and coldly, "that you have placed yourself in a situation which enables you to arrive at the knowledge of such a fact."

"In other words, you are displeased with my presence. I did not expect to be told so in plain language by a relative, and by one whose destiny it probably is to call me by a more endearing name than that of cousin."

Emily was too well acquainted with Hallam to ask any explanation of his strange words; neither did she care to hear more. She was on the point of rising to leave the spot, when

Hallam, divining her intentions, placed his arms across the door, as if to prevent her departure.

"You leave not here," said he, "until you have heard me, and have taken choice between two evils."

"I will call for help," replied Emily, rising to her feet, and frightened by his ambiguous threats.

"You may call, but there will be none to answer."

"Where is brother James?" cried Emily, in a wild voice.

"If you make the attempt to call for brother James, he will be as powerless as you are; but you need not be unnecessarily frightened," he said, noticing her expression of horror. "No harm has happened to him, and it depends upon you whether any will or not."

"For the sake of a poor wretched girl, do not torment me thus; I can not endure much now. If you are determined to detain me by force, tell me at once your meaning."

"You will hear it soon enough. I have no desire to tantalize you, though; I will, therefore, keep you in suspense no longer. I came here, then, to ask you, gentlemanly and decently to be my *wife*."

Emily made no response. She was surprised, but waited to hear more concerning this extraordinary proposition. Hallam continued:

"You do not seem to like the manner in which I woo. May be I am not as ardent as some of your lovers used to be. But I should suppose by this time you would begin to be displeased with that kind of courtship, since it has terminated so unfortunately. I will go at it in a business-like style. I presume you can have no objection to my suit now? All obstacles are removed. *He*—you know who I mean—will never turn up again in an unexpected place. He died this time, without a doubt; I saw the last clod thrown upon the rebel's grave; I saw him stand upon the scaffold—I saw the trigger tapped—and I saw him drop."

"O God, have mercy on me!" cried the wretched girl, trembling from head to foot. "Walter," she continued, turning to him with a pitiable look, "if you are human, let me go. I am nothing but a miserable woman, standing, too, upon the brink of the tomb. I will not trouble any one long with my existence. For the sake, then, of your honor and manhood, do not trample a dying woman under your feet."

"You are not near dead, Emily. But we will not argue that question; and, as I have not much time to tarry, I will make my proposal like a hasty lover, and then hear your answer. I ask you again if you will be my wife?"

"I would die first!" she replied, changing her manner, while her eyes were flashing with indignation.

"Very well, then; there are only two alternatives: you must become my wife or be a *beggar*—may be worse than that. You are at liberty to take your choice. I will add that, in case the first desirable event should take place, in five minutes after the ceremony is performed I will never see you again. I will swear to this, for your consolation. We will even put it in the marriage contract, if you wish. I want you to be only a *nominal* wife."

"For what reason do you desire this?" asked Emily, astonished at such a strange proposition.

"If you can not discover a reason, I will tell you. I do not care about keeping it a secret now. You are in my power anyhow; and I would as soon as not you should understand the whole subject from beginning to end. By your father's will, it is provided that in case you die without heirs your whole property shall descend to your husband. Is not that a sufficient reason?"

"Suppose I do not consent to such an arrangement?"

"I think it quite probable you will consent to it when you know all. I am making you a reasonable and a kind offer; I will not interfere with you or your property until your decease, which, you say, will not be long. You can enjoy all the privileges you now have; and may even choose another lover if you want to. The only difference there will be in this slight change, you will be Mrs. Hallam instead of Miss Burrell. If you refuse, your property may be confiscated, and something worse than that may happen."

"Explain yourself more fully," said Emily, in blank astonishment.

"I will," replied Hallam, drawing forth a paper from his pocket; "for I want you to understand the matter clearly. By this document, I am authorized to arrest you and your brother, and carry you to Washington to be dealt with."

"For what?" asked Emily, now beginning to comprehend the plot.

"For high treason—for disloyalty—for assisting a rebel spy in an attempt to escape from a fate he justly deserved."

"Brother James had nothing to do with that transaction; I alone am guilty of that crime."

"There is proof that he did. He is implicated anyhow; and it may happen that, if he is put on trial, the evidence against him will be much stronger than you anticipate. The probability is that he will leave the world in much the same manner Winston did."

"You are the instigator of this unjust proceeding, Walter Hallam."

"That is neither here nor there," replied Hallam, "and is not the question. I have laid the facts in the case before you. You can govern yourself accordingly. I would respectfully suggest that the first-mentioned alternative is the most efficient mode of putting an end to this ugly matter. I assure you, that if you marry me, the proceeding shall be stopped at once, and you will remain just as you are till the day of your death, with the exception of the change in your name."

Poor Emily thought he was the coolest, most unmitigated villain she had ever read of even in the annals of fiction.

"Does brother James know aught of this?" she at length asked.

"He does not. I thought it unnecessary to inform him until your decision should be obtained. He need not know any thing about it, if you will marry me quietly. In fact, I would rather not tell him; for it is a slightly unpleasant piece of business. But let me hear your decision. My time is short."

"As for myself," replied Emily, "I would let you do your worst. You could not deprive me of many days, even if you should put me to death; but, to save my brother, I will make another proposition, which may suit you as well. My fortune seems to be your only object. If, then, you will put a stop to this proceeding, I will give you my property at my death, which will not be long off."

"I am too shrewd for that, Emily: 'a bird in the hand is worth two in the bush.' I will not allow you to cheat me in that style. What assurance have I that I would ever get your property? This may be another one of your schemes to fool me—another display of your excellent diplomacy. Mine is the best plan."

"I will bequeath every cent of it to you, and with it my curse. I would swear to this by all my hopes of heaven."

"I tell you this will not do; you need not talk about it. I like your father's will much better than any you could make. By his I will come into undisputed possession of the property. Yours might be too easily broken; I might have a long and troublesome law-suit about it; besides, you might be prevented by some unforeseen contingency from making it."

"I will make it now—to-day."

"I will not hear to it," said Hallam, angrily. "You tried to foil me once, and you might do it again. I have no confidence whatever in your promises. I give you only the two alternatives. I will get half your property anyhow. So choose."

"Then," said Emily, "do as you please. I would not, if I could, degrade myself by such an unholy alliance, and thus become a partner to your villainy. You can do as you like; I think it an impossibility that such wickedness can prosper. You will be brought to justice some time; if not in this world, you will be summoned to answer for it before that dread tribunal from which no offender escapes."

"It would be best, Emily, to reconsider your decision. I am now compelled to carry out my plans. The matter stands thus: you must marry me, or else see your brother hanged."

"I do not believe you. Brother has done nothing to arouse even a suspicion of his loyalty. He can prove his innocence. If he can not—if you have by bribery and falsehood destroyed his character, and are determined to bring him to the untimely end you name—I believe God will arrest the iniquitous proceeding, and send upon you a dreadful retribution adequate to your crimes. Sin brings its own reward, even in this life, and you will not escape unscathed the vengeance of offended heaven."

"You can not frighten me from my purposes by such ecclesiastical blarney. I can not now retreat. That would certainly be worse than to proceed. I ask you again to reflect upon the step you are about to take. It is a matter of vital importance to you. You have only to choose between a nominal marriage and *beggary*, if not death."

"Persuasion is in vain," said Emily. "I would prefer ten thousand deaths to a marriage with such an unnatural ingrate. Brother's influence has raised you from obscurity to what little celebrity you have obtained. If this last act of villainy is a sample of your gratitude, go on; but you will be punished, Walter, you will be punished, as much as you may mock the God that gives you life."

"Have you decided, Emily, irrevocably?"

"I have told you so more than once."

"Then I call you to witness that you are responsible for all the consequences that may follow. In the name of the United States, I arrest you for disloyalty."

He stepped back into the avenue, and motioned with his hand. In a few moments a dozen Federal soldiers stood by his side. Hallam re-entered the bower.

"Come, Emily; I have no time to tarry. We must be off."

"You will let me make some arrangements, will you not?"

"Yes, certainly; we will go to the house for your brother; he will accompany you as a fellow-prisoner. Come."

Emily arose and followed him to the house. Walter, knowing the irascible nature of Colonel Burrell, stationed his soldiers in the hall. He then told Emily to see her brother, and give him such information as she thought proper, or send him into the hall. She went to the Colonel's room and related briefly what had taken place, not concealing Walter's proposal, and then she commenced making preparations to return to Washington. Colonel Burrell immediately went into the hall, his eyes flashing like those of an enraged tiger.

"Hallam, what in the h—ll means this proceeding?" said the Colonel, advancing close to Walter, who shrank back a step or two by the side of the Yankee soldiers.

"It means that you are a prisoner, by the proper authority. You can see it if you wish."

The Colonel looked at him for a full minute with an expression of wild ferocity. He appeared to be at a loss for words to express his boiling anger.

"I always thought," he at length hissed through his clenched teeth, "that you were a d—d villain. Now I know it. You are at the bottom of this —— proceeding. You want Emily to marry you, do you? Why, G—d d—n your brazen impudence, I would see her dead first! Yes, by ——, I would see her sunk to bottomless h—ll first!" he bawled in a hoarse voice, and then paused for a moment, overcome by the intensity of his fearful wrath.

"It is useless, sir," said Hallam, taking advantage of the temporary cessation of maledictions, "to resist lawful authority. You are called upon by the Government of the United States to answer certain charges alleged against you. I suggest that your proper course would be to submit quietly."

"Answer charges! What sort of charges, you d—d scoundrel? They are nothing but your infernal lies. But you shall repent this; by the living G—d, you shall repent it!"

"Stop your d—d nonsense, Colonel Burrell," interrupted Hallam; "I have heard enough of it. You are a prisoner, and if you have not sense enough to see the propriety of yielding submissively, then I will use the means necessary to enforce silence and obedience to the orders of the government. I will give you one hour to make preparations for your departure. Your abuse of me does not mend the matter, and will not prevent your arrest. You must go. If you behave yourself with becoming dignity, you shall be treated with the respect due to your rank. If you do not, I must deal with you as a common criminal!"

Colonel Burrell was a sensible man, and he saw that Hallam was right. He therefore calmed the tumult of his revengeful feelings as well as he could, and requested to be allowed to remain until next day, in order to have a carriage repaired to convey his sister to the depot, which was some distance off. Walter agreed, and waited till the morning dawned, when the whole party set out for the Federal capital. The route lay up the river bottom. Hallam with his guard followed the carriage, in which were seated Colonel Burrell and his sister. Emily appeared to look upon the proceeding with indifference, and gazed upon the objects without as calmly as if she were paying a visit, and would soon return. The trials through which she had passed seemed to have tranquilized her feelings, and she awaited this new ordeal with Christian patience, well-assured that whatever might be the result to herself and her brother, justice would finally triumph over fraud, treachery, and villainy. But Colonel Burrell did not view the matter with such feelings of resignation. Black anger clouded his frowning brow, and he meditated fearful revenge upon Walter Hallam.

"I will make the villain repent," said the Colonel, talking more to himself than to Emily. "I will yet make the d—d whelp curse the day he was born! Who would have thought he could be such a devil?"

"I am sorry to hear you talk so, brother. You do not at all improve your condition by such unnecessary profanity. You do yourself more harm than any body else."

"I can not be like you, Emily; I wish I could. But every time I think of the base ingratitude of that d—d—— I do n't know what to call him, it turns my breast into a miniature hell."

Emily did not say any thing more. She thought it useless to talk to her brother in his present state of feeling. So the carriage rolled on, and the incumbents kept silent. They were now about ten miles from Colonel Burrell's residence. Just as the carriage had made a sudden turn in the road, Hallam was considerably surprised to see several Confederate soldiers, only about a hundred yards ahead. They were on horseback, and he supposed them to be guerrillas. He quickly spurred in front of the carriage, followed by the larger portion of his guard.

"Who are you?" demanded Hallam.

"The advanced guard of a Confederate brigade," was the deliberate reply. "Who are *you?*"

Hallam was at a loss for an answer. He thought of taking to flight. But one of the Confederates saw how the matter stood.

"I summons you all to surrender," said the soldier. "Our command will be here in ten minutes, and you can not escape."

"I am not to be fooled in this way," replied Hallam. "I will wait ten minutes, and if it be not as you say, then you must surrender. I will not yield to four or five guerrillas."

"Very well," replied the Confederate, "we will give you ten minutes; but if you attempt to escape, we will fire on you."

They did not wait long. A cavalry brigadier-general with his escort rode up. Walter Hallam looked at the officer with indescribable terror depicted on his countenance. He was trembling from head to foot. The officer returned the look in silence.

"In the name of God, who are you?" cried Hallam, terrified beyond all control. "Are you living or dead?" The General made no reply. "For God's sake, speak! Am I talking to a ghost?"

"Whom have you in that carriage?" asked the officer, without replying, and riding up to the door of the vehicle, which was about thirty yards distant.

Emily's eyes met those of the General; she started in amazement; then, with a slight scream, fell fainting upon the seat. Colonel Burrell was so much astonished and alarmed at this unexpected convulsion of his sister that he did not at first notice the cause of her fright. The General hastily dismounted and hastened to the carriage door. Colonel Burrell now looked into his face.

"My God! who is this?" exclaimed the Colonel, in fear and amazement as great as Hallam's.

But the General appeared too much interested in the young lady to answer questions. He motioned to one of his escort for a canteen, and then sprinkled water in Emily's face. Presently she rose to a sitting posture.

"Henry is it you, or am I dreaming? Are you a ghost? Tell me quick, for pity's sake."

"It is I, my dear Emily, living and in good health. You may be certain I am no ghost."

Colonel Burrell extended his hand, and warmly grasped that of General Henry Winston.

"I was certain you were a ghost, because I was told you were buried. I welcome you back from the grave. But come into the carriage; I will leave you and Emily to talk it all over."

Colonel Burrell very soon vacated his seat in the carriage, and Henry Winston seated himself by Emily's side. We can not describe the meeting between the lovers, so we will leave them and follow Colonel Burrell. He moved to where Walter Hallam was still sitting upon his horse.

"Now, Hallam," said Colonel Burrell, "I challenge you to fight me on the spot. I must have your life, or you must have mine. Nothing but blood will wipe out the insult you have offered me. Dismount, and let us get through with it."

"I beg to remind you," replied Hallam, "who and what we are. We are both prisoners, and will hardly be allowed the liberty you ask. Otherwise I would accommodate you."

"I can never be satisfied till I fight you," replied Colonel Burrell. "You have acted the d——d rascal, and proved yourself a scoundrel of the deepest dye. You must now fight me, or add cowardice to your other vices."

"No man has ever had grounds to call me a coward yet, and I'll be d——d if you shall do it. If these Confederate gentlemen will allow us the privilege, I will fight you with pistols, at the distance of ten paces."

The matter was briefly explained to the Confederates, who very readily agreed to witness a duel between two Yankees. In fact, it was great sport to them; and a couple quickly volunteered their services to act as seconds to the belligerents. The ground was very soon measured off.

"Gentlemen," said one of the seconds, unbuckling his belt, and producing two navy pistols, "here is a pair of barkers that never fail. They are sure to fire, and rarely miss the mark. I've killed many a *blue gentleman* like you two with these same black dogs. They are so used to this kind of work, I can hardly keep 'em quiet whenever they git thar peepers on a Yankee. They have never missed a *blue* mark; and I will tell you, for your mutual consolation, that if you will only hold steady hands, you will both have the pleasure of seeing each other fall. All the difference between 'em is in name—one is called Jeff Davis and the other Bob Lee. Any objections to 'em?"

"None," replied both duelists.

"Then take your positions," continued the soldier, giving each a pistol. "I suggest that, since one of the parties goes on a crutch, we count a little different from the old style, to give both a fair chance. I will count three, and while I am doing this you are to aim, but you are not to fire till I've counted four or five."

"You are for having us both killed," said Hallam.

"Why, d--n it," replied the Confederate, "what do you fight for but to kill? If you are not going to kill or be killed, you may as well throw down the pistols and take *squirt-guns*. I'm disinterested—perfectly so; I only want to see fair play. But, to be certain that justice will be done, I would rather see both of you killed. The proposition I make is as fair for the goose as for the gander. Will you agree to it?"

"I will," answered Colonel Burrell.

"So will I," said Hallam, who could not now back down.

"Then be ready," said the Confederate, stepping back a few paces to the front of the combatants. "One—two—three—four—five!"

Between "two" and "three" Walter fired. He had determined to violate the agreement, and kill his antagonist before "three" could be pronounced, and thus run little risk. But his haste and treachery proved dear; for the Confederate kept on counting, and when he said "four" Colonel Burrell deliberately fired. The ball passed through Hallam's heart. Without a groan, he fell back to the earth a corpse. The first report attracted the attention of Henry and Emily; they both looked forth in time to see Colonel Burrell fire and Walter fall. The General sprang from the carriage and rushed to the spot.

"What means this?" he asked.

"All fair, General, all fair," replied the second. "Two of these *blue* gentlemen desired, it seems, to settle an old difficulty, and we had the kindness to accommodate 'em. That one lying there was no doubt a scamp, and old Bob Lee has punished him very severely for his rascality."

General Winston looked upon his fallen enemy. He could not but think the punishment was just, and said not a word.

"Now, General Winston," said Colonel Burrell, offering his hand, "I am done with the Federal Government. I have been unjustly treated by the officials at Washington. They seem to have suspected my loyalty. Henceforth they shall have no room for suspicion, because I shall take a bold stand in favor of the South. If you will receive me into your command, I will endeavor to make amends for the damage I may have done."

"I accept the offer of your services with pleasure, Colonel Burrell; and may the God of justice enable us to achieve the independence of our down-trodden country; and may you live to see the Southern Confederacy take her true position among the proud nationalities of the earth."

Emily heard it all. With streaming eyes she bent upon her knees, and poured out to just heaven the gratitude of a thankful heart. When General Winston returned to the carriage he was touched at the sight. She rose.

"I thank God, my dear Emily, you have learned to pray. Have you not found it, in all your trials, a source of consolation far above any thing furnished by this earth?"

"I cried unto the Lord with my voice, and he heard me out of his holy hill," was all the reply she made.

CHAPTER XXVII.

"All's well that ends well."

READER, we must now omit the events of several gloomy months. The memorable war of 1861 is ended. The dark days of bloodshed and suffering have passed away, and we can now look forth upon the wide-spread havoc occasioned by the political storm which has swept over the face of the "sunny South." Many sad monuments of its fury meet the eye upon every hill-top and in every valley; around nearly every fireside there is a vacant chair; from nearly every household some loved one has disappeared, and gone down to the "republic of dust and ashes," a martyr to an unsuccessful but a high and holy cause. Many, many a bitter tear will be shed to the memory of these dead heroes, when all physical traces of the disastrous war have disappeared. They fought with more than Spartan courage; they endured hardships with more than Roman firmness; they fell with more than the professed patriotism of Brutus; but all in vain! The Confederate flag, that once proud emblem of a struggling nationality, droops—tattered, torn, stained with blood—over a hundred thousand patriot graves, that lie scattered from the confines of the "Old North State" to the wild regions of Texas. They are to be seen on the plains of Manassas—upon Tennessee's soil—around Atlanta—in the marshes of Florida—upon the high hills of Vicksburg—along the banks of the "Father of Waters"—throughout every state of the lamented but "*so-called*" Confederacy.

> "Their loveliest mother earth
> Enshrines the fallen brave;

In her sweet lap who gave them birth
They find a tranquil grave."

And there let them sleep till the last trump shall sound, when they shall come forth from the bloody tomb and lay down their honors at the foot of the great Throne. The South may be stripped of her wealth, she may be trampled upon and insulted, but she can not be robbed of her noble dead. She will remember them with affectionate regard till North, South, East, and West have sunk beneath the black waves of never-ending oblivion.

Southern Confederacy! we bid thee a fond, an affectionate, a sorrowful farewell. Adieu to all thy promised greatness and grandeur. Like a bright, flashing meteor, did thy holy light temporarily obscure the red glare of the torch of despotism. But now thou hast disappeared, and the darkness is intense. The star of thy destiny is set in blood, to rise no more. Yet that same star once rose high in the political firmament, and threatened by its brightness to eclipse the splendor of all surrounding nations. The sacred principle which gave rise to thee is suppressed. The fair temple of liberty erected upon thy soil is demolished, and the beautiful goddess, shrieking over thy darkened ruins, has winged to heaven a returnless flight. Celestial goddess! when thou sittest in paradise, pour into the ears of Washington the tale of southern wrongs. Tell him that the Declaration of Independence, which he fought to sustain, is held in contempt; that the Constitution, which his wisdom helped to frame, is trampled in the dust; that the government which he first administered has become a despotism, and no longer secures "peace and happiness," but it has destroyed the prosperity of eight millions of people. Tell him that the Old Dominion which gave him birth lies bleeding at every pore, reduced to ruin by foreigners and abolitionists. Tell Andrew Jackson that Tennessee is a conquered province; that her citizens have lost the right of free suffrage; and that she is ruled with a scepter of steel. Tell John C. Calhoun that South Carolina has been prostrated, bruised, beaten, humbled by Dutch, Irish, northerners, and Africans; and that she can never send a member to fill the place he occupied in the senate unless he swears to plant his foot upon her bleeding neck, and sell her birthright to free negroes. Tell Daniel Webster that Massachusetts has degraded herself; that she will soon be a race of mulattoes; that she has abolished the worship of liberty, and bows to the black Baal of Africa. Tell all this, Goddess of Liberty, and Washington, and Jackson, and Calhoun, and Webster will weep tears of blood, even in heaven.

Confederate States! farewell—a long farewell! The holy sisterhood of states, held together by the silken chords of mutual trust and love, is broken. Ye must sever the union of your choice, baptized with the blood of your noblest sons. Let it go: it is the downfall of the only true republic under the broad canopy of heaven. Return to the "glorious Union" that will bind you to her affectionate breast with bonds of brass and iron. Lay aside your ancient pride and dignity, accept such terms as ye can get from the new "*miscegenated*" monarchy, and drink down the wormwood and gall of humiliation; swallow down the bitter pill of defeat; stand by the "best government the world ever saw;" give up your wealth to rapacious conquerors; recognize and sustain that noble "higher law than the Constitution;" abolish forever "the sum of all villainies;" place the heaven-favored African in his true sphere above the white race; worship the golden calf of Ethiopia; do all this, and may the God of Israel pity your social and political degradation!

It now remains for us to acquaint the reader with the destinies of those who have figured in these pages, and our task is done. We will first proceed to gratify a natural curiosity in regard to the remarkable escape of General Winston. We can not do this better than by quoting an extract from a Washington newspaper, which is as follows:

"Our readers will recollect our account of the execution of Henry S. Winston, the celebrated rebel spy, a few weeks ago. The vast multitude present on the occasion will, no doubt, be surprised to learn that the prisoner who was hanged and buried is now alive and safe in Dixie. It happened that the spy did not die; and, while the crowd supposed him to be struggling in the agonies of death, he was comfortably *swinging by the arms*. The whole contrivance was one of the most ingenious tricks of modern times, and sounds more like romance than truth. Since the prisoner's escape, the whole plot has come to light. It would furnish to our novelists a most excellent foundation for a thrilling story.

"When the first report that the spy was alive reached the city, the grave in which he had been buried was opened, and what was at first suspicion soon became an indisputable fact. It was now observed that the coffin was much larger than was necessary, and that at the head there was no plank at all; but this opening was concealed by the lining. The grave was dug on the side of a hill, and communicated with a *sink-hole* sufficiently large to admit the body of a man. It is a little strange that this circumstance aroused nobody's suspicion at the time. It was supposed, though, to be the result of accident.

"It is probable, therefore, and such must have been the case, that no sooner did the *dead* man hear the first clods of earth rattle over his head, than he quietly cut the lining of his coffin, and then respired freely while he was being buried alive. That night he must have crept through the sink-hole and made his escape.

"As soon as all this was discovered, the authorities arrested the provost marshal, as it was thought that the contrivance would have been a failure without his assistance; but this officer proved his entire innocence. He stated that, a short time previous to the execution, a man by the name of Dick Grover called in his office and proposed to become executioner, giving as a reason that Winston was a personal enemy, and he desired the pleasure of tying the rope around his neck. The provost had no objection, and agreed to the proposition. The authorities had the city thoroughly searched; and fortunately, though accidentally, Grover was discovered. This man is a hardened villain. He swore that he was privy to the whole plot, but that he would be d—d if he would tell any thing unless he were guaranteed a full pardon. He stated that there were many engaged in it, and some of them officers. The authorities thought best to grant what he asked, as no clew could be obtained by which any other person could be implicated without his confession. From his statement it appears that Dr. Vernon, who, up to this time, was above suspicion, was the chief actor. Some of the guard on duty at the time state that Vernon had a long interview with the spy during his confinement, which, however, excited no suspicion, as the surgeon was known to be strictly loyal. In the prisoner's cell an old book was found, from which the plan was taken. It contains an account of a contrivance similar to that which Vernon and his accomplices practiced with such complete success. Vernon, however, improved on the original plan by the addition of the burial ceremony.

"Grover states that a broad, strong, leathern belt was bound around the spy, immediately under his arms, and to this was fastened a piece of rope, like that which was tied to the gallows. It came out at the victim's ear, and contained a loop at its end. The noose, or hang-knot, was very ingeniously constructed. It concealed a stout iron hook, which was so carefully wrapped that it had the appearance of being a part of the rope. When all was ready for the execution, Grover adjusted the rope, and then pulled over the prisoner's head a black cap, which was also made to correspond to the other machinery, and conceal the operation of the curious contrivance. While every body supposed he was re-arranging the noose, after the cap was on, he was fastening the loop to the iron hook. No sooner, therefore, did the prisoner drop through the trap-door, than one end of the noose pulled out by the sudden jerk, and was concealed under the cap. Any body would have sworn that the man was hanging by the neck. He acted his part to perfection, and the whole multitude was completely deceived. After swinging some twenty minutes, he was pronounced dead by Dr. Vernon and another surgeon bribed to secrecy. The corpse was then buried, as we have already stated. It is a strange circumstance that nobody recollected who these surgeons were. Both were in disguise. Bribery must have been resorted to on an extensive scale. Grover himself was paid no less than one thousand dollars for his participation in the affair.

"Vernon and his assistants seem to have suddenly decamped. At all events, not one of them can be found. Grover was making arrangements to leave the city when he was apprehended. No doubt the whole party will be amply rewarded when they reach the land of Dixie, if they are not already there. We understand that Winston, for his shrewdness and risk in running the gauntlet, has been promoted to a brigadier-generalship. So much for this, the most remarkable escape on record."

We will not disappoint the reader's expectation by stating that Henry and Emily did not reach the zenith of earthly happiness, pictured in all delightful stories, in a *happy marriage*. The ceremony was performed, on a bright

Sabbath morning, one week after their unexpected meeting in the road. It is needless to say that they were a happy pair.

The next day the brigade of General Winston commenced its march to the South. After some few difficulties, not worthy of notice, it reached the State of Mississippi. General Winston left his beautiful bride in the town of Holly Springs, and immediately commenced military operations in his native state. He was, in a short time afterward, ordered with his command to Virginia, where he served till the close of the war. His brigade made a mark which will stand out in bold relief amid the annals of the unfortunate Confederacy. When this war for separation terminated, General Winston did not deem it compatible with his personal safety to remain in the United States. The reader will not, therefore, be surprised to learn that he landed at Havana, in July, 1865, in company with that noble patriot, of whom Kentucky may well be proud, the gallant General John C. Breckinridge. We may add that Colonel Burrell and Emily, who had now entirely recovered her health, were in the crowd. May all these self-exiled patriots find that peace and quiet in a foreign land which was refused them in their own! May every blessing of kind heaven attend them in their new homes!

Poor Colonel Ellsworth fell in the very first battle in which he was engaged for the defense of southern honor. He was a noble-hearted man, and deserves the gratitude of all true southern patriots. *Requiescat in pace.* Let him rest with all other Confederate heroes, who have spilled their blood for liberty, under the drooping folds of the Confederate flag. It is their winding sheet. Glorious banner! we lay thee down, blood-stained, with emotions ineffable. Thy "stars and bars" are destined no more to wave over the southern land. Thou art furled forever!

Honored flag! we take a mournful leave of thee in the following beautiful lines of an American poet—a just tribute to the cause of which thou art the emblem:

> "Take that banner down; 't is weary—
> Round its staff 't is drooping dreary:
> Furl it, fold it, let it rest;
> For there 's not a man to wave it,
> For there 's not a sword to save it,
> In the blood that heroes gave it;
> And its foes now scorn and brave it:
> Furl it, hide it, let it rest.
>
> Take that banner down; 't is tattered—
> Broken is its staff, and shattered;
> And the valiant hosts are scattered
> Over whom it floated high.
> O, 't is hard for us to fold it,
> Hard to think there 's none to hold it,
> Hard that those who once unrolled it,
> Now must furl it with a sigh.
>
> Furl that banner—furl it sadly;
> Once six millions hailed it gladly,
> And ten thousand, wildly, madly,
> Swore it should forever wave—
> Swore that foeman's sword should never
> Hearts like theirs entwined dissever;
> And that flag should float forever
> O'er their freedom or their grave.
>
> Furl it, for the hands that grasped it,
> And the hearts that fondly clasped it,
> Cold and dead, are lying low;
> And that banner, it is trailing,
> While around it sounds the wailing
> Of its people, in their woe.
> For, though conquered they adore it;
> Love the cold dead hands that bore it;
> Weep for those who fell before it;
> Pardon those who trail and tore it:
> O, how wildly they deplore it,
> Now to furl and fold it so!
>
> Furl that banner; true 't is gory,
> But 't is wreathed around with glory,
> And 't will live in song and story,

Though its folds are in the dust:
For its fame, on brightest pages,
Penned by poets and by sages,
Shall go sounding down the ages—
　Furl its folds though now we must.

Furl that banner, softly, slowly;
Furl it gently—it is holy,
　For it droops above the dead:
Touch it not, unfurl it never;
Let it droop there, furled forever,
　For its people's hopes are fled!"

THE END.

www.ingramcontent.com/pod-product-compliance
Lightning Source LLC
Chambersburg PA
CBHW022121290426
44112CB00008B/761